From Gandhi to New Gandhi

Ah, how tell a tale so drear?
Sad as death what thou shalt hear
Of great Ajax, undone quite,
Smit with madness, in the night.
Look within and see the floor
Reeking with his victim's gore;
Slain by his own hand there lies
His ungodly sacrifice

Tecmessa in Sophocles' *Ajax*
(Translated by Francis Storr)

From Gandhi to New Gandhi

A Political Odyssey through Ghosts and Resurrections

Piyush Srivastava

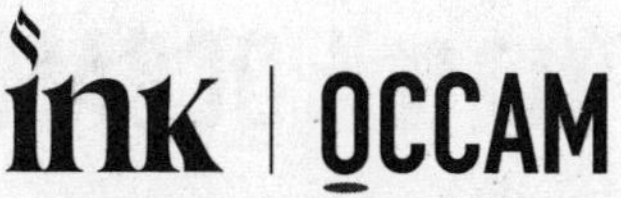

ISBN: 978-93-6547-242-4

First published in India 2025
This edition published 2025

BluOne Ink Pvt. Ltd
A-76, 2nd Floor, Sector 136, Noida
Uttar Pradesh 201301
www.bluone.ink
publisher@bluone.ink

Printed and bound in India by Thomson Press India Ltd.

Kali and Occam are imprints of BluOne Ink

Contents

Chronology

Chapter 1: Mahatma Gandhi

- **2 October 1869**: Gandhi was born.
- **1887**: He passed his matric examination.
- **29 September 1888**: He reached Tilbury Docks in Southampton on his way to study law in London.
- **10 June 1891**: Gandhi was called to the bar and became a qualified barrister.
- **24 May 1893**: Employed by Dada Abdullah, a Gujarati businessman, Gandhi reached South Africa.
- **7 June 1893**: Gandhi was thrown off a train at Pietermaritzburg station in South Africa for refusing to move from the first-class compartment, an event that shaped his future activism.
- **1894**: Leo Tolstoy's *The Kingdom of God is Within You* was published.
- **1896**: Gandhi returned to Bombay but failed to get clients at the high court.
- **12 October 1896**: He first met Bal Gangadhar Tilak in Durban.
- **December 1896**: Dada Abdullah called Gandhi back.
- **10 February 1908**: He was beaten up by some Pathans in South Africa.

- **1910**: Gandhi established Tolstoy Farm near Johannesburg, a cooperative colony for civil resisters.
- **9 January 1915**: Gandhi returned to India from South Africa, marking the end of his 21-year stay.
- **4 February 1916**: Banaras Hindu University was founded.
- **9 May 1916**: Ambedkar presented his research paper at Columbia University.
- **26 December 1919**: Swami Shraddhanand addressed the Congress session in Amritsar.
- **14 January 1920**: Gandhi made a statement that Tilak believed everything was fair in war.
- **28 January 1920**: Tilak replied to Gandhi's statement.
- **28 December 1923 – 1 January 1924**: The Congress's thirty-eighth session was held in Cocanada (Kakinada), Andhra Pradesh.
- **7 November 1925**: Madeleine Slade, also known as Miraben, reached Sabarmati Ashram in Ahmedabad.
- **6 December 1931**: Gandhi stayed with Romain Rolland in Villeneuve, Switzerland, for five days.
- **November 1933**: Madan Mohan Malaviya invited Nehru to address the students at Banaras Hindu University. Nehru targeted Hindu Mahasabha in his speech.
- **1934**: Bhai Parmanand's memoir titled *The Story of My Life* was published.
- **1933 – 1934**: Bhai Parmanand became the president of the Hindu Mahasabha.
- **June 1934 – February 1935**: Nehru wrote his autobiography in prison.
- **1 August 1936**: N.C. Kelkar stated that Gandhi had created a 'mystifying aura' around himself and was working on an agenda to 'destroy the legacy of Tilak'.

- **30 – 31 December 1937**: The nineteenth Hindu Mahasabha session was held in Karnavati, Ahmedabad.
- **12 April 1939**: Maulvi Syed Golam Sarowar Husseini raised an agitation in Noakhali against the behaviour of a Hindu teacher towards his Muslim pupil.
- **29 December 1939**: Savarkar asked Mahasabha members at its twenty-first session in Calcutta why educated people were not joining them.
- **17 October 1940**: Gandhi launched Individual Satyagraha (Vyaktigat Satyagraha).
- **8 July 1943**: Ambedkar shared an interesting figure on religious dynamics in security forces which was presented before the House of Commons.
- **10 October 1946**: Muslim League leader, Husseini called on the Muslims in Begumganj Bazar, Noakhali, to kill Hindus.
- **6 February 1947**: Gandhi visited Raipur of Noakhali.
- **17 February 1947**: Khalilur Rahman, a religious interpreter, met Gandhi in the village of Devipur in Noakhali.
- **2 March 1947**: Gandhi went from Noakhali to Patna.
- **3 April 1947**: He stated that he would ask 'those who were against his holding the prayer meeting not to come, or if they did, they should come by themselves and kill him if they wanted to'.
- **May 1947**: He stayed in Delhi's 'Bhangi Nivas'.
- **1 – 2 May 1947**: He talked to Manu and Rajendra Prasad in Bhangi Nivas.
- **17 July 1947**: Gandhi approved the proposal for partition.
- **15 August 1947**: India gained independence from British rule.
- **August 1947**: J.B. Kripalani resigned as Congress president.

- **9 September 1947**: Gandhi came from Calcutta to Birla House and lived there until his assassination.
- **9 December 1947**: Gandhi explained why he was living in Birla House instead of a 'Bhangi' colony.
- **18 January 1948**: Over one hundred leaders, including Nehru and Patel, signed a seven-point pledge in Hindi and Urdu that they would protect Muslims and convinced Gandhi to suspend his fast.
- **20 January 1948**: Madanlal Pahwa exploded a bomb near Gandhi and was arrested.
- **29 January 1948**: Nehru boastfully stated in Amritsar that he would finish the RSS.
- **30 January 1948**: Mahatma Gandhi was assassinated by Nathuram Godse at Birla House in Delhi during his evening prayer meeting.
- **2 February 1948**: M.S. Golwalkar was arrested.
- **4 February 1948**: The RSS was banned by the government.
- **12 February 1948**: Gandhi's special mourning day was observed.
- **16 February 1948**: Govind Ballabh Pant spoke positively about Gandhi in the UP Legislative Council.
- **19 – 21 March 1948**: The Socialist Party held its sixth Annual Conference independently at Nasik.
- **6 August 1948**: Golwalkar was granted bail.
- **17 – 23 October 1948**: Golwalkar met Patel to discuss lifting the ban on the RSS.
- **13 November 1948**: Golwalkar was rearrested.
- **6 November 1948**: Arun Chandra Guha pointed out in the Constituent Assembly that Ambedkar found no occasion to refer to Gandhi or the Congress.
- **June 1949**: The draft of the RSS constitution was sent to the home ministry.

- **11 July 1949**: The ban on the RSS was lifted.
- **12 July 1949**: Golwalkar was released.
- **18 February 1953**: Sheikh Abdullah wrote to Shyama Prasad Mookerjee about Praja Parishad.
- **20 March 1957**: Pant spoke negatively about Gandhi in the Rajya Sabha.
- **30 January 1961**: Rajendra Prasad inaugurated the National Gandhi Museum in New Delhi.
- **12 November 1964**: Satyavinayak Puja was held in Poona to welcome Gopal Godse and his two accomplishes in Gandhi's murder.
- **14 November 1964**: Newspapers reported Gajanan Vishwanath Ketkar's speech, stating he knew Godse would kill Gandhi.
- **25 November 1964**: Ketkar surrendered in Madras.
- **21 July 1965**: Ketkar filed his bail plea in the Bombay High Court.
- **30 September 1969**: The report of Justice Jivanlal Kapur's Commission on Gandhi's assassination was released.
- **2004 – 2014**: Manmohan Singh-led United Progressive Alliance was in power.
- **24 December 2014**: The Modi Government awarded the Bharat Ratna to Madan Mohan Malaviya.
- **15 August 2022**: Modi took the names of Savarkar, Gandhi, Subhas Chandra Bose, and Ambedkar in his Independence day speech from the Red Fort.

Chapter 2: Vinayak Damodar Savarkar

- **12 September 1837**: The Red Hill Railroad was opened in Madras.
- **1 January 1880**: New English School was founded in Poona.

- **5 July 1880**: Barindra Kumar Ghosh was born in London.
- **28 May 1883**: Savarkar was born in Nasik district.
- **24 October 1884**: The Deccan Education Society was established in Poona.
- **1 April 1889**: K.B. Hedgewar was born.
- **22 June 1897**: Damodar Hari, Balkrishna Hari and Vasudeo Hari shot at two plague officers, Walter Charles Rand and his escort Lt Ayerst. Ayerst died immediately. Rand passed away on **3 July 1897**.
- **22 January 1901**: Savarkar's Mitra Mela opposed Queen Victoria's mourning session after her death.
- **7 October 1905**: He was removed from Fergusson College for burning foreign clothes in Poona.
- **9 June 1906**: Savarkar left Bombay for London.
- **1 October 1906**: Aga Khan III led the Muslim Deputation (Shimla Deputation of thirty-five influential Muslims).
- **30 April 1908**: Khudiram Bose and Prafulla Kumar Chaki attempted to assassinate Magistrate Douglas Kingsford.
- **2 May 1908**: Aurobindo Ghosh and many other revolutionaries were arrested.
- **10 November 1908**: Kanailal Dutt was hanged.
- **8 June 1909**: Babarao Savarkar was sentenced to life imprisonment.
- **1 July 1909**: Madanlal Dhingra assassinated Sir William Hutt Curzon Wyllie.
- **17 August 1909**: Dhingra was hanged at Eatonville Jail in London.
- **6 May 1909**: Aurobindo was acquitted, but several revolutionaries were sentenced to death.
- **11 December 1909**: Their punishment was later reduced to life imprisonment, and they were sent to Andaman Cellular Jail.

- **13 November 1909**: Mohanlal Pandya hurled a bomb on Viceroy Lord Minto.
- **21 December 1909**: Anant Laxman Kanhere shot dead Jackson, the district collector of Nasik.
- **19 April 1910**: Kanhere was hanged.
- **1 July 1910**: Savarkar was extradited from London to India.
- **8 July 1910**: Savarkar attempted to escape by jumping into the sea.
- **22 July 1910**: He was brought to Bombay.
- **26 December – 29 December 1910**: The twenty-fifth Congress session was held at Allahabad.
- **30 January 1911**: Savarkar received his first life transportation sentence for the murder of A.M.T. Jackson.
- **17 June 1911**: Vanchinatha Iyer assassinated Robert Ashe, district collector of Thirunelveli.
- **11 July 1911**: Savarkar was imprisoned in the Cellular Jail, Andaman, until 2 May 1921.
- **26 June 1915**: Revolutionary Sachindranath Sanyal was arrested again and given a life sentence on 14 February 1916. He was sent to Andaman Cellular Jail on 18 August 1916.
- **February 1920**: Sachindranath Sanyal was released from Cellular Jail.
- **13 October 1921**: Jamnadas Dwarkadas forwarded Savarkar's letter appealing for the release of his brothers to Sir William Henry Hoare Vincent.
- **November 1921**: The Prince of Wales visited India.
- **1922**: The Democratic Swaraj Party was formed.
- **31 July 1924**: The Bombay Legislative Council advocated the removal of all restrictions on Savarkar.
- **3 February 1925**: The first electric passenger train ran between Victoria Terminus and Kurla, Bombay.

- **10 December 1925**: Sanyal was rearrested for his involvement with the Hindustan Republic Army (later known as Hindustan Socialist Republican Army).
- **30 October 1928**: Lala Lajpat Rai was injured while protesting against the Simon Commission and died seventeen days later.
- **2 January 1929**: The Muslim Conference, chaired by Aga Khan III, passed Jinnah's fourteen-point demands.
- **8 April 1929**: Bhagat Singh and Batukeshwar Dutt bombed Delhi's Central Assembly.
- **1930**: D.N. Pritt represented Bhagat Singh, Sukhdev, and Rajguru in court.
- **23 March 1931**: Bhagat Singh, Sukhdev, and Rajguru were hanged.
- **26 March 1931**: The Karachi session of the Congress was held.
- **9 June 1931**: Revolutionary Hari Kishan Talwar was hanged.
- **22 July 1931**: Vasudev Balwant Gogate shot at Sir Ernest Hotson in Poona.
- **4 January 1932**: Gandhi Day was observed in Bombay when he was arrested there.
- **26 April 1934**: Wamanrao Chavan fired at a British officer at Dhobi Talao in Bombay.
- **10 May 1937**: Savarkar was released from all restrictions.
- **1937**: Gogate was released from prison.
- **1 August 1937**: Savarkar joined the Hindu Mahasabha and the Democratic Swaraj Party.
- **9 October 1939**: Savarkar met Lord Linlithgow to express Hindu support to Britain during World War II.
- **16 January and 19 January 1941**: The Intelligence Bureau expressed concern over the Mahasabha's call for

'direct action' on the Pakistan issue during a meeting in Delhi.

- **December 1942**: The Kanpur session of the Hindu Mahasabha was held.
- **July 1943**: Subhas Chandra Bose formed the Rani of Jhansi Regiment of the Indian National Army in Singapore.
- **22 March 1945**: Gandhi wrote to Savarkar to offer condolences for the death of his brother.
- **15 December 1946**: The Barshi Maharashtra session of the Hindu Mahasabha was held.
- **December 1947**: IB Inspector A.S. Balkundi of Ahmednagar sent his report on Madanlal Pahwa. It was endorsed by M.K. Sinha, deputy director, on **14 January 1947**.
- **4 May 1948**: The trial court of Atma Charan at Red Fort first convened.
- **27 May 1948**: The chargesheet in Gandhi's assassination case was submitted.
- **21 June 1948**: Badge turned approver and was granted a pardon.
- **10 February 1949**: Atma Charan's court passed the judgment.
- **21 June 1949**: The High Court of East Punjab passed its order in Gandhi's murder case.
- **15 November 1949**: Apte and Godse were hanged in Ambala jail.
- **1952**: Atma Charan was appointed as a judge of the Allahabad High Court.
- **26 February 1966**: Savarkar passed away after twenty-five days of atmaarpan (dedicating the soul).

- **25 June 1975**: Indira Gandhi imposed internal Emergency.
- **6 November 1978**: Shah Bano's husband pronounced triple talaq to her.
- **20 May 1980**: Indira Gandhi praised Savarkar in a letter to Pandit Bakhle.
- **1986**: The Rajiv Gandhi government enacted the Muslim Women (Protection of Rights on Divorce) Act, overturning the Supreme Court's order in the Shah Bano case.
- **February 1986**: The gate of Babri Masjid was opened for Hindus.
- **July 1988**: The Rajiv Gandhi government introduced the Anti-Defamation Act, which was withdrawn after two months.
- **26 May 2014**: Narendra Modi became the Prime Minister of India.
- **28 November 2019**: Uddhav Thackeray became the Chief Minister of Maharashtra with the support of Congress.
- **23 March 2023**: Manoj Sinha stated that Gandhi did not study law.

Chapter 3: Jawaharlal Nehru

- **1716**: Pandit Raj Kaul of Kashmir settled in Delhi under Mughal Emperor Farrukhsiyar.
- **1857**: Lachchminarain Nehru and his son Ganga Dhar Nehru were uprooted from Delhi during the 1857 revolt.
- **6 May 1861**: Motilal Nehru was born in Agra.
- **1881 – 1882**: *Anandmath* was serialized in *Banga Darshan*, a Bengali journal.
- **1886**: Motilal Nehru started practising law.

- **14 November 1889**: Jawaharlal Nehru was born.
- **May 1905**: Jawaharlal went to Harrow.
- **9 June 1906**: Savarkar left for London.
- **24 June 1906**: Savarkar arrived in London.
- **1907 – 1908**: Jawaharlal began thinking about joining politics.
- **October 1907**: Jawaharlal joined Trinity College, Cambridge.
- **December 1912**: Jawaharlal first attended the Bankipore Congress session.
- **December 1916**: Jawaharlal first met Gandhi during the Lucknow session of the Congress.
- **13 April 1919**: The Jallianwala Bagh massacre took place.
- **24 April 1919**: Robert Williams, Robert Smillie, and George Lansbury wrote against the Jallianwala Bagh massacre in the *Daily Herald*.
- **14 November 1919**: A sub-committee for the Jallianwala Bagh inquiry was formed.
- **12 December 1919**: M.R. Jayakar reached Lahore to join Madan Mohan Malaviya to discuss the Jallianwala Bagh carnage.
- **13 February 1920**: Jayakar returned to Lahore to show the printed copy of the Jallianwala report to party leaders.
- **Mid-February 1920**: Jayakar again met with party leaders at Sewa Ashram, Nagwa, in Banaras.
- **11 March 1920**: Gandhi wrote to Jayakar about the evidence in the Jallianwala Bagh report.
- **May 1920**: Nanak Singh's collection of poems on the Jallianwala Bagh massacre was published.

- **5 June 1920**: Gokaran Nath Misra wrote to Jayakar to draft a petition regarding the Punjab massacre. Jayakar refused to do so.
- **8 July 1920**: The British newspaper *Morning Post* launched the 'General Dyer Fund'.
- **12 February 1922**: Gandhi called off his Non-Cooperation Movement.
- **1 January 1923**: Das and Motilal established the Swaraj Party.
- **30 April 1925**: Jawaharlal wrote to Jayakar to pay the dues of the Jallianwala fund.
- **24 November 1931**: Swaraj Bhawan was transferred to the Jawaharlal Nehru Memorial Fund.
- **4 July 1928**: Jawaharlal wrote to Jayakar not to make the fund scam a legal issue.
- **25 October 1937**: Jawaharlal met Tagore in Calcutta to discuss the controversy surrounding 'Vande Mataram'.
- **October 1937**: The Congress accepted 'Vande Mataram' after making some cuts.
- **20 October 1937**: Jawaharlal wrote to Subhas Chandra Bose stating that he was reading an English translation of *Anandmath*.
- **1 March 1938**: Jinnah wrote in the *New Times of Lahore* that 'Vande Mataram' was unacceptable to Muslims.
- **16 April 1938**: Jinnah addressed the All-India Muslim League in Calcutta and opposed 'Vande Mataram'.
- **1 July 1939**: Gandhi wrote in *Harijan Sewak* that he wouldn't 'risk a single quarrel over singing "Vande Mataram" at a mixed gathering'.
- **April – September 1944**: Jawaharlal wrote *The Discovery of India* while imprisoned at Ahmednagar Fort prison.

- **6 December 1946**: Nirmal Kumar Bose informed Gandhi that Tagore believed 'Jawaharlal was a truer representative of modern India than Gandhiji'.
- **20 December 1946 – 1 January 1947**: The Srirampur Congress meeting was held.
- **1947**: The Jammu Praja Party of Kashmir was formed.
- **1950**: Jawaharlal took over from Purushottam Das Tandon as Congress president. He had previously held the position from 1929 to 1930 and from 1936 to 1937.
- **24 January 1950**: The Constituent Assembly of India adopted 'Vande Mataram' as the national song.
- **21 October 1951**: The Bharatiya Jan Sangh was founded in Delhi.
- **April 1952**: Harivansh Rai Bachchan left for Cambridge.
- **July 1954**: Bachchan returned from Cambridge.
- **January 1955**: Jawaharlal left the post of Congress president.
- **15 July 1955**: Jawaharlal was awarded the Bharat Ratna.
- **December 1955**: Harivansh Rai Bachchan joined as officer on special duty (OSD) in the foreign ministry.
- **September and December 1956**: Two train accidents occurred during Lal Bahadur Shastri's tenure.
- **February 1959**: Indira Gandhi took over from Uchharangrai Navalshankar Dhebar as Congress president.
- **1 May 1960**: Maharashtra was formed, with Bombay as its capital.
- **1962**: Rajendra Prasad received the Bharat Ratna.
- **27 May 1964**: Jawaharlal passed away.
- **12 October 1964**: Gopal Godse, Vishnu Karkare, and Madanlal Pahwa were released.
- **1965**: The Shastri government instituted the Jawaharlal Nehru Award for International Understanding.

- **22 March 1965**: A commission was formed under Gopal Swarup Pathak to probe Gandhi's assassination.
- **21 November 1966**: The Justice Kapur Commission was formed when Pathak was made a central minister.
- **1971**: Indira Gandhi was awarded the Bharat Ratna.
- **1974**: Dev Kant Barooah coined the slogan 'India is Indira, Indira is India'.
- **1975**: Barooah became Congress president.
- **1977**: Mrityunjay Prasad was elected as a Janata Party member of Parliament.
- **6 April 1980**: The BJP was founded.
- **1986**: The Indira Gandhi Peace Prize was instituted by the Rajiv Gandhi government.
- **1991**: Rajiv Gandhi was awarded the Bharat Ratna and Indira Gandhi Peace Prize.
- **21 May 1991**: Rajiv Gandhi was assassinated in Sriperumbudur.
- **20 May 2014**: Modi reached the Parliament as prime minister.

Chapter 4: Nathuram Godse

- **15 May 1942**: Rashtra Dal's first camp was held in Poona.
- **25 March 1944**: Savarkar launched *Agrani*, a Marathi newspaper.
- **1 August 1944**: Savarkar founded the Hindu Rashtra Dal.
- **9 July 1947**: An article published in *Hindu Rashtra* stated, 'the motherland was vivisected; the vultures tore pieces of flesh', as mentioned by the Kapur Commission.
- **2 October 1947**: Mahatma Gandhi told his associates he didn't wish to live for 125 years.

- **3 December 1947**: Ketkar declared in a meeting in Poona that 'Gandhism-cut[type of]-false-Nationalism' was 'Enemy No. 1'.
- **25 January 1948**: A Hindu Mahasabha procession was taken out in Delhi for Arya Samaj's anniversary.
- **27 January 1948**: V.G. Deshpande, Digvijaynath, and Prof. Ram Singh attended a Hindu Mahasabha meeting in Delhi.
- **31 January 1948**: An intelligence report abstract mentioned by the Kapur Commission noted that a Hindu Mahasabha procession in Delhi celebrated the anniversary of Arya Samaj, and Swami Dharmanand said that Gandhi's fast had spoiled the 'show' aimed at removing Muslims from Delhi.
- **5 March 1948**: Sardar Vallabhbhai Patel suffered a heart attack.
- **10 February 1949**: The last hearing in the Gandhi assassination case was held at the Red Fort court.
- **15 December 1950**: Patel passed away.
- **1952 – 1956**: Morarji Desai served as the home minister of Bombay.
- **1 May 1960**: Nagarwala was appointed the first inspector general of police of Gujarat.
- **24 November 1964**: The district magistrate of Poona ordered Ketkar's detention.
- **23 September 1969**: Mahant Digvijaynath passed away.
- **18 March 1974**: J.P. launched 'Sampoorna Kranti' movement from Patna.
- **1980 – 1990**: Gopal Godse worked for the Hindu Mahasabha in Delhi.
- **March 1998**: Murli Manohar Joshi became the HRD minister.

- **26 November 2005**: Gopal Godse passed away.

Chapter 5: Narendra Modi

- **31 March 1946**: Gandhi wrote about his association with rich people in an article published in *Harijan Sewak*.
- **11 August 1947**: Jinnah addressed the Constituent Assembly of Pakistan.
- **10 September 1947**: It is claimed that the Karachi police registered a case against eighteen Hindus, including L.K. Advani, for hatching a conspiracy to kill Jinnah.
- **17 September 1950**: Narendra Modi was born.
- **30 May 1964**: *Hindustan Standard* wrote: 'After Nehru, Desai and Shastri in Close Race'.
- **29 June 1967**: Indira Gandhi formed a committee on cow slaughter with M.S. Golwalkar as one of its members.
- **7 April 1975**: Morarji Desai started a fast at his residence in New Delhi for election in Gujarat.
- **25 June 1975 – 21 March 1977**: India was under the Emergency.
- **20 September 1979**: Khushwant Singh interviewed Indira Gandhi during Janata government.
- **31 October 1984**: Indira Gandhi was assassinated.
- **July 1988**: Rajiv Gandhi's government introduced the anti-defamation bill.
- **25 September 1990**: Advani started his Rath Yatra from Somnath.
- **23 October 1990**: Advani's rath was stopped in Bihar.
- **21 May 1991**: The LTTE assassinated Rajiv Gandhi.
- **May – July 1999**: The Kargil conflict took place.
- **26 February 2003**: Abdul Kalam unveiled a portrait of Savarkar in the Central Hall of the old Parliament building.

- **October 2001**: Narendra Modi became the Chief Minister of Gujarat after the resignation of Keshubhai Patel.
- **27 February 2002**: The Godhra train burning incident occurred, followed by communal riots in Gujarat. Modi's government faced criticism for its handling of the riots.
- **4 June 2005**: Advani visited Jinnah's mausoleum in Karachi.
- **7 June 2005**: Advani stepped down as BJP chief, but withdrew his resignation four days later.
- **31 December 2005**: He finally resigned from the post of BJP president.
- **1 December 2007**: Sonia Gandhi called Modi '*Maut ka Saudagar*'.
- **26 May 2014**: Narendra Modi was sworn in as the fourteenth prime minister of India.
- **8 March 2019**: Modi laid the foundation stone of the Kashi Vishwanath Corridor.
- **18 May 2019**: Modi went into a cave in Kedarnath.
- **23 May 2019**: Modi won a second term as prime minister.
- **26 March 2021**: He spoke in Dhaka about his role in the creation of Bangladesh.
- **22 January 2024**: Modi performed the Ram temple consecration.
- **3 February 2024**: Advani was nominated for the Bharat Ratna.

Chapter 6: Rahul Gandhi

- **14 June 1857**: Maulvi Liyaqat Ali looted gold from the fort of Allahabad.
- **13 April 1918**: Richard Burdon Haldane delivered his speech on 'Challenges to Democracy'.

- **August 1931**: Gandhi attended the Second Round Table Conference in London.
- **March 1942**: Indira Gandhi married Feroze Gandhi.
- **1952 and 1957**: Feroze Gandhi won elections as a Member of Parliament.
- **19 June 1970**: Rahul Gandhi was born.
- **1981 – 1983**: Rahul attended Doon School, Dehradun.
- **31 October 1984**: Indira Gandhi was assassinated by her bodyguards in New Delhi.
- **1989**: Rahul joined St Stephen's College, Delhi.
- **6 December 1992**: The Babri Masjid was demolished.
- **1994**: Rahul Gandhi graduated with a BA degree from Rollins College, Florida.
- **1995**: Rahul Gandhi enrolled at Trinity College, Cambridge.
- **20 March 2007**: Rahul Gandhi said in Deoband, Saharanpur that Babri Masjid would have been saved if someone from his family were prime minister at that time.
- **14 January 2009**: Rahul Gandhi and David Miliband stayed overnight in huts in the Amethi district during a visit.
- **December 2017 – July 2019**: Rahul Gandhi held the position of president of the Congress.
- **20 July 2018**: He hugged Modi in Parliament.
- **2 March 2021**: Rahul admitted that the Emergency was a mistake.
- **7 September 2022**: His Bharat Jodo Yatra started from Kanyakumari.
- **8 January 2023**: Congressmen called Rahul a tapasvi on social media during his Bharat Jodo Yatra.
- **9 January 2023**: Rahul Gandhi's Bharat Jodo Yatra passed through Haryana.

- **16 January 2023**: He told a gathering in Tanda, Hoshiarpur, that 'India is a land of tapasvis, but the government is targeting them'.
- **17 January 2023**: He stated at a news conference in Hoshiarpur that he would never visit the RSS office, 'even if you cut my throat'.
- **30 January 2023**: He addressed a rally in Srinagar during the Bharat Jodo Yatra.
- **March 2023**: Rahul lost his Lok Sabha membership.
- **August 2023**: Rahul's Lok Sabha membership was restored.

1

Mahatma Gandhi

On the Path of Buddha

I visited Gandhi Smriti and Darshan Samiti on Tees January Road in New Delhi on 21 January and again briefly on 4 February 2023. This road, previously known as Albuquerque Road, holds profound significance as the site where Nathuram Godse assassinated Mahatma Gandhi on 30 January 1948.

The name 'Tees January' suggests that the country pauses here on that fateful date. However, I can't shake the feeling that this naming choice was born of a mechanically creative mind rather than a genuine emotional connection to Gandhi or his ideology. I grew up hearing that Gandhi would always remain relevant. My purpose in visiting the site was to feel the truth of this sentiment.

Both times I visited, I observed about twenty to thirty foreigners, mostly elderly, along with a dozen school students accompanied by their teachers. A few Indian men, seemingly from outside Delhi, were also present, passing time while waiting for their evening trains. The tourists chatted quietly among themselves, pointing at the pictures and reading the captions on the walls. Meanwhile, the students used their phones to capture images of Gandhi, perhaps to preserve a piece of the experience.

There were about a dozen and a half staff members—caretakers, managers, gardeners, and labourers. I rarely saw them smile, and when they did, it seemed forced. Maybe silence is the usual atmosphere here; perhaps some still mourn Gandhi's death, or at least pretend to.

As I walked towards the spot where Nathuram shot Gandhi three times, a particularly alert woman on the staff stared at me. Her gaze met that of an expressionless nurseryman mowing the lawn, who gave me a sharp look for about thirty seconds before resuming his work. I am sure it was not intentional, and they didn't mean to make me uncomfortable. It seemed like they admired the foreign tourists, eagerly guiding them and showing them where to go at every step.

Gandhi, or Bapu (father), still resides in the land of his birth even in death, though he was killed for his ideology. The picture frames on the walls of the Smriti (memorial) seem as if they are pleading with Bapu to remain. One frame reveals a text: 'Gandhiji spent his life to send out the message of truth, non-violence and communal harmony, and even gave up his life for it. His message is relevant more than ever in these times of intolerance and religious fanaticism.'

Another frame holds a quote by Albert Einstein: 'Generation to come will scarce believe that such a one as this ever in flesh and blood walked upon this earth', followed by a line added by someone, perhaps a past manager of the Smriti: 'This generation has assured Einstein that future generations shall never forget the Mahatma.'

We don't know how long such graffiti will remain on the walls of these centres. Some Gandhians have alleged that the photographs by French lensman Henri Cartier-Bresson, capturing the immediate moments before and after Mahatma Gandhi's murder, were removed from the walls of the Smriti and relegated to the dark, cluttered cellar under the pretext of being digitized. The digital pictures were later displayed on a screen without captions, disconnecting them from the memories they were meant to preserve.

There was an unverified allegation that Narendra Modi, motivated by his obsession with digitization and under pressure from crony capitalists eager to monetize everything, had visited the Smriti three months prior to this incident and suggested those changes. The Modi government refuted the accusation, but the suspicion lingered, especially given that Modi is a follower of Vinayak Damodar Savarkar, the prominent proponent of Hindutva ideology. Savarkar was arrested on conspiracy charges related to Gandhi's murder and was later acquitted due to a poor investigation by the government under Gandhi's close ally, Jawaharlal Nehru.

While Gandhi now seems to be diminishing in significance within his own land, Savarkar's name appears to be gaining prominence. The June 2022 issue of *Antim Jan* (*The Last Man*), a Hindi magazine published by the Smriti, praised Savarkar, making a clear political statement that times were changing.

Critics of Savarkar believe that he might have faced rearrest following Justice Jivanlal Kapur's Commission report on Gandhi's assassination, but I have no doubt that he would have been released once more due to the lack of conclusive, clinching evidence.

The report relied primarily on statements from politicians and government officers who were careerists, eager to advance their own interests, or from individuals believed to be closely or distantly associated with the murderers.

Incidentally, Savarkar had passed away three years before the Kapur panel completed its investigation.

In 2013, while working on a film for Yann Arthus Bertrand, a French director and producer, I spent about two weeks at an upscale hotel on Buddha Marg in Kushinagar, India. Kushinagar is the site where Gautam Buddha is believed to have renounced his body. His teachings evolved into a religion that transcended the Indian subcontinent, spreading to many other countries. Ironically, however, his ideology struggled to survive in his own homeland.

During my stay at the hotel, I observed something peculiar. The Indian staff appeared trained to show less respect to Indian guests, focussing instead on catering to Buddhists from countries like China, Japan, Korea, and other places. Foreign Buddhists were warmly welcomed in the hotel's restaurant, while Indian guests were relegated to a common dining area, separate from the foreign visitors. This was ostensibly because the Buddhists valued complete privacy during meals.

Despite their veneration of Buddha, these foreign Buddhists seemed to harbour disdain for Buddha's countrymen, that is, Indians, who had historically rejected his teachings and tried to assimilate him into Hinduism by declaring him the ninth incarnation of Lord Vishnu. Another Hindu narrative sought to blur Buddha's identity further by claiming that Lord Brahma appointed Tathagata as a teacher after his enlightenment in Uruvela, now modern-day Bodh Gaya.

Buddha's Middle Path arose from his disillusionment with the Hindu way of life, which he perceived as trapped between indulgence and self-mortification. Similarly, Gandhi's journey of self-discovery and atonement began 8,000 km away from India, in South Africa, but found its ultimate resolution at home.

The compassion of Buddha was echoed in Gandhi's principle of non-violence. However, their approaches differed in certain respects. For instance, Gandhi did not oppose the killing of animals if they posed a threat to human life, while Buddha, according to tradition, died of dysentery after consuming pork, embodying his adherence to acceptance over rejection. Gandhi's weapon of 'fast unto death' was inspired by Jainism, but Buddhists considered such acts as the ultimate form of violence against the self. Despite their differences, the similarities between Buddhism and Gandhism were more apparent to the common man.

Western scholars continue to look to India to understand how and why the country managed to expel Buddhism without significant upheaval. This raises a troubling question: Will we fail to notice the disappearance of Gandhism? Some argue that this process is already underway.

Despite his deep understanding of history, Bapu became vulnerable by rejecting conventional forms of revolution, such as war and bloodbath. Instead, he chose the methods of non-violence and Satyagraha. This idealism, much like Buddha's Middle Path, was both his strength and Achilles' heel.

In the words of Romain Rolland, the French writer and Nobel laureate, Gandhi 'distrusts majorities and fears "mobocracy" and the unbridled passion of the populace. He feels at ease only in a minority.'[1] I am unsure whether Rolland, Gandhi's biographer, considered the deeper Indian tendencies when he concluded his book with the belief that 'either Gandhi's spirit will triumph, or it will manifest itself again, as were manifested centuries before, the Messiah and Buddha.'[2] I wonder how Gandhism will endure when Buddhism, despite being a 'hundred times more realistic than Christianity' according to Nietzsche, did not survive in its land of origin.[3]

A segment of India has already been focussed on moving away from Gandhi. Nathuram Godse's younger brother, Gopal Godse, noted that 'India had turned its back on Gandhi' and 'had come close to embracing Nathuram's vision' by the time of the Mahatma's assassination.[4]

One day, I asked my driver, who was resting in the cab, to join me for lunch at the restaurant in the Kushinagar hotel. However, the staff refused to let him in, citing the belief that the foreign Buddhists abominate Indian drivers and servants. The receptionists kept apologizing when I shouted at them. It was the dictate of a shrewd hotelier, but to me, it seemed to have become a practice that had evolved into a tradition over time.

Buddhism migrated from its land of origin under pressure from casteist forces resistant to change 2,500 years ago. These same forces continue to disparage Gandhi today.

Unlike Buddha, who unequivocally rejected the caste system, Gandhi did not openly denounce it. However, his practices on the ground often contradicted the Vedic diktats. Gandhi shared meals with those at the lowest levels of India's social hierarchy and encouraged major industrialists to contribute to their welfare.

In his philosophy of non-violence, Gandhi selectively engaged with Hindu epics, Ramayana and Mahabharat.

These texts, despite being steeped in stories of war and mass destruction, present the overarching theme of the 'victory of the righteous over evil', achieved through extreme violence. However, Gandhi held the Gita in particular esteem, viewing it as an authentic religious text that resonated deeply with both the heart and the mind. He viewed the conflict in the Gita as a metaphor for inner human struggle. While he believed that knowledge of religious texts was important for students, he argued that mere awareness of scriptures and actual behaviour according to their teachings are two different things. This perspective troubled Hindutva zealots, who were accused of being anti-religion despite their claims of upholding and defending it.

We may overlook the fate of Buddhism, but are we not setting the stage to expel Gandhism from India?

A plaque at the Smriti, featuring paintings of Bapu by artist Upendra Maharathi, reads, 'After Buddha, Gandhi has been the greatest inspiration for artists in India.' This may be true, but what about the diminishing space for Gandhi in the current atmosphere? This decline can partly be attributed to the inherent rejection embedded in his views—rejection of divisiveness, inequality, and the exploitation of power—which conflicts with the ideologies gaining prominence today. Another significant reason is that his prominent followers did not match his stature of piety; instead, they displayed superficial harmony with him for their own agendas.

For example, Ghanshyam Das Birla, the prominent Indian industrialist, wrote to Gandhi from Pilani on 11 June 1924: '[Suppose] somebody kills another for the good of society, will that be an act of violence?'[5] This was in response to a letter Gandhi had sent him about non-violence. Birla's letter appears to be an attempt to engage with Gandhi to secure socio-economic benefits in the future. It seems that Birla, along with many others, failed to fully grasp the foundations of Gandhi's non-violence, despite being in close proximity to him for years. Such proximity was indeed a privilege, but it did not foster a genuine commitment to the principle of non-violence. In the end, there was hardly any leader around Gandhi who was truly aligned with him.

Gandhism was in danger even during Gandhi's lifetime, and the threat has deepened now. Successors of both crafty and self-styled Gandhians, as well as anti-Gandhians, have come together, creating a cacophony that drowns out his ideas.

If Gandhi were to vanish from India, there is a possibility that he might persist in an isolated corner as an incarnation of some god. For example, a family in a village in the Raigarh district of Chhattisgarh has had a statue of Gandhi in their home since 1957. Their ancestor, Nanhu Dai, was an MLA from Sarangarh. In Andhra Pradesh, farmers in a village in Srikakulam worship Gandhi during the kharif season. A temple dedicated to Gandhi was built by Hampanna Sahukar in a village in Yadgiri district, Karnataka, in 1948. The followers of Jatra Oraon, who led the Tana Bhagat Movement against land revenue in Ranchi district and was arrested by the British police, worship Gandhi in Ranchi, Lohardaga, and Gumla districts.

Such isolated instances, however, do not have a significant impact in a country where the names of many gods change every 200 km. The presence of statues of Gandhi or acts of worship towards him in some villages suggests that he holds the potential to be revered in a manner similar to divine incarnations.

The idea of Gandhi's vanishing reminds me of an incident in Jhansi where Bundelkhand University organized a book fair in March 2023. Pradeep Jain Aditya, a close associate of Rahul Gandhi, led a sit-in with his supporters, demanding the removal of Gopal Godse's book *Gandhi Vadh Kyon* (Why Gandhi Was Slain) from the fair. Aditya, who had been appointed as a minister of state for rural development in Manmohan Singh's second government with Rahul Gandhi's blessing, claimed that the book was banned. However, the ban on the book had been lifted two decades ago, and it sold over a hundred copies at the fair. Notably, Gandhi's *An Autobiography or The Story of My Experiments with Truth* was not available.

It was an open secret that the testimonies presented by the Godse brothers in court or in their writings to justify their act of killing Gandhi were scripted and re-scripted by others. Nevertheless, merely basking in the reflected glory of Bapu or suppressing a book or two authored by the Godses will not save Gandhi's legacy unless his ideology is actively invoked and practised.

The Congress Party today shows little genuine interest in Mahatma. Instead, it only evokes his assassination to extract as many electoral gains as possible.

The killers' purpose was fulfilled to some extent when they created a political illusion of anti-Muslim and anti-Pakistan sentiments within India's lifeline. Ironically, those who labelled themselves as Gandhians at that time were the ones who misused and abused his legacy. They have since grown in prominence.

The Hindu Mahasabha leaders advocated for a war against Muslims and Pakistan, believing that eliminating Gandhi was necessary to achieve their goals. The so-called followers of Gandhi, who acted as stooges, made their task easy.

Vincent Sheean, an American journalist, examined the assassination and stated that it was intended to remove an obstacle to war: 'It was thought by Godse and his fellow conspirators that only Gandhi was preventing war between India and Pakistan, a war which, they considered, India would inevitably win, thus reuniting the country by force.'[6]

We find ourselves in a similar situation, reviving this game after seven decades. Many are seeking pleasure in the miseries of Muslims and Pakistan. Anyone who is part of the social dynamics here, or a keen student, can uncover the vicious truth beneath the surface.

There is a shop in the Smriti where pocket watches, similar to the one Gandhi used to keep, and other items from power looms are sold. I attempted to interact with the saleswomen, telling them that the price of the watch (Rs 700), which was out of fashion, was too high for the common man. They looked at me blankly, as if they were not really present. I knew they were not responsible for setting the price. Whether animate or inanimate, everything in the Smriti seems to convey a numbing indifference. Someone later informed me that the price of the watch was Rs 250 before 2014.

There were also one or two tourist guides in the Smriti explaining to the students why Nathuram killed Bapu. 'Godse was angry with Gandhiji because he had agreed to India's partition. Gandhi and Godse were both patriots, but the latter believed the former was outdated and sought to advocate a second partition of the country,' one guide said.

The denouncement of Gandhi is not always unconscious or the result of ignorance. Sometimes, it is a carefully crafted plan, even at the cost of ridicule, which the rumourmongers do not mind. They believe in repeating a lie a hundred times to make it seem like the truth.

Manoj Sinha, lieutenant governor of Jammu and Kashmir and a follower of Hindutva ideology, stated in a programme in Gwalior on 23 March 2023, 'Few people know; even the educated people have the misconception that Gandhiji had a degree in law. Gandhiji didn't have any degree. However, nobody can say today that Gandhiji was not educated.'

Some people responded to the misinformation by sharing a letter of recommendation by D. Edward, a judicial officer at the Inns of Court, verifying Gandhi's law examination, as well as his certificate from the Bar at Inner Temple, London, on social media. Sinha may not have ever visited the Smriti or read Gandhi's *An Autobiography or The Story of My Experiments with Truth*, where Gandhi states, 'I passed my examination, was called to the bar on the 10th of June 1891, and enrolled in the High Court on the 11th.'[7] It is also possible that Sinha knew the truth but was instructed to spread the falsehood.

Gandhi arrived in London in September 1888 and returned in June 1891 but abandoned his legal career after two years when he found it 'immoral'.[8] He once said to Manu, his secretary, 'I regret having become a barrister, and if you believe me, I am not even conscious of being one.'[9] Nonetheless, the blabbermouths don't look beyond their targets. They are so focussed on sending their own messages that they do not entertain or accept others, making it impossible to correct them. They are boastful and poor listeners.

I felt a definite sense of sadness at the Smriti during both my visits, but the place was not entirely lifeless, perhaps because the labourers were constantly at work and one or two gardeners were busy decorating the greensward. Movement is important in a theatre.

Gandhi spent his last 144 days at the sprawling property of Ghanshyam Das. The place was previously known as Birla House. At the time, there were demands from some Hindus for him to stay in poorer localities where the most deprived people lived, who were also the worst victims of communal riots following India's partition. Gandhi explained to the poor riot victims why he was staying at the businessman's farmhouse. His excuse, albeit a weak one, is displayed on a wall at the Smriti. He said a friend had written to him that 'many poor people could not come to attend the prayers on the Birla House grounds'. Gandhi stated:

> They asked me why I was not staying at Bhangi Colony as before. I had given the reason on my arrival at Delhi … When I arrived … Delhi was like a dead city. The riots had just broken out and the Bhangi Colony was full of refugees. Sardar [Vallabhbhai] Patel therefore, had decided to put me up at the Birla House instead … My main object in staying in Delhi, is to give to the Muslims whatever comfort I can. That object was served better by my staying at the Birla House. Muslim friends felt safer in coming here than in poor quarters of Delhi. Moreover, it was much easier for the members of the cabinet to come to see me at the Birla House, as most of them were staying close by. They are very busy men and going to the Bhangi Colony could require much more time than coming to the Birla House.

Gandhi had stayed at 'Bhangi Nivas', a house in a slum, during the first week of May 1947. Maybe the Hindu victims of violence residing in poor colonies could have reached Gandhi at Bhangi Nivas in large numbers with their problems, which Mahatma wanted to avoid.

Incidentally, his use of the slang 'Bhangi' reminds me of Savarkar, who also used it casually in his prison diary. Gandhi freely used the word 'Bhangi' in his conversations at Bhangi Nivas with Manu and Rajendra Prasad.[10] Hindi scholars claim that it was the only term in use at that time and that Savarkar or Gandhi had little choice. However, it was not an acceptable term among the lowest castes.

Gandhi's last meeting was with Sardar Vallabhbhai Patel, who held the dual positions of deputy prime minister and home minister of India. They met from 4 p.m. to 5 p.m. on 30 January before Gandhi went to prayer. At 5.17 p.m., Nathuram Godse shot him in the chest and abdomen with a small black Beretta pistol.

Gandhi had been warned about the threat but he opposed frisking every visitor. Despite this, it is hard to reconcile the circumstances. Moreover, a teenage refugee from Pakistan had already demonstrated his intentions by exploding a bomb near Gandhi's prayer site ten days before Nathuram's final attempt to kill him.

Either Jawaharlal Nehru and Vallabhbhai Patel must have believed there was no serious threat to Gandhi's life or they were naïve given their new positions. Gandhi would not have feared death, but the lack of accountability from Nehru's government in addressing dangerous activities in Delhi and other parts of the country points to an unsettling oversight that we have often overlooked.

Nehru had been boastful just one day earlier when he had declared in Amritsar, 'We'll finish the Sangh at its root.' He was referring to the Rashtriya Swayamsevak Sangh (RSS), an offshoot of the Mahasabha.

Many ideologues and leaders of the RSS frequently cite this remark of Nehru, based on newspaper reports from the time, to highlight the first prime minister's intense animosity towards them. M.G. Vaidya, the first RSS spokesperson, once wrote: 'A thoughtless bullet from a pistol of Nathuram Godse killed Mahatma on January 30, 1948 and the then government got a God-given opportunity to malign, abuse and try to destroy [the Sangh].'[11]

A text-picture on the wall of the National Gandhi Museum, located near Rajghat about 20 km from Gandhi Smriti, reads: 'My head is reeling. And yet I must finish it . . . I am afraid I shall have to keep late hours today.' Gandhi told this to Abha, his walking stick. Finally, when Bapu rose to go to bed, he recited a verse by Nazir to her:

Hae bahar-e-bagh duniya chand roz
Dekh lo iska tamasha chand roz.
(The spring of the garden of the world lasts few days;
Watch its pomp while it ends.)

Gandhi completed the draft of a new constitution for the Congress Party during the night and handed it to his personal secretary, Pyarelal Nayyar, in the morning.

The constitution, published later as 'His Last Will and Testament', stated:

> [The] Congress in its present shape and form, i.e. as propaganda vehicle and parliamentary machine, has outlived its use . . . For these and other similar reasons, the A.I.C.C. resolves to disband the existing Congress organization and flower into a Lok Sevak Sangh [Public Servant's Organization].

He further added that a Congress worker should be 'a habitual wearer of Khadi' and 'a teetotaller'.[12]

Acharya Jugal Kishore, the then general secretary of the Congress and a confidant of Jawaharlal, claimed a few days after the Mahatma's assassination that he had only recommended certain changes to the party's constitution and never intended to dissolve it.

Gandhi placed great emphasis in the new organization's constitution on empowering villages through the panchayat system. However, when the Constituent Assembly debated the Constitution of India, Arun Chandra Guha of West Bengal pointed out:

> The learned Dr. Ambedkar in his long and learned speech has found no occasion to refer to Gandhiji or to the Congress . . . The Gandhian and the Congress outlook has been that the future constitution of India would be a pyramidal structure and its basis would be the village panchayats. According to Dr. Ambedkar, the villages have been the ruination of India, the villages have been the den of ignorance.[13]

Only nine months had passed since Gandhi's death. Nehru did not offer his views on this.

The Last Successful Failure

Hindi poet Harivansh Rai Bachchan shared his views after the Congress Party formed its government in most provinces in 1937. He believed that the Congress had gradually become disconnected from the masses and was making decisions unilaterally. The party later resigned in protest when Viceroy Lord Linlithgow involved India in the Second World War without consulting the Congress.

According to Bachchan, the Congress had 'started taking wrong steps from here', referring to the moment when the party resigned in protest. He saw Gandhi's non-cooperation and Satyagraha movements, which were initially mass movements, as having lost their momentum. Bachchan stated:

> They had called the entire country to take part in it and the countrymen participated ... The Individual Satyagraha [*Vyaktigat Satyagraha*] left the country alone. Didn't Gandhiji realize or accept that his grip over the masses was loosening? The Muslim League and the British government took advantage of it and consolidated themselves against the Congress.[14]

It was considered discourteous for believers in non-violence to say bluntly during Gandhi's time that he was failing in some way, but it was becoming increasingly evident.

Nirmal Kumar Bose, Gandhi's secretary in Noakhali and Patna, gently expressed that Bapu stood with the Muslims in Noakhali (now in Bangladesh) despite being insulted by those he was siding with.[15]

Bose recounted that Khalilur Rahman, a local Muslim leader, told Gandhi in the village of Devipur that the conversion of Hindus should not be taken seriously, as it was merely a ruse to save their lives. Gandhi was not convinced and asked Rahman whether saving a life by sacrificing faith was acceptable. Gandhi further added that 'as a religious preceptor, he had taught Hindus to lay down their lives for their faith, rather than give it up [out of] fear.' Gandhi grew impatient and, in an almost angry tone, told Rahman that if he ever met God, he would ask Him why someone with such views was ever made a religious preceptor. 'The divine became silent, and after an exchange of courtesies, left.'[16]

Gandhi's first journey to South Africa was one of self-discovery and the pursuit of truth within himself. A.W. Baker, a solicitor in Pretoria, attempted to persuade him to convert to Christianity. Gandhi countered by asking how he could join a new religion when he was completely ignorant of his own.

Earlier, when Dr Josiah Oldfield of Lady Margaret's Hospital in Bromley, London, asked Gandhi, 'Why not accept Christianity?' Gandhi replied, 'I would not care to study Christianity without having studied my own religion first.'[17]

Gandhi's spirituality was appealing, but it was not the case that all Muslims or all Hindus were willing to listen to him. While Gandhi appeared to lean towards the Muslims, they never fully accepted him as a Mahatma, partly because his approach was perceived as contrary to core Islamic practices.

Bose recalled how Muslims began opposing Gandhi's presence in Noakhali and demanded that he leave:

> Beginning from the chief minister [Huseyn Shaheed Suhrawardy] of Bengal down to the lowliest educated and politically conscious Muslims in Noakhali, everyone demanded that Gandhiji should go to Bihar and take up the

cause of the Muslim sufferers there if he were to prove his claim of impartiality.[18]

There were many factors contributing to the growing hatred between Hindus and Muslims, which eventually culminated in communal violence. One incident involved Kshitish Babu, a schoolteacher from Lamchar, Noakhali, who allegedly called a Class 7 student 'haramjada' (bastard). Maulvi Syed Golam Sarowar Husseini, a local Muslim League MLA, agitated against this incident. Many similar occurrences were reported in the area in 1939.

As the Congress Party did nothing to protect the Hindus in the district, its leaders began to join the Hindu Mahasabha out of frustration.

The simmering discontent erupted into full-fledged violence seven years later when Sarowar delivered a violent, anti-Hindu speech at Begumganj Bazar. He quoted verses from the Quran and incited the crowd to kill the kafirs. 'This was followed by violent assaults of Muslim mobs on Hindu properties, the killings of hundreds of Hindus and the rape of their women.'[19]

Gandhi had gone to Noakhali at the personal request of Muriel Lester, a journalist and his old Quaker friend. She had informed Gandhi that she had 'met Hindu widows who watched their husbands being butchered by Muslims' and that 'before their husbands could be cremated, those widows were dragged off to be "converted" and "married" to the same killers'.[20]

Mentioning such details is painful, but it is necessary to understand the context, as the seeds of Gandhi's assassination were sown there. This seed was planted in several locations over many decades, including London in 1909 when Madanlal Dhingra assassinated Sir William Hutt Curzon Wyllie, an apolitical aide-de-camp for Lord George Hamilton and secretary of state for India. Gandhi condemned the assassination in harsher terms than Sultan Mohammed Shah Aga Khan III, the forty-eighth imam of Nizari Ismaili sect.

Gandhi drew the attention of those who worshipped violence in Britain and India by calling Curzon's murder 'most detestable'. Savarkar openly protested any condemnation of the killing at a memorial service convened by Aga Khan III in London.

Opposed by the Muslim leaders of Bengal, Gandhi travelled from Noakhali to Bihar. Many historians believe that his presence in Noakhali helped bring the two hostile communities together. This view stems from Gandhi's success in uniting poor Hindus and Muslims at his rural meetings, where they gathered around him and shared the stories of massacres. His ability to listen patiently to the people likely had a positive impact. However, the story of his struggles for acceptance in the region remains of great interest to researchers. Bose states:

> The opposition to Gandhiji's stay in Noakhali began to take a vulgar turn towards the end of February 1947. The roads over which he walked from village to village were deliberately dirtied every day, while Muslim audiences began to boycott his meetings.[21]

Gandhi was resolute, having already embraced self-mortification, but he was apprehensive about the threat to his life. He confided to Manu while travelling from Patna to Delhi in a third-class train compartment on his way to meet Mountbatten, 'When I decided to go to Noakhali, I had resolved to do or die there and had sent away all my companions. But I allowed you to join me in this sacrifice.'[22]

Back in Delhi, no one was concerned about his life or death but required his consent for the partition of British India. They knew that Mountbatten was the key to bringing Gandhi back.

On 17 July, Jawaharlal and Jinnah, the premiers-in-waiting of to-be-carved-out India and Pakistan, respectively, approved Mountbatten's proposal. Gandhi 'realized too late that his closest comrades and disciples were more interested in power than principles, and his own vision had long been clouded by the illusion that the struggle he led for India's freedom was a nonviolent one'.[23]

It was widely believed that Mountbatten followed the advice of Nehru, his friend V.K. Krishna Menon and Lady Edwina. 'They all agreed that Gandhi was a saint, but saints should never indulge in practical politics or govern a nation …'[24]

Gandhi knew he had created something remarkably significant in his quest for freedom and unity. He was aware that his efforts would remain etched in public memory for a long time. Though he was not blind or weak within, there were times when he felt helpless.

Reflecting on the unregulated enrolment of volunteers in the Congress Party, Gandhi noted that even criminals had joined its ranks. He preferred to reject success achieved through wrongful means, such as violence, and advocated for combating evil with compassion. However, he also admitted, 'We would have failed to enrol even one man or woman if we had expected them to follow the norms of non-violence the way I follow.'[25]

Despite this, he observed that the number of 'goons' was less than those genuinely committed to the freedom movement. This was possible because of the principle of non-violence adopted by the Congress Party, which aligned with the sentiments of the masses.

'The rise of goondaism is a warning for all of us to be alert and look for its remedies. The only way I find is to follow the principle of non-violence with total discipline,' he wrote in *Young India* on 7 May 1931.

'A non-violent struggle can be taken forward with the help of just one satyagrahi and can't continue with the support of even lakhs of non-satyagrahi,' Gandhi stated in the same publication.

The positive impact of Gandhi's struggles became evident much later in Noakhali.

Gandhi travelled from house to house and village to village in Noakhali, meeting people, listening to them and encouraging them to abandon anger and embrace empathy. Occasionally, he asked Manu to sing '"*Vaishnavajana to tene kahiye*" substituting Christianjana, Parsijana, Sikhajana, Muslimjana and Harijanjana for Vaishnavajana in the repetition of the first line, and he too joined in the song'.[26]

However, some, like Rahman, did not understand this message and believed they could deceive Gandhi. Many perpetrators saw Bapu's efforts as a sign of weakness and continued to engage in violence.

However, the Ambika Kalinga Charitable Trust, founded in 1946, was renamed the Gandhi Ashram Trust in 1975. This change indicated that some people in Noakhali still cherished Gandhi's memory, even after more than three decades. Whether they followed his teachings, however, was a different matter.

Back in Delhi, Gandhi held interfaith prayers, during which passages from the Quran were recited. On one occasion, a youth shouted, 'Stop it', and then chanted, 'Victory to Hinduism'. The police intervened and removed him.[27] This incident became a recurring disruption at his prayers.

Gandhi realized, after boarding the train at Patna railway station, that Manu had secured an additional compartment from the government to prepare his food. He scolded her and instructed the stationmaster at the next stop to make the compartment available to general passengers.

Manu wrote:

> He looked out of the window and asked me to look also. I sensed that I had committed some mistake. I looked out and saw passengers hanging on to the footboards. I got a gentle rebuke. 'Did you ask for this second compartment?' he questioned me. 'Yes, Bapu,' I replied. 'I asked for it as I thought you would be disturbed by my heating the milk on the primus, cleaning the vessels, etc.
>
> Bapu dubbed it a 'lame excuse' and said, 'This is what is called blind [undiscerning] love. You do know that to save me from trouble the government offered me a special train if I did not want to go by plane. How many trains would be held up and what a lot it would cost to run a special train? How can I tolerate it? I am very cost minded. You asked only for a second compartment, but had you asked for a saloon you would surely have got it.
>
> 'Now the only way of repentance is to remove all the luggage into this compartment and to request the station-master to see me at the next station,' Bapu told her.[28]

There are many such captivating stories about Gandhi, but his stay at Syed Mahmud's palace and his meeting with Abdul Aziz, an ailing Muslim League leader in Patna, led to some Hindus becoming disenchanted with him.

On 1 March 1947, Bose recorded an interaction between Gandhi and an interviewer. When asked how victims could forgive perpetrators after losing their loved ones, Gandhi responded that Bihar had been more severely affected than Noakhali:

> Did they want Muslims to take dire vengeance for the Hindu atrocities there? [. . .] From this, they should learn to forget and forgive if they do not wish to descend to the lowest depths of barbarity. Bravery refuses to strike; it would suffer all infliction with patient cheerfulness.[29]

In recent years, some leaders have urged people not to buy from Muslim stalls or shops. This sentiment has roots in a past where Muslims were accused of killing Hindu men, abducting their women, forcibly converting them to Islam and boycotting Hindu traders. Additionally, Muslim labourers refused to work in Hindus' fields.

When Gandhi toured Raipur in Noakhali, he advised that violence or boycotts were isolated incidents and should be forgotten, suggesting that the government should address such issues.[30] After Independence and the Partition, when Muslims in Delhi reported similar incidents, Gandhi promptly referred them to ministers for resolution.[31]

Some senior leaders critically analysed Gandhi's actions and awaited his downfall. Mukund Ramrao Jayakar, a Congress-Swaraj-Party-Hindu Mahasabha leader from Bombay, claimed that Gandhi's 'theories threw apples of discord'. He further added:

> Types of vituperation, personal invective, unjust judgments, wild scandalmongering were invented, the likes of which had hardly been seen before. Newspapers and journals, professing sympathy with Gandhi's doctrine, hurled denunciation at his critics, full of the grossest falsehoods and malignant lies; and Gandhi had frankly to confess his impotence to check this undergrowth of venal and abusive journalism.[32]

Jayakar believed Gandhi's decline began after the Second Round Table Conference and noted that British leaders were apprehensive that 'Gandhi was perhaps a Mussolini, a Lenin or a Hitler'. They found him 'politically vague, spiritually obscurantist, nothing difficult to manage'. Jayakar, an admirer of Savarkar, tried to diminish Gandhi's contribution by asserting that 'Gujeratis' claimed 'Gujerat would win freedom for India'.[33]

The ideas of Savarkar or Godse were already influencing attitudes around Gandhi before and after Partition. Some protesters maintained respect for Gandhi, but many did not. Gandhi often ignored or dismissed such disrespect, relying on his personal tendency to discount others' views or suppress them with the force of his intellectual authority.

Jayakar was not the only prominent figure trying to undermine Gandhi's ideas and revive the Poona School of thought, which had been propounded by Bal Gangadhar Tilak as a form of radical nationalism. Narhar Vishnu Gadgil, a public works minister in Nehru's government, openly expressed his disdain for Gandhi. He couldn't hide his anger toward Gandhi when given the opportunity to write about governance. He noted that the mosques left behind by

Muslims who migrated to Pakistan were 'occupied by many refugee Hindus' and 'the Muslims went on agitating for her evacuation …' The victims of Partition and the riots were 'squatting in filthy tents near gutters and in slums …'[34]

Gandhi began fasting on 13 January 1948 to advocate for aid to Pakistan. Five days later, over one hundred leaders—from Nehru and Patel to Abdul Kalam Azad and Prasad, along with the heads of every party in Delhi—signed a seven-point declaration in Hindi and Urdu. According to Gadgil, they promised to 'live in Delhi like brothers and in perfect amity', taking 'the pledge that we shall protect life, property and faith of Muslims', but he also criticized the consequences of Gandhi's actions, stating, 'We paid fifty crores of rupees to Pakistan because of Gandhiji's fast, although Pakistan owed us three hundred crores. Our philosophy is one-sided goodness. We don't believe in tit for tat, but in pat for tat.'

Gadgil further claimed that it was because of gestures like these by Gandhi that Madanlal Kashmirilal Pahwa threw a bomb at one of his prayer meetings. Muslims in Delhi would attend Gandhi's prayer at Birla House, and instead of participating, they would narrate 'exaggerated tales of injustices done to them, and Gandhiji would send them to us'—the ministers—to help them.[35]

As Gandhi was brought to the elevated platform in Birla's garden two days later, he said, 'I have no doubt that one who is an enemy of the Muslims is also an enemy of India.' A bomb exploded about fifty yards away from him, causing part of a wall to collapse. Fortunately, no one was hurt. Gandhi urged the people to remain seated. The next day, he remarked, 'I believe that Rama is my only protector. If he wants to end my life, nobody can save me even if a million men were posted to guard me.'[36]

After his arrest, Pahwa told the police that he didn't like Gandhi's talk of a truce between Hindus and Muslims. His friends—Godse, Narayan Dattatraya Apte, Gopal and Digambar Ramchandra Badge—were present at Birla House during the explosion but managed to slip away unnoticed.

It was not the first time Gandhi left everything to Rama. As a child, he had relied on the gods when he feared ghosts and spirits. However, after his assassination, his words were twisted to suggest that his death was inevitable.

By then, Gandhi's votaries, who had become powerful political leaders, were well aware that Hindu communalism was in opposition to the Muslim League. During the last two years of his life, Gandhi faced daily opposition from both sides, as neither was averse to using violence to achieve their goals.

On one occasion, Gandhi acknowledged this tension, saying that he would ask 'those who were against his holding the prayer meeting not to come or if they did, they should come by themselves and kill him if they wanted to'.[37]

Bapu had once expressed his desire to live for a century and a quarter, but in 1947, he told his associates that he had lost all interest in such a long life due to the continuous conflicts surrounding him.

The government had either become indifferent or concluded that the old man was irrelevant, having lost political significance after Partition and the formation of the new government. Whatever their reasoning, the reality was that nothing was done on the ground to prevent the act of terrorism against a lonely symbol of non-violence.

The way substantial room has been created over the last two decades for Savarkar to re-emerge makes many of us question who the true visionary was. Was it really Gandhi? Or was he destined for martyrdom, leaving the nation in the hands of those whom Nehru, Patel, and the Congress Party blamed for his death?

The gate of the Smriti and the remaining part of Birla House, still known by that name, stand side by side. When I visited the Smriti, I tried peering through the gaps between the locked gates of the milky-white bungalow, which showed no signs of life, except for a peacock perched on the terrace railing. When I revisited the place, the peacock was also gone.

A few days before my first visit to the Smriti, I was standing at a tea stall in Lucknow with some friends, discussing Gandhi, when a man in his early thirties, dressed in a navy-blue suit, suddenly shouted, 'No, please, no Gandhi.'

Amused, I asked the man, who looked like a corporate executive, 'Do you dislike Gandhi?' His response reminded me of my experience at the hotel in Kushinagar, where the staff seemed reluctant to allow Indians into the same restaurant as foreign guests. Perhaps this was because they resented those who had expelled Buddha from India. Similarly, this man seemed intent on pushing Gandhi out.

There was tension on his face. 'I don't like him. He agreed to create Pakistan. I like Modi, who wants to capture Pakistan and make it part of India again.'

I responded, 'Sir, Modi unexpectedly turned his prime ministerial aircraft toward Lahore to celebrate Nawaz Sharif's birthday. What do you think about that?'

I further explained how on his way back from a two-day trip to Russia, Modi broke all protocols and diverted his official IAF Boeing 737 to Lahore's Allama Iqbal International Airport on 25 December 2015. From there, he took a helicopter to Raiwind, on the outskirt of the city, where the then Pakistani prime minister's bungalow was located.

'*Mard hai wah* [He is a real man],' the man replied angrily, moving his right hand adorned with a golden bracelet. 'He is planning to assimilate Pakistan into India. He will correct Gandhi's mistakes.'

He finished his tea, glanced at the tea stall keeper, and said, '*Likh lena* [note it down].'

Then he left, despite my desire to engage with him further. From the reactions around us, I realized he had suddenly gained many admirers.

India had already begun to unlearn Gandhi soon before Independence, but in the last two decades, it has become fashionable to embrace ideological emptiness. We have not only failed to learn how to question our democracy but also become incapable of criticizing our heroes in the flesh due to our contempt for learning. Instead, we have learned to abuse both our democracy and our heroes at the slightest conflict of opinion or due to our own deep ignorance or the shifting political discourse. It didn't happen overnight. It unfolded with the rise of political ambition in the *soi-disant* Gandhians.

Bose, the secretary of Mahatma in the 1940s, was arguably the first to publish a book that detailed Gandhi's controversial experiment with brahmacharya (celibacy), making it easier for the Mahatma's critics to attack him. Yet, he still held the highest regard for Bapu. He wrote: 'Gandhi's life had been like the Ganges in its influence upon the life of India ... And the river of life which Gandhi represented had its origin in the heights of the Indian Himalayas.'[38]

Today, we can see with our own eyes and fully grasp the truth in Mountbatten's words. He was right when he suggested that Gandhi's assassination was a mockery of India's freedom. In a radio broadcast on Gandhi's special day of mourning, he said:

> The death of Mahatma Gandhi came with the shock of a personal bereavement to millions of people in every part of the civilized world ... Gandhiji, the man of peace, the apostle of Ahimsa, died by violence, as a martyr in the struggle against fanaticism—that deadly disease that has threatened to make mockery of Indian freedom.[39]

The Mahatma had experienced failure before. He had withdrawn his Non-Cooperation Movement after the Chauri Chaura incident. In response, leaders like C.R. Das, Motilal Nehru, Srinivasa Iyengar, and others advocated entering the legislative council as a strategy to obstruct the British government from within. One such proposal by Das was defeated at the Gaya session of the Congress. However, Das eventually formed the Congress-Khilafat Swarajya Party on 1 January 1923, with Motilal as its secretary. Narasimha Chintaman Kelkar, Suhrawardy, and Subhas Chandra Bose were among its leaders. Gandhi never supported this idea, but his views were ultimately ignored.

The Swarajya Party was formed despite the apprehension of many leaders that it would disintegrate the Congress. Acharya Kripalani, Congress president in 1946 and 1947, noted that some leaders' decision to enter the council was seen by many as a threat to the unity of the Congress.

While Das, Motilal, and Vithalbhai discarded Gandhi's core ideas and sought a larger political influence in government, the Congress remained committed to its policy of non-violence and non-co-operation. They also resolved to continue boycotting the legislatures.

A special session of Congress was called in Delhi in the third week of September 1923, with Maulana Abul Kalam Azad as president. Here, the pro-changers, the Swarajists, seemed to have won their point. But, at the annual session in Cocanada in December 1923, under the presidency of Mahomed Ali, the Congress re-endorsed the policy of non-co-operation, reaffirming the decision to boycott the legislatures. The Swarajists then organized themselves into a party within the Congress and contested elections with resounding success. Kripalani further observed that Gandhi could sense the crisis in the party and eventually mellowed down a bit to keep the flock together.[40]

He wrote:

> He was unwilling to express any view without first discussing the matter with the leaders of the Swarajya Party. In Young India he merely expressed the view that his faith in the old programme was unshaken. He met Motilal and Das towards the end of May 1924. Neither party could convince the other.[41]

In the last week of June, Gandhi convened a meeting of the All-India Congress Committee (AICC) in Ahmedabad, where a resolution was passed requiring elected members to donate ten tolas of self-spun yarn in lieu of the annual party fee of four annas. Kriplani stated, 'The other resolution sought to debar those who did not believe in the policy of boycott of courts and legislatures ... These resolutions were strongly objected to by the Swarajists. Led by Motilal and Das, they walked out of the AICC.'[42]

The situation changed quickly after the death of Das in June 1925. Motilal returned to the Congress, and Gandhi relaxed the rules he had set for the party's office bearers. He also agreed to provide better representation for the Swarajists in Congress.

Frankenstein's Monster

Mountbatten, Nehru, and Patel arrived at the Smriti soon after Gandhi was killed. Mountbatten suggested preserving his body, similar to Vladimir Lenin's. His son, Devdas, supported the governor-general's idea, but Pyarelal insisted that Gandhi's last wish was to be cremated immediately after his death. Despite his alleged bias towards a particular community, Bapu, the ardent Hindu, practised his faith both in life and in death.

In 1927, a friend asked Gandhi why the majority of Indian students in schools were unfamiliar with Hinduism and the Bhagavad Gita, given the claim that India was a spiritually advanced nation. Bapu rigidly supported religious education, even though it wasn't widely reflected in everyday life.

Nathuram had read religious texts, but he adopted the myopic politics of religion and caste that India embraced before independence, accepting it as his superiors interpreted. His vision was blurred, and his actions and words suggested he couldn't differentiate between criticism and diatribes. This mindset became more prevalent among a segment of the population with the rise of right-wing movements across the country.

Jawaharlal and other followers of Gandhi were distant from such discussions. Their politics left no corner for spirituality or religion, leaving Gandhi isolated.

Nehru sometimes appeared critical of Gandhi, seemingly for the sake of being critical. However, his autobiography reads like the story of his closeness to Gandhi and his prominent presence in Gandhi's life. He was sending a message to the masses that he was aligned with the political Gandhi. Nehru wrote his autobiography while in prison, and it was first published in 1936. Gandhi was among the first to read it. In the book, Nehru conveyed that, despite not always understanding or agreeing with Gandhi, he never felt uncomfortable following him.

Godse, along with his mentors and colleagues, was partly religious, partly political, but entirely pro-violence. Their belief taught them to eliminate those they criticized. They failed to distinguish between passion and patricide, with their sense of judgment between good and bad buried in a fit of rage.

Even Savarkar acknowledged the philistine attitude within his group. At the twenty-first Mahasabha session in Calcutta, he said:

> It has come to my notice that a very large section of English-educated Hindus hold back from joining the Hindu Mahasabha [and they are] totally unconcerned about it under the erroneous idea that it is an exclusively religious organization, something like a Christian Mission. Nothing could be far from the truth.[43]

Savarkar was actually referring to those with a balanced education, something his own team lacked, as they were devoid of argumentative ideas. He failed to understand that a truly balanced or scientific education would reject the notion of killing.

Gandhi might have lived a few more years and died a natural death if his assassins had an education that guided their minds in the right direction. However, we often shy away from admitting that Gandhi might also have survived if Nehru's government hadn't mishandled the incidents leading up to his murder.

Jawaharlal shouldn't be excused by his statement:

> As for Gandhiji himself, he was a very difficult person to understand; sometimes his language was almost incomprehensible to an average modern person. But we felt we knew him well enough to realize that he was a great and unique man and a glorious leader, and having put our faith in him, we gave him an almost blank cheque, for the time being at least.[44]

It was not because Gandhi was 'incomprehensible'; it was because Nehru was indecisive. He couldn't determine whether he was making a comical error by aligning with Gandhi or if he was shaping his political career. What exactly was he trying to achieve by giving Gandhi a blank cheque?

Did Nehru believe that the rise of the Mahasabha signalled the end of his own political prominence, which led him to stick with Gandhi? Or was he carefully manoeuvring against the Mahasabha to please both the educated elite and the poor, who supported Gandhi? Did he trust Bapu's method of silence to frustrate such elements? Ultimately, did he or his colleagues, in the process, hasten Gandhi's end?

When Madan Mohan Malaviya invited Nehru in 1933 to address the students at Banaras Hindu University, he targeted the Hindutva party because he felt that 'the new aggressive leaders of the Mahasabha had pushed him [Malaviya] out'.[45] Nehru's excuse for attacking the Mahasabha was not entirely honest, as he knew Malaviya's rigid rightist ideology. He targeted the Mahasabha because he saw it as a possible political obstacle to his success in the future. The fact remains that Malaviya's sons and grandson have also adhered to the same ideology. Although he distanced himself from the organization after becoming involved in the affairs of BHU, he did not abandon the ideology. Malaviya later played a significant role in establishing the RSS in the heartland.

Nehru attacked the Mahasabha with intense political bitterness. The Mahasabha was not particularly strong, but Nehru also fostered an opposition within it, ultimately creating a problem of his own making, a Frankenstein's monster.

Surprisingly, Bhai Parmanand, president of the Hindu Mahasabha from 1933 to 1934, was never a staunch critic of Gandhi. In fact, he leaned towards Gandhi, as reflected in his memoir, *The Story of My Life*. He also exchanged cordial letters with Nehru, for whom political survival was more important than Gandhi.

This situation recalls the year 2000, when K.S. Sudarshan became the RSS sarsanghchalak, while Atal Bihari Vajpayee of the BJP served as the prime minister. The RSS created an illusion of opposition to the BJP by criticizing it for delays in constructing the Ram temple at Ayodhya. Nehru's history, as this book describes, is filled with instances of his proximity to Hindutva leaders. However, every hero needs an antagonist, and Nehru lacked a strong political rival that could generate sympathy for him across India. This could be one of the reasons why he chose to continuously target an organization with pan-India presence but which was relatively weak in strength, in order to maintain his image as a hero.

Balakrishnan Shivram Moonje made significant efforts to revive the Mahasabha and later supported the RSS with the goal of promoting militarization. His ambition to transform India—a country of farmers—into a militarized society led him to serve as a medical officer in the British forces during the Boer War in South Africa, driven by a clear ideological direction. He even met Benito Mussolini in Italy to study the militarization of society. As noted, 'It was he who gave the momentum to the thought of the Indianization of the Army in India.'[46]

Later, Nehru targeted the RSS for the same reasons he had previously criticized the Mahasabha. While neither the Mahasabha nor the RSS posed a serious challenge to the Congress at that time, it was evident even to Nehru's critics that these organizations had the potential to grow and eventually challenge the largest political party of the time. However, the reality on the ground was not as appealing as he portrayed it.

By 1933, the Mahasabha had been relegated to the margins, and the RSS was still in its infancy. Nehru kept both organizations in the limelight through his speeches, aware that several offshoots had emerged due to the weakening of the Mahasabha, first under Savarkar, and then under Syama Prasad Mookerjee, who became its head in 1942 and later served as the industry and supply minister in Nehru's interim government.

It suited the politics of the Congress Party to view the Mahasabha and its affiliates in isolation, preventing a comprehensive discussion of the truth. More precisely, it is a historic fact that the Congress Party effectively gave birth to the Mahasabha with the emergence of the Muslim League.

The movement against the first partition of Bengal was launched in 1905, and in October 1906, the British government sent a Muslim delegation, known as the Shimla Deputation, led by Aga Khan III. They met with the then viceroy, Lord Minto, and demanded a separate Muslim electorate and representation in the viceroy's council. The idea of a Muslim party was first proposed in Dhaka in 1905 and was formally established there as the All India Muslim League in 1906.

In response, Lala Lalchand convened a Hindu convention in Lahore in 1907 and co-founded the Punjab Hindu Sabha with U.N. Mukerji in 1909. Both were closely associated with the Arya Samaj and active in the Congress. They wanted the Congress to form Hindu committees without delay.

Malaviya organized the first meeting of the Hindu Mahasabha in Allahabad in 1910 under the aegis of the Congress. He remained a prominent member of both the Congress and the Mahasabha throughout his life. The organization's name was changed to Sarvadeshak Hindu Sabha in 1915 and to Akhil Bharatiya (Bharat) Hindu Mahasabha in a meeting held in Haridwar in 1918–19. L. Sukhvir Singh served as its general secretary, and Pandit Dev Ratan Sharma was the secretary. Sharma had attended the Congress session in Lucknow in 1916 and was disillusioned by the pact between the Congress Party and the Muslim League.

The Mahasabha established branches across the country in the following years but had only a handful of supporters.

Most of its activities were confined to Poona, Bombay, and Nasik during the 1930s under the supervision of Moonje. He was a member of both the Congress and the Mahasabha until Tilak's death.

The condition of the Mahasabha is reflected in the words of Vijay Kumar Pujari, a prominent member and leader within the organization, who was eager to revive the group in the mid-1940s:

> There is a mountain of works before the Hindu Mahasabha. But the Hindu Mahasabha of today doesn't have energy to lift this mountain... The Mahasabha should oppose the government, the Congress and the [Muslim] League regularly. A strong organization is required for this work.[47]

He added that the 'Hindu public has never lagged behind in supporting a karmyogi' and so the Mahasabha can become an 'effective organization' when its leaders 'jump in the karmashetra'.[48]

The crisis Pujari referred to was due to Savarkar overshadowing everything in the Mahasabha, including both its overt and covert activities. The conspiracy against Gandhi was only one of the issues that came to public knowledge.

The poor public perception of the Mahasabha leaders is evident from Gadgil's reaction. He expressed his surprise when his friend informed him that Nathuram Godse had shot Gandhi. Gadgil remarked, 'Jedhe was informed that Godse was given a ceremonial send-off from Poona when he left for Delhi. I said that he should have told me earlier.'[49]

Gadgil had expected the killer to be a refugee from Pakistan. Keshavrao Marutrao Jedhe was a peasant leader who intermittently aligned himself with the Congress.

A Savarkar or a Godse emerges not only from a lack of proper education but also from feeling helpless in the face of someone whose influence is too great for their voices to be heard. Nehru was adept at exploiting this dynamic. He did so effectively from behind Gandhi's politeness, which was more acceptable to the masses than any of Gandhi's more vocal denigrators or acolytes.

Gandhi's critics initially sought to undermine his stature to bring him down to a level where he could be compared with his flaccid critics. To this end, they tried various tactics. One such tactic involved a false report that appeared in a section of the press during Gandhi's participation in the Second Round Table Conference. The report claimed that 'Gandhiji has got huge funds, running into millions of pounds, secretly deposited with friends, and the Congress is after this money. It [the Congress] is afraid that if Gandhiji retires from its membership it might lose these hoards.'[50]

Further, Nehru mentioned a report by Glorney Bolton in his book, noting that the leaders in Mooltan, the ferry, 'knew that there was a conspiracy against Mr Gandhi within the Congress Working Committee'.[51]

He was referring to Tej Bahadur Sapru and Jayakar, who were fellow travellers with Gandhi. Sapru was briefly associated with the Congress but later joined the Indian National Liberal Federation and the Mahasabha. Occasionally, he would also work with Gandhi.

Bolton, the author–journalist and fellow passenger, stated, 'They [Sapru and Jayakar] never disguised the fact that Mr Gandhi was in their words, "muddle-headed". It was worth winning a "muddle-headed" leader when he could bring with him a million "muddle-headed" followers.'[52]

All their attempts to undermine Gandhi failed over the years. The final effort was to prove that Gandhi was behind the creation of Muslim Pakistan and that their demand for a Hindu India was being overlooked.

At the nineteenth Hindu Mahasabha session in Ahmedabad, Savarkar said, 'Let us bravely face unpleasant facts as they are. India cannot be assumed today to be a Unitarian and homogeneous nation but on the contrary, these are two nations in the main, the Hindus and the Muslims in India.'[53]

When the Congress interpreted this remark as Savarkar's acceptance of the two-nation theory, Ambedkar took responsibility for defending the Mahasabha leader. He explained:

> Although there are two nations in India, India shall not be divided into two parts, one for the Muslims and the other for the Hindus; that the two nations shall dwell in one country and shall live under the mantle of one single Constitution; that the Constitution shall be such that the Hindu nation will be enabled to occupy a predominant position that is due to it and the Muslim nation made to live in the position of subordinate co-operation with the Hindu nation.[54]

Earlier, Ambedkar shared an interesting figure presented by the secretary of state for India before the House of Commons. According to this figure, the Indian Army constituted of 50 per cent Hindus and Gurkhas, 34 per cent Muslims, 10 per cent

Sikhs, and 6 per cent Christians.[55] Ambedkar noted that while this was a wartime composition, the Muslims proportion in peacetime was 'somewhere in the neighbourhood of 50 per cent'.[56] The Dalit thinker explained, 'Mr Savarkar does not admit that the Hindu Mahasabha has started to counteract the Muslim League.'[57]

Assuming that Hindustan (United India) would be an independent nation, Ambedkar quoted Savarkar, 'The Moslem minority in India will have the right to be treated as equal citizens, enjoying equal protection and civic rights in proportion to their population.'[58] It seemed strange why Ambedkar elaborated on Savarkar, who supported Hindu dominance in which one caste was considered superior to another.

Ambedkar found 'frankness' and 'boldness' in Savarkar's theory compared to the 'irregularity' and 'vagueness' that characterized the 'Congress declaration about minority rights'. He wrote, 'Mr Savarkar's scheme has at least the merit of telling the Muslims, thus far and no further.' After explaining Savarkar's position, Ambedkar also called Savarkar's theory 'illogical' and 'most dangerous'.[59]

In the introduction to his book *Pakistan or the Partition of India*, Ambedkar wrote, 'I have an open mind, though not an empty mind.' However, it is clear that he preferred Savarkar over the Congress. In a lengthy lecture at Columbia University in 1916, Ambedkar didn't mention India's slavery but focussed on the freedom of scheduled castes from oppression.

Gandhi never created any confusion regarding the concept of two nations or two communities within one or two countries. He consistently opposed the partition and was often heard saying it would be done 'over my dead body'.[60]

The creation of Pakistan was essentially a negation of Gandhi's principle of non-violence. Gandhi once addressed the question of Pakistan:

> [If] someone asked him under threat of violence to admit such a claim … he would ask the aggressor what was really meant by the demand and, if he were really satisfied that it was something worth striving for, then he would have no hesitation in proclaiming from the housetop that the demand was just.… [However, he would] offer non-violent resistance … if the demand were backed by force.[61]

Nothing extraordinary occurred except for the Great Rajputana Famine when Gandhi was born to Karamchand Gandhi, the prime minister of the princely state of Porbandar in the Kathiawar sub-province of Gujarat, and his wife, Putlibai. Being from the Bania caste, Mohandas' parents followed Jainism within the Hindu religion. He was the youngest of three brothers and a sister.

His elder brother Lakshmidas held an Indian law degree and joined Porbandar's financial services. His second brother, Karsandas, served in the police force in Rajkot. The family moved to Rajkot when Mohandas was seven. After studying in a vernacular school until the age of ten, he enrolled in Rajkot's Kathiawar High School (also known as Alfred High School) for matriculation. He married Kasturba, the daughter of Porbandar merchant Gokuldas Makanji, at the age of eleven.

After matriculation and a brief period of disillusionment at Samaldas College, Bhavnagar, Gandhi travelled to Tilbury Docks on the Thames in Southampton, London, to pursue a law degree. He completed his studies, attempted to practise at Bombay High Court for two years, and then left for South Africa in 1893 to handle business cases for Dada Abdullah and Company. Abdullah was a wealthy Gujarati merchant in Natal, a former province. The first case was against Dada Abdullah's merchant cousin, Tyeb Haji Khan Muhammad, in Pretoria, Transvaal. During his journey from Durban to Pretoria, Gandhi experienced the famous incident where a white man and a railway guard threw him off the first-class compartment at Pietermaritzburg.

Gandhi returned to Bombay in 1896 and stayed there for a few months before Dada Abdullah called him back. He went to South Africa with his wife and sons Harilal and Manilal. Ramdas and Devdas were born there. He returned to India on 9 January 1915 after his successful integration into public life in South Africa.

A close examination of history suggests that India's journey from Nehru to Modi represents an odyssey from the first to the second death of Gandhi. Gandhi was assassinated during Nehru's tenure as prime minister. While Gandhi had faced critics in past, it is only since Modi became prime minister that he has faced a massive onslaught from Hindutva forces.

Gandhi shaped Nehru into an educated, polished, and ambitious leader, balancing various extremes—intellectual and practical, right and left, communists and capitalist, and even Gandhism and Savarkarism, or Gandhi and Godse.

While Gandhi was ideologically rigid in his personal life, casting aside his own son, Harilal, at the slight deviation, he mentored Nehru, who was also under the care of his father, Motilal Nehru.

Bapu had no qualms about taking Nehru under his wing at Motilal's request, even though Motilal led an Anglicized lifestyle that included drinking. Gandhi, on the other hand, had told Harilal that it was better to die than to consume alcohol. When Harilal informed him that a doctor had recommended limited doses of liquor, Gandhi's stance remained uncompromising.

Gandhi justified his preference for Nehru over his own son by stating, 'A disciple is more than a son. Discipleship is a second birth. It is a voluntary surrender.'[62]

The truth remains that a guru is nobody without a disciple, and every disciple in the making seeks a guru.

It was a unique time. Whether guru or disciple, leader or follower, they all knew they were part of a history that would never be forgotten. It was no coincidence that many prominent leaders of the time—Bal Gangadhar Tilak, Gandhi, Savarkar, Nehru, Aga Khan III, and Jayakar—were writing essays, autobiographies, and memoirs. They were aware that they were part of a great historical narrative and sought to immortalize themselves as key figures.

The journey of most of these leaders from death to prominence began soon after they were gone. But Savarkar remained largely forgotten or dormant until the late 1990s, when Vajpayee, an RSS swayamsewak, became prime minister of India. He and his party members began frequently mentioning the Hindutva icon in their speeches. In 2003, towards the end of his tenure, Vajpayee placed a portrait of Savarkar in the Central Hall of Parliament, directly opposite Gandhi's portrait.

Under Modi, Savarkar's legacy reached the masses. During his speech from the ramparts of the Red Fort on the seventy-fifth anniversary of India's independence, Modi mentioned Savarkar alongside Gandhi, Subhas Chandra Bose, and Ambedkar.

Nehru knew how to immortalize himself. With several books already to his credit, he also initiated the trend of portrait politics in India to satisfy his own ego. It was an un-Gandhian act.

A faded letter from an undersecretary of the then ministry of states, dated 17 May 1948, addressed to artist K.S. Kulkarni, reads:

> I am desired to confirm the order conveyed to you on the fourteenth instant while you visited this ministry for the supply of oil paintings of Mahatma Gandhi, [unreadable], Pandit Jawaharlal Nehru, [unreadable], Sardar Ballabh Bhai Patel. It would be appreciated if the supply could be expedited.[63]

The paintings were intended for the rooms of the secretaries. The urgency for the portraits of the recently assassinated Father of the Nation was an opportunity for others to display their own images. It was an easy way to align oneself with the greatness of Gandhi by pulling him down to their level. This trend continued unabated.

Jawaharlal's daughter, Indira Gandhi, and her sons, Rajiv Gandhi and Sanjay Gandhi, have had hundreds of institutions, buildings, and roads named after them across India. This has been a major point of criticism from the RSS,

BJP, and Modi, who argue that the Congress Party focussed on glorifying a single family. This criticism resonated with voters during the 2014 elections when Modi urged them to make India 'Congress-free'.

Engrossed in the 'New Gandhis'—from Indira and Feroze to Rahul—the Congress Party had already expedited the process of purging the real Gandhi.

As Mahatma Gandhi's influence diminishes in the present day, Savarkar's prominence grows. A dispensation that had no hero of its own adopted him to reshape and customize.

It is also notable that many leaders mentioned in this book—such as Vishnushastri Chiplunkar, Tilak, Moonje, M.S. Golwalkar, Keshav Baliram Hedgewar, Gadgil, Savarkar, Godse, and many others—were Brahmins from Maharashtra or nearby areas. The Hindu Mahasabha leaders were primarily Chitpavan Brahmins, while the RSS leaders were from the Deshasth or Karhade Brahmin sub-castes. Together, they comprised 2.39 per cent of Maharashtra's population in 1931 and were known for their prudence. They quickly transitioned from Sanskrit to English during British rule to maintain their social leadership.

The Chitpavans rose to prominence in the early 18th century during the Peshwa era. They counted Nana Fadnavis and Nana Saheb among their notable figures and were recognized for their distinctly fair complexion, comfortable lifestyle, and light greenish-brown eyes.

Gopal Krishna Gokhale, Gandhi's political mentor, was also a Chitpavan, but he transcended this background, influenced by his English education and personal direction.

As a result, his disciple, Gandhi, reciprocated with complete surrender to him.

Kelkar states, 'The moment Gandhiji heard of Gokhaleji's death, he took a vow to go barefoot for one whole year. It caused him great inconvenience, but he stuck to it until the vow had run its course.'[64]

Gandhi's dedication to Gokhale, rather than to Tilak, became a source of jealousy for the Poona lobby, which had become the stronghold of Hindutva due to the presence of such leaders and their regular intellectual activities.

It was no surprise, then, when Gandhi received an anonymous letter urging him to remain an admirer of Tilak rather than Gokhale (both of whom had already passed away by that time). Gandhi responded in an article:

> The letter, moreover, admonishes me not to lose heart in the prosecution of the Swaraj programme [of Tilak], and finishes off by accusing me of imposture in claiming to be politically a disciple of Gokhale. I wish correspondents would throw off the slavish habit of writing anonymously. We, who are developing the Swaraj spirit, must cultivate the courage of fearlessly speaking out our minds.[65]

'Discipleship, however, is a sacred personal matter,' Gandhi wrote, explaining how he felt a distance when meeting Dadabhai Naoroji, 'he seemed to be too far away' from him.

Before seeking support in India, Gandhi had already concluded that he had to stick to the method he had applied in South Africa. While most Indian leaders admired his work there, they didn't see it as immediately useful for their own purposes in India. They had doubts about its long-term success.

In 1896, Gandhi sought support for his mission in South Africa from several leaders. He met Justice Mahadev Govind Ranade, Badruddin Tyabji, and Pherozeshah Mehta in Bombay, Tilak, Ramkrishna Gopal Bhandarkar, and Gokhale in Poona.

Gandhi wrote:

> It was different with Gokhale, I cannot say why. I met him at his quarters on the college ground. It was like meeting an old friend, or better still a mother after a long separation. His gentle face put me at ease in a moment. His minute inquiries about myself, and my doings in South Africa at once enshrined him in my heart. And as I parted from him, I said to myself, 'you are my man'.[66]

On their second meeting, Gandhi observed:

> He simply 'took me in hand', and began to fashion me. He was concerned about how I spoke, dressed, walked and ate. My mother was not more solicitous about me than Gokhale … It was really a case of love at first sight, and it stood the severest strain in 1913. He seemed to me all I wanted as a political worker—pure as crystal, gentle as a lamb, brave as a lion and chivalrous to a fault.[67]

Gokhale was someone who could quickly forfeit his esteemed position in society. Gandhi wrote about an encounter between Gokhale and a sanyasi who accused him of not being 'sufficiently proud of Hinduism'.

'Mahatma Gokhale raised his brows and in a voice that would have pierced the heart, replied: If Hinduism consists in doing as you say [boasting that the Hindus are superior and in looking down on the Mussalmans] then take it that

I am not a Hindu. Please go and leave me alone', Gandhi quoted Gokhale. 'The mission [of service to my country], which I have undertaken under orders, I cannot give up at bidding. It would be well if I can keep popular opinion on my side while performing my duty; but it would matter little even if I am not so fortunate as to have the support.'[68]

Many years after Gandhi was gone, the government wanted to convert the place where he had breathed his last into a museum, but Ghanshyam Das Birla refused to allow this, citing his personal memories with Mahatma.

His memories were indeed illustrious. He became a member of the Central Legislative Assembly of British India in 1926 and president of the Harijan Sewak Sangh in 1928 with Gandhi's blessings. His father, Baldeodas, had already amassed a fortune in the opium trade before diversifying the family businesses.

In a letter to Ghanshyam Das in 1925, Gandhi wrote about the Marwaris or Kathiawaris, 'I would like to add for your information that in Gujarat, there is no dearth of competent or heartless Shylocks.'[69]

Gandhi's views were shaped not only by his own intellect but also by his daily exposure to the suffering of hundreds of people. He was acutely aware of the hoarding of goods by the emerging trading class across India.

He developed a sensibility to the fact that large-scale production of goods in one place was a major cause of crises in the country. In contrast, he advocated for local, smaller-scale production. Gandhi explained this in an article in *Harijan*:

> Even if we agree that mechanical production on a large scale would fulfil the demand of the society then too it would be area centric. Its distribution would be a daunting task. But the distribution would be easy if the production is done where it [the produce] is required. There would be little scope for cheating.[70]

While most industrialists supported large factories, Gandhi believed such a system would lead to unhealthy competition in the market: 'With this, direct and indirect exploitation of the villages will start. This is the reason we should concentrate on self-sustenance of the villages, where manufacturing and production is done.'[71]

Gandhi knew his advocacy of self-sustained villages would hurt certain interests. His concerns about the rise of extreme greed with centralization of production (as opposed to village-level production) were validated in the years that followed.

It is said that one of Ghanshyam Das's sons, K.K. Birla, agreed to sell part of the area in the mid-1960s, while his father was still alive, for a hefty sum and a few acres of land elsewhere in the National Capital. The government was under pressure due to frequent campaigns and movements by students at Delhi University to convert the site into a public place and develop the museum dedicated to Mahatma Gandhi.

Ghanshyam Das was a visionary, whom Gandhi took to the Second Round Conference in London as a representative of the industries. His descendants continued to influence the ruling dispensations through their business ventures, one of which was a newspaper that helped a section of the family network with powerful national and international leaders. This connection earned them a dedicated route in Delhi to avoid the usual traffic jams.

In a letter to Ghanshyam Das in 1924, Gandhi explained why he trusted him and others: 'I do not trust anybody blindly. But it is our duty to have faith in mankind…'[72] Another letter from Gandhi to Ghanshyam Das in the same year indicated that the businessman was gradually trying to involve himself in the leader's affairs, a quality typical of many non-Gandhians of the time.

'Your complaint is about three things: First, my absolving of the Swaraj Party from the charge of aspiring to office, my granting a testimony to Suhrawardy and thirdly, my endeavouring to secure Congress presidentship for Sarojini,' Gandhi wrote, while adding that Sarojini Naidu had 'delivered good to the country' and that 'I stand witness to her courage'.[73]

Gandhi had a very personal space, which perhaps only Nehru (besides his assistants) could occasionally intrude upon. Ghanshyam Das must have received encouragement in this regard, as Gandhi often asked him for, or accepted from him, funds for movements related to untouchability or even for the Muslim University in Aligarh.

Ghanshyam Das or Nehru and many others were not exactly followers of Gandhi; they followed him because he had an entire universe at his command.

Love and Betrayal

In 1908, Gandhi was beaten by a group of Pathans, led by Mir Al'am and his aides, in South Africa. This occurred after he agreed to a proposal from Jan Christian Smuts, a South African statesman, to settle a racial dispute. The attackers left him bleeding profusely and unconscious. Joseph J. Doke, a minister from the Johannesburg Baptist Church, later described Gandhi as the 'chief asset of the Indian cause'.

He recalled, when he was brought to office, 'he was helpless and bleeding, the doctor was cleansing his wounds, the police officers watching and listening beside him, while he was using what little strength he had to insist that no action should be taken to punish his would-be murderers'.[74]

At this point, discriminatory laws had already been enacted against Indians in various parts of South Africa. In 1894, the Natal Municipal Corporation proposed disenfranchising Indians altogether. By the end of 1895, Gandhi recognized that he was about to become embroiled in a struggle against the South African governments, which was openly hostile to Indians. In an appeal, he sought to instil confidence in the government, stating that 'Indians were proud to be under the British Crown.'[75]

Paul Power states:

> When the Boer War began at the end of 1899 and again during the Zulu revolt early in 1906, [Gandhi] led Indian community in offering to provide stretcher teams. The British authorities accepted and after the hostilities commended Gandhi and his associates for their performance.'[76]

However, Gandhi did not volunteer out of humanitarian concerns but 'as a means of showing the loyalty of his people and improving his bargaining position'.[77]

In 1906, the Natal Municipal Corporation introduced a bill that would disenfranchise Indians, claiming they had no parliamentary tradition. Simultaneously, the Transvaal government passed the Asiatic Amendment Act, which required the re-registration of Indians. As per Power, the proposal sparked widespread discontent and led the Indian community to send Gandhi to London to petition for the withholding of royal assent for the bill. However, the Transvaal government pressed ahead with their plans. New Indian immigrants were excluded from the registration process, while existing residents were required to register, undergo fingerprinting, and carry passes.

Gandhi responded by leading a protest to defy the new registration law, declaring that 'non submission to the registration law was the only honourable step'.[78]

He was arrested for the first time in November 1907 and sentenced to two months in jail. Over the next six years, he was imprisoned on three more occasions. However, the source of much of the discontent towards him stemmed from his agreement with Smuts on 30 January 1908. According to the terms of their settlement:

> Indians should register voluntarily, not under any law; that the details to be entered in the new certificates of registration should be settled by the government in consultation with the Indian community; and that if the majority of Indians underwent voluntary registration, the government should repeal the Black Act and take steps to legalizing the voluntary registration.[79]

Previously, Gandhi had argued that only criminals should be required to give fingerprints, a stance which led some Indians, particularly the Pathans, to oppose the settlement. They reminded him of his own argument against fingerprinting. Additionally, some Indians who had previously entered the Transvaal illegally, and were involved in smuggling others in without proper documentation, opposed the truce as well.

On one occasion, as Gandhi was en route from his Satyagraha Association office to the registration office, Al'am stopped him and launched the attack. Al'am knew Gandhi personally and had often sought his advice. Suspicious of Gandhi's intentions, he threatened others with consequences if they proceeded with registration.

Al'am and his group were later punished, though Gandhi played no part in the legal proceedings.

Despite the opposition, Gandhi managed to convince the majority of Indians to comply with the registration. He had earned their trust, which was further cemented when he returned the money given to him by local Indians to represent them in London in 1906 and 1909, instead donating it to public funds. His act of selflessness impressed many, and local Indians remarked, 'He is poor because he will be poor.'[80]

In South Africa, Gandhi delved deeply into passive resistance, renaming it Satyagraha in 1906. Leo Tolstoy viewed it as the realization of his own philosophy of non-resistance. Gandhi had read *The Kingdom of God is Within You* by Tolstoy and immediately became his student. Tolstoy admired the spirit of love in Gandhi, who set up an ashram in Johannesburg and named it 'Tolstoy Farm'.

The letters they exchanged in 1909 and 1910 reflect their bond over a common cause. Gandhi explained his non-violent struggle, while Tolstoy shared how Russians had begun refusing military service. This stood in sharp contrast to the ideas of Tilak, Moonje, Savarkar, the Mahasabha, and later, the RSS.

E. Stanley Jones, an American missionary, wrote about Gandhi's influence on him: '... a little man, who fought a system in the framework of which I stand, has taught me more of the spirit of Christ than perhaps any other man in the East or the West.'[81]

On a midsummer day in 1907, C.F. Andrews observed 20,000 Indians in Durban, South Africa, prepare for passive resistance. They gathered to address many issues, including the inhuman poll tax of three pounds imposed on every Indian over the age of thirteen, without which they would remain indentured. Andrews noted 'the behaviour of the crowd and their attitude towards Mahatma Gandhi, their leader'. He noted:

> [My] thoughts went back to the Gospel story for an analogy. He [Gandhi] was there, in the heart of that multitude that pressed upon him. They had come to him without anything to eat; and he was busy providing for their needs … The crowd would never leave him even for a moment and his patience was inexhaustible.[82]

It was a miracle that such a man listened to Gokhale and returned to India to continue the battle he had started there.

Smuts, Transvaal colonial secretary and later minister of the interior, breathed a sigh of relief when Gandhi left South Africa and said, 'The saint has left our shores, I sincerely hope, forever.' But thirty years later, Smuts wrote, 'It was my fate to be antagonistic [to] a man for whom even then I had the greatest respect.'[83]

On his way back from the Second Round Table Conference, Gandhi stayed with Romain Rolland in Villeneuve, Switzerland, for five days. 'The Swiss peasants still tell the story of Romain Rolland's frenzied search for goat milk for his strange friend from India!'[84]

Rolland won the Nobel Prize in Literature in 1915, nine years before he noticed Gandhi and more than three decades before he wrote the Mahatma's biography.

Rolland, who was in touch with Gandhi through letters, introduced Madeleine Slade to him. Slade lived at Sabarmati Ashram in Ahmedabad to learn spinning and weaving. Later, India knew her as Miraben.

The attention Gandhi received around the world was rare. However, most of those involved in establishing the New English School, the Deccan Education Society, and Fergusson College in Poona —such as Chiplunkar, Tilak, Gopal Ganesh Agarkar, and many others —bore the weight of cultural purity, a burden they had yet to shed. They were wary of Gandhi's practical purity.

Interestingly, we can accept Jayakar's claim that Tilak didn't know, until Gandhi became a prominent leader, that he was a Vaishya, having assumed he was a Jain. But why did Tilak view Gandhi through the lens of caste? And what prompted Jayakar to mention this in his memoir? They could never accept Gandhi, given his non-Brahmin background, as their leader.

On 25 June 1934, a bomb exploded near a car outside a hall in Vishrambaug, Poona, where Gandhi was scheduled to address a meeting. The attackers mistakenly believed Gandhi was in the car. Some people were injured in the attack. Gandhi later stated that he had forgiven the strangers who had attempted to take his life. This was how Gandhi was welcomed in a city where enlightenment seemed to come through new English education but ultimately resulted in Maharashtrian hegemony.

Kelkar, on the sixteenth death anniversary of Tilak, claimed that Gandhi had created a 'mystifying aura around himself' and had pursued an agenda to 'destroy the legacy of Tilak'.[85]

Tilak never agreed with Gandhi's ideas. He had doubts about the practical implication of *Nishkriya Virodh* (Passive Resistance) or Satyagraha. 'He may have appreciated [it] from spiritual viewpoint, but never accepted it as a politician.'[86]

A statement by Gandhi appeared in *Young India* on 14 January 1920, claiming that 'Tilak believed everything was fair in love and war.'[87] Tilak responded to Gandhi's remark and wrote:

> I feel sorry that you have written in Young India that I believe everything is fair in politics. I am writing to you to tell you that you have not presented my view in your article properly. Politics is a game of worldly people, not of the sadhu-saints...[88]

Gandhi didn't pursue the matter further, as he had already made his view on the subject public a year earlier when he asked Swami Shraddhanand to address a political meeting.

At the Congress session in Amritsar in 1919, Shraddhanand addressed questions about whether a sanyasi should participate in political movements. He claimed that the victims of British rule in Punjab had encouraged him to take up the responsibility given to him. The other reason Shraddhanand cited was, '[The] Veda gives me direction to do my duties while living for hundred years without getting involved in the worldly life.'[89]

Shraddhanand began his speech with Vedic mantras to promote the 'pure Indianisation of the Congress'.[90] Gandhi likely disapproved of this indirect Hinduization of the Congress, but he chose not to react to it.

Despite their differences, Mahatma never harboured ill will towards the Hindu leaders. Nehru, however, did not emulate this trait of his mentor, as his political ambitions, insecurities, and calculations led him to take a different approach.

In the United Provinces, there was Govind Ballabh Pant, a self-styled Gandhian who never truly followed Gandhi. Intellectuals in Ayodhya blame him for exacerbating the Ram Temple–Babri Masjid issue to secure the support of the Mahasabha against the socialists.

A story circulates about a senior British officer who told Pant that he had warned a tehsildar he would be transferred if he failed to control communal violence in his area. The tehsildar managed to suppress the unrest by force within days.[91] Pant believed in a harsh approach to governance—ruling the masses by instilling fear in them. This approach was entirely contrary to Gandhian principles. Pant made no effort to address the root cause of violence in people's minds; instead, he merely suppressed it temporarily. Nevertheless, Pant recounted this story with admiration for the British officer.

Pant served as premier of the United Provinces and later as chief minister of Uttar Pradesh before becoming India's minister of home affairs. He had the backing of Nehru and Patel. Despite being a nominal Gandhian, Pant's preference for Sanatan over others was well known.

Gandhi had rejected this kind of discourse. In his letter to Malaviya on 24 February 1933, Gandhi pointed out the 'difference of outlook' between them and dismissed the possibility of productive 'discussion between the Sanatanists and reformers'.

The Congress contested the 1937 elections in the province under the leadership of Acharya Narendra Dev, and it was clear that he would be the premier. However, Nehru fielded Purushottamdas Tandon and announced that Tandon would be the head of the province if they won. Many members rejected this proposal, and Pant emerged as the final choice of the Congress leadership.

Ten years later, Gandhi wanted Dev to succeed Kripalani, who had resigned as president of the Congress. Gandhi had also offered this position to Dev in the 1930s. In 1947, Gandhi believed a Congress socialist would be more suitable for the role, as he didn't want the position to merely serve as a rubber stamp of power. Nehru did not oppose Dev's candidacy directly, but Patel and Pant did. Gandhi sent a letter to Dev through Pant, suggesting that Dev withdraw his candidacy to avoid an election. However, Pant withheld the letter and succeeded in isolating the true socialists, who posed a potential threat to him or Nehru politically. While Gandhi shared an emotional bond with Nehru, his search for an intellectual equal remained unfulfilled.

Gandhi first encountered Dev in 1926 at Kashi Vidyapith, Varanasi. Struck by Dev's brilliance, Gandhi asked Sri Prakash, a nationalist leader, 'How is it that you have kept such a jewel of a man hidden from me and have never spoken to me about him?'[92]

However, any closeness between Gandhi and Dev could have unsettled Nehru. Moreover, Dev never concealed his ideological differences with Gandhi.

After Gandhi's assassination, Dev remarked that Gandhi knew the masses 'intimately'.[93] Even earlier, despite their differences, Dev did not oppose Gandhi's principles of non-violence. In many of his speeches, he argued that while Gandhi advocated the 'socialisation of the means of production',[94] he feared that it might lead to class struggle and violence.

The socialists, including Dev, advocated transforming the Congress into a liberal or labour party. They believed this 'transformation of the National Congress into a Socialist Congress will help to galvanise the country into a new mood of creative venture'.[95]

However, in March 1948, the Congress amended its constitution to prevent dual membership, effectively forcing socialist leaders to choose between the Congress and their party. As noted in a paper presented at the Indian History Congress in 2002: 'The sole object of this amendment was to create such a condition in which the parties working within or outside the Congress should dissolve themselves or merge with the Congress.'[96]

After Gandhi's assassination, the Socialist Party decided to part ways with the Congress. They held their sixth annual conference independently in Nasik in March 1948. Prominent leaders, including Ram Manohar Lohia, Achyut Patwardhan, Ashok Mehta, Jayprakash Narayan, Yusuf Meherally Merchant, Kamla Devi Chattopadhyay, and Aruna Asaf Ali, participated in the conference. In his address, Dev criticized the 'vast disparity between what the Congress stands for and what the Congress governments wanted to do'. He condemned the presence of 'rank communalists' in the government and highlighted Patel's assurances to 'the capitalists by telling them that Shanmukham Chetty is their representative'. Chetty was a pro-British and anti-Congress leader from the South. Dev alleged that Chetty and Patel favoured private enterprises while Jawaharlal focussed on establishing public sector industries. Chetty, who became India's first finance minister, was accused of obstructing an investigation into tax evasion by mill owners. Jawaharlal ultimately forced him to resign on 15 August 1948.

Dev believed that Congress leaders, except Gandhi, were indifferent to the issues affecting the masses. He lamented the rise of corruption and capitalism, which, in his view, were of no concern to most Congress leaders. In his tribute to Gandhi, Dev noted that he was the only leader who had 'faith in the Indian masses'.[97] In the same conversation at Nasik, Dev also criticized Nehru, stating, 'He wants the Leaguers to disband the League and join the Congress. He welcomes Hindu Mahasabhaites into the Congress. He pats the RSS and welcomes them too.'[98]

Earlier, in 1934, Dev and other socialist leaders had formed the Congress Samajwadi Party within the Congress. However, by 1948, they were forced to resign from the Congress, making their party independent. As a young man, Dev admired Tilak, but as he matured through and deepened his studies, he gravitated toward Marxism.

The by-elections of June 1948 were crucial for the Mahasabha, which sought to launch a campaign against the Babri Masjid in Ayodhya–Faizabad. Pant assisted them by fielding Baba Raghav Das from the Congress. Das stirred religious sentiment and defeated Dev. A Poona-born Brahmin, Das openly advocated for the removal of the masjid, which led to the resurgence of the issue.

By 1951, Nehru had softened and did not wish to oppose Dev. Ironically, he still allowed Pant and his followers to field Madan Gopal, who won the election.

During a debate in the UP Legislative Council sixteen days after Gandhi's death, Pant remarked:

> What an irony of fate, how strange that a Mahatma who gave his all for the cause of ahimsa, who put an end to terrorism

> in his own country and converted revolutionaries into a non-violent lot, that same Mahatma fell a victim to violence at the hands of one of his compatriots and so-called co-religionists.[99]

The outspoken politician praised Gandhi, but his remarks exaggerated Gandhi's achievements, claiming he had 'put an end to terrorism' and 'converted revolutionaries into a non-violent lot'. Gandhi did want to end all violent means of struggle and hoped to convert revolutionaries to non-violence, but he ultimately failed in this regard.

Pant later spoke in the Rajya Sabha, saying:

> I am sorry that this suicidal and fatal doctrine of two nations should be favoured and supported by some of those who know the great disaster and catastrophe that it had caused in our country before and at the time of partition and ever since.[100]

This theory was promoted against Gandhi primarily by the Mahasabhaites, with Pant furthering it.

Pant was prominent when Abhinandan Mishra, also known as Abhiram Das, a Hindu Mahasabha sadhu in Ayodhya, forcibly entered the Babri Masjid on the night of 22–23 December 1949 and installed an idol of Lord Rama there. Raghav Das and Mahant Digvijaynath, also known as Swaroop 'Nanhoo' Singh, the mahant of Gorakhnath Temple in Gorakhpur and president of the Hindu Mahasabha in the province, had orchestrated this operation well in advance.

The situation today might have been different if Narendra Dev had won the election from Faizabad, his home constituency, pushing the Hindutva leaders to the margin.

Dev began his political career in 1916, inspired by Tilak. However, his extensive studies eventually led him to reject religious ideology in favour of working towards a classless society.

Pant was known for his desire to establish 'Sanatana dharma' and Nehru had an opportunity to align himself with this goal by allowing it to begin in Ayodhya.

As the Congress gradually sidelined all its leaders except the Nehrus and the New Gandhis, the Bharatiya Janata Party embraced them posthumously, including Patel, Pant, and Malaviya, as its icons. They became known as the 'maximum-hero party in the world'. The Modi government awarded the Bharat Ratna, India's highest civilian honour, to Malaviya on the eve of his 153rd birth anniversary. Pant had received this award during his lifetime from the Nehru government.

Malaviya practised law for a few years starting in 1893 before dedicating himself to social work. His family's knowledge of Hindu scriptures and his close association with karmkand earned them the prefix Pandit.

When Annie Besant, Raja Darbhanga Rameshwar Singh, and Malaviya decided to establish Banaras Hindu University, they received overwhelming support. Malaviya became the third vice-chancellor following Sir Sunder Lal and Sir P.S. Sivaswami Iyer. His son, Govind Malaviya, served as the sixth vice-chancellor of BHU, and his grandson, Giridhar Malaviya, was the chancellor. He and his descendants have consistently supported Hindutva. It is said in Varanasi that Madan Mohan Malviya used separate utensils for Besant.

Besant had made Banaras her home, founded the Central Hindu College, and transferred it to BHU in 1917.

Much before founding the All India Hindu Mahasabha, Malaviya was associated with the Prayag Hindu Samaj, established in Allahabad in 1880. He was also involved with Bharat Dharm Mahamandal, formed in 1887 in Haridwar, with Raja Darbhanga as its patron.

Although Malaviya did not approve of violence, he facilitated RSS activities at the university, where Golwalkar completed his BSc and MSc in 1927 and 1929, and taught zoology for three years before returning to Nagpur. Hedgewar was a frequent visitor to BHU and was always a welcome guest.

Prabhakar Balwant Rao Dani, also known as Bhaiyaji, studied at BHU and founded a wing of the RSS there.

Gandhi never spoke out against Malaviya, Pant, or Digvijaynath, as he was reluctant to condemn anybody easily. However, he did not learn from the murder of Shraddhanand.

Shraddhanand wrote to Gandhi, noting that Muslim leaders frequently quoted the Quran to justify their positions and suggested they could use the same verses against Hindus when the time came. In 1923, Shraddhanand left the Congress Party and joined the Mahasabha but grew disillusioned and departed after two years, criticizing the organization for pursuing a 'narrow political ambition'. As a liberal in many ways, he was particularly upset when Dalits were barred from speaking on the dais at Mahasabha meetings in Varanasi, which were presided over by Malaviya.

Shraddhanand's Hindu Shuddhi Sabha, founded in Agra on 13 February 1923, continuously worked to reconvert Muslims and Christians to Hinduism.

A major controversy erupted in 1926 when Asghari Begum, a woman from Karachi, arrived in Delhi with her two children and nephew to meet Shraddhanand. They were converted to Hinduism, and Asghari was renamed as Shanti Devi. Her father, Maulvi Taj Mohammad Khan, and her husband, Abdul Halim, filed a case against Shraddhanand. However, Shraddhanand won the case as Shanti Devi herself had no complaint against him. Infuriated, Abdul Rashid shot Shraddhanand dead in his home in Naya Bazar, Delhi. Despite being unwell, Shraddhanand had agreed to meet Rashid, who claimed he wanted some clarity on religion.

Notably, Tabassum, a prominent radio artist and actor, was one of the children who had arrived in Delhi with Asghari.

During the Congress session in Guwahati on 26 December 1926, Gandhi urged people not to mourn for 'a hero among heroes, the bravest of the brave'. He added, 'Every one of us might wish for such a death ... He greets it as a friend. Let us all be brave enough to die the death of a martyr, but let no one lust for martyrdom.'

Gandhi exonerated the killer, stating, 'I don't regard him as guilty of Swami's murder. Guilty indeed are all those who incited feelings of hatred against one another.'[101] Malaviya supported Gandhi's resolution.

In contrast, Bhagat Singh, known for his clarity of thought, had great contempt for Malaviya, In an article titled 'Acchoot da Sawaal (Question of Untouchability)', published in *Kirti* in June 1928 under the penname 'Vidrohi', he wrote:

> Our country is very spiritual but we hesitate in giving the status of human to a human ... A known social reformer like Pandit Malaviyaji, known for his soft corner for the untouchables, first agrees to be garlanded by a sweeper in public but later considers self to be polluted till he bathes and washes those clothes.

Gandhian Religion

A few days ago, I was told that 'he [Gandhi] is a Buddhist'. Not long ago, a newspaper described him as 'a Christian Mohammedan'—an extraordinary mixture indeed. Others imagine that he worships idols and would be surprised to find a shrine in his office or a statue of 'Gunputty [Ganpati] among his books'. 'I question whether any system of religion can absolutely hold him.'[102]

Mohandas's first encounter with religion came when his old housekeeper Rambha suggested he repeat Ramanama to ward off unease, as he was afraid of ghosts and spirits. He would also read the Ramayana (Ramcharitmanas) of Tulsidas and the Bhagavat at home.[103] Later, it became a practice at Sabarmati Ashram to recite the Ramcharitmanas with music playing in the background. However, the Rama of the Hindu epic was not his personal hero. His Rama had no definite form.

Gandhi once remarked that he laughed when someone objected to his chanting Ramanama, arguing it was meant only for Hindus. Non-Hindus opposed his chanting, which included inspirational passages from Tulsidas's epic in the Awadhi dialect.

A section of Brahmins, in particular, and upper-class Hindus across India, in general, were displeased with Gandhi for holding them responsible for perpetuating the system of untouchability. For instance, while addressing a gathering in Mayavaram (Mayiladuthurai), Tamil Nadu, on 2 May 1915, after meeting members of the Panchama (lowest caste), Gandhi highlighted their plight. He explained that the community members told him they lacked access to drinking water and other essential supplies and were actively prevented by upper-caste Hindus, particularly Brahmins, from buying or holding land.

'Is this a part of Hinduism?' he asked the audience, which included members of other upper castes. He added, 'If the Brahmins themselves consider they are holding high position by penance and posterity then they have themselves much to learn; then they will be the people who have cursed and ruined the land.'[104]

Every time Gandhi heard stories of atrocities against the lower castes, he became deeply agitated. However, over time, he tempered the harshness of his words while continuing to challenge such injustices.

Gandhi wrote:

> No, there is only one omnipotent and omnipresent God. He is named variously, and we remember Him by the name, which is most familiar to us. My Rama, the Rama of our prayers, is not the historical Rama, the son of Dasharatha—the King of Ayodhya . . . He is the eternal, the unborn, the one without a second. Him alone I worship, His aid alone I seek, and so should you . . . He belongs equally to all. I, therefore, see no reason why a Mussulman or anybody should object to taking his name. But he is in no way bound to recognize God as Rama. He may utter to himself Allah or Khuda so as not to mar the harmony of the sound.[105]

Later, Gandhi clarified:

> I have accepted all the names and forms attributed to God as symbols connoting one formless, omnipresent Rama. To me, therefore, Rama described as the Lord of Sita, son of Dasharatha, is the all-powerful essence whose name inscribed in the heart removes all suffering—mental, moral and physical.[106]

Gandhi was engaging his followers in a religion without form, but the name he used was borrowed from a text exclusively devoted to Hindus. This approach made it easier for his critics on both sides to challenge him.

At Sabarmati Ashram, after the recitation of Ramanama, Gandhi would read passages from the Gita and explain them. Other attendees, mostly children, would present religious songs from Hindu texts. Recognizing that Muslims were apprehensive about his chanting of Ramanama, he incorporated prayers from all religions into his practices. This move, however, was equally controversial, drawing criticism from both Hindutva supporters and Islamists.

Nehru noted in his autobiography:

> Gandhiji, indeed, was continually laying stress on the religious and spiritual side of the movement. His religion was not dogmatic, but it did mean a definitely religious outlook on life, and the whole movement was strongly influenced by this and took on a revivalist character so far as the masses were concerned.

Nehru added that his father and many other senior Congress leaders approached political problems purely on a political plane. Even he himself admitted to being 'troubled sometimes at the growth of this religious elements in our politics, both on the Hindu and the Muslim side'. Reflecting further, he wrote, 'Even some of Gandhiji's phrases jarred upon me ... his frequent reference to Ram Raj as a golden age which was to return.'[107]

Gandhi also established specific rules for his ashram, which were followed diligently. These included vows of purity, purity of palate, ahimsa, and non-theft. The vow of purity of palate stipulated that 'one must not eat or drink for the sake of any pleasure to be derived from the food but merely to keep oneself alive and fit for one's work'.[108] The vow of non-theft meant 'if you have more than you need while others have less than they need, you are a thief'.[109]

In contrast, Savarkar's Rama was a warrior—a figure of fear and an attacker who could see through the ages.

Nathuram Godse adhered to the religion that Savarkar promoted and saw Gandhi as a representation of Ravana. He published caricatures in his Marathi newspaper *Agrani*, depicting Mahatma as the ten-headed demon with arrows aimed at him.

Godse, like any Chitpavan, came from an orthodox family. Despite his lack of formal education, Savarkar respected him. Savarkar was constantly seeking devoted followers, and Godse was in search of a sense of identity. After completing some minor tasks for Savarkar, Godse, in August 1938, persuaded the Mahasabha to take direct action on the jizya issue. The Nizam of Hyderabad, Mir Osman Ali Khan Asaf Jah VII, had imposed the community tax on non-Muslims, and reports of atrocities against Hindus in parts of the province had begun to surface. While the Hyderabad State Congress led a peaceful protest, the Arya Samaj adopted a more aggressive stance, alleging that Hindu rights were at risk. Godse joined the Arya Samaj and escalated the protest.

The Congress withdrew from the protest in December. Godse was jailed but was soon released after the Nizam rescinded his decision.

Gandhi evolved significantly over time. None of the ideas he adopted were originally his, but he practised them in his own life. He studied various theories and applied them to himself when they resonated with them. The writings of Henry David Thoreau (1817–62), an American transcendentalist, served as one of his guides. Gandhi read Thoreau's essay on civil government resistance and the concept of civil disobedience. In 1907, he published Thoreau's ideas in *Indian Opinion*, his newspaper in South Africa.

Gandhi's concept of Sarvodaya (progress of all) was inspired by John Ruskin (1819–1900), a British author who wrote 'Unto This Last', a treatise on economics. Gandhi translated it in 1908 under the title 'Sarvodaya'.

Ultimately, all these ideas merged into the 'Rama' of Mahatma. Yet, he ignored the writing on the wall that the mythical narratives, which had been his tools for truth, were being distorted to promote violence against him and undermine his commitment to non-violence.

Savarkar described Lord Rama's war with the demons, initiated at the invitation of Guru Vishwamitra, as a conflict fought on both political and religious fronts. He wrote, 'And at that time those gods and god-like emperors, too, considered it the holiest religious duty to show upper-savage cruelty to beat down the cruelty of the Rakshasas, to be arch-devils against the devils.'[110]

For one, Rama was eternal and peaceful; for the other, He was cruel in order to restore peace. Gandhi could not have been unaware that his almighty Rama was a relatively new entrant and the least accepted form of the deity. The Rama of Ramayana or Ramcharitmanas—peaceful or violent—was the singular figure for Hindus. They learned of Him through books or kathas and pravachans, but they were not taught to question or analyse Him.

Arthur Anthony Macdonell, a Sanskrit scholar, observed the two extremes in Indian religion, saying:

> In her literature, philosophy, art and regulated life there is much that is worthless, much also that is distinctly unhealthy; yet the treasures of knowledge, wisdom and beauty, which they contain, are too precious to be lost. Every citizen of India needs to use them, if he is to be cultured modern Indian.[111]

For common Hindus, it was difficult to understand Gandhi's religion. Savarkar made it simpler. He quoted Shivaji as saying that he would, 'fight to a finish and establish Hindavi Swaraj … essentially a Hindu movement in the defence of Hindu Dharma for the overthrow of the alien Muhammadan domination, for the establishment of an independent, powerful Hindu Empire'.[112]

Such desperate writing arose because Gandhi's personal popularity outside Maharashtra had undermined Savarkar's socio-political influence, leaving him struggling to remain visible.

For Savarkar, a Hindu was more than just someone living in Hindustan. He was a proponent of Hindutva, a concept previously advocated by Tilak in an article published in *Chitramayjagat*. Savarkar's vision of the country was 'not only a fatherland but also a holy land'.[113]

He asserted that 'Mohammadan or Christian communities possess the essential qualifications of Hindutva' but 'they don't look upon India as their Holy land'.[114]

Savarkar elaborated:

> These are the essentials of Hindutva: a common rashtra [nation], a common jaati [caste] and a common sanskriti [culture]. All these essentials could be best summed up by stating in brief that he is a Hindu to whom Sindhustan is not only a *pitrabhu* but also a *punyabhu.*[115]

As some Hindus feared violence when independence was about to be declared, Gandhi arrived in Calcutta ahead of time. He was prepared to return to Noakhali, but the leaders of Bengal urged him to stay, assuring him they would manage the other areas.

Manu recalled an incident on the afternoon of 14 August, while Bapu was staying at Haidari Mansion, Beliaghata. A group of young men dissatisfied with Mahatma confronted him, accusing him of being 'an enemy of the Hindus' and claiming he had only come 'because a few Muslims [had] been killed in last three or four days'.

In response, Gandhi smiled and said:

> You are all youths. But to me you are like children. Even my youngest son Devadas is older than every one of you. Why can't you realize that I, a Hindu by birth, a Hindu by action, can never be an enemy of the Hindus?[116]

The youths likely remained unconvinced of his devotion to Hinduism.

Hindutva's Love for Gandhi

Otherwise loyal to Nehru, Gadgil showed sympathy towards the RSS when it was banned. Despite being a self-proclaimed Gandhian, the former minister admitted to assisting the RSS during its time of crisis. He wrote:

> I didn't consider the ban unjust in view of the reports we had about the activities of its various centres in the country. But that did not mean we considered everyone in the RSS as guilty ... The friends and supporters of the RSS in Delhi used to meet Vallabhbhai and me often. In 1949, one of them, Maulichand Sharma, saw me and I told him to go and see Vallabhbhai who was then in Dehradun. He went and met him. He met Mr D.P. Mishra, the home minister of central province also. There was some correspondence between the head of the RSS, Golwalkar and the Government of India. The ban on the RSS was lifted later on and many detenus were released.[117]

Following Hindu tradition, the Sangh suspended all activities for thirteen days after Bapu's murder, gradually resuming its works after 13 February.

In the introduction to Golwalkar's *Bunch of Thoughts*, M.A. Venkata Rao wrote:

> This era commenced roughly with the emergence and work of Raja Rammohan Roy in the beginning of the last century and has continued to the present day through the life effort of notable thinkers in many fields like Ramakrishna and Vivekananda, Swami Dayananda, Sri Aurobindo and Lokmanya Tilak, Gandhi and Tagore, Dr Hedgewar, and

> Veer Savarkar. These are only typical names and do not exhaust the galaxy ...[118]

Rao also noted:

> Mohandas Karamchand Gandhi introduced a powerful leaven into this maelstrom of ideas, impulses and images having many elements congenial to the spirit of Indian Culture. Thus, the national liberation movement of M.K. Gandhi derived power from the cultural heritage indwelling in the sub-conscious mind of the people.[119]

The original RSS ideologues didn't express their dislike for Gandhi as openly as some of their followers do today.

Nana Deshmukh, one of the founding members of the Bharatiya Jan Sangh, claimed that Gandhi visited the Sangh camp in Sewagram in 1934. During his visit, Gandhi asked the volunteers who were sitting in a queue, about their castes and was pleased to find both Brahmins and Dalits seated together.[120]

Bhai Parmanand wrote that he was fortunate to meet Mahatma during his lectures in Durban. 'His simple life and asceticism left a deep impression on me.'[121] He noted that the secret of Gandhi's 'phenomenal success' lay in the 'magnanimity of his heart, which made him always love the Muslims ... In Mahatma Gandhi, we have a unique figure of a man who, while he loves the Hindus, loves the Muslims even more.'[122]

In February 2024, the Akhil Bharatiya Vidyarthi Parishad (ABVP), the student wing of the RSS, protested at the gate of the National Institute of Technology, Calicut (Kozhikode), against a professor of mechanical engineering who had posted on social media that Godse 'saved India'. The protesters claimed that they have always rejected Gandhi's assassin.[123]

The pran-pratishtha (bringing life to an idol) of Rama in Ayodhya in January 2024—one of the most significant events in India's religiously divided history—was, in theory, an opportunity for the RSS to sideline Gandhi. Yet, its sarsanghchalak, Mohan Bhagwat, invoked Gandhi, stating:

> We have to behave in a coordinated manner with each other, which is the first truth of religion. Compassion is the second necessity, which includes services and charity … Earn from both hands, keep the minimum for self and return the rest through services and charities. There is need for purity and it requires control [on self] . . . Gandhiji used to say that earn for everybody and spend on everybody.

It was not that the RSS needed to reference Bapu at this moment. Bhagwat only mentioned Gandhi when he realized that something inappropriate was unfolding, which was not acceptable to the Sangh. Acharya Govind Dev, a sadhu, had nearly equated Modi with God in his speech, prompting Bhagwat to intervene. He invoked Gandhi's principles to emphasize the canonization requires a solid foundation.

Furthermore, as sarsanghchalak, Bhagwat is worshipped by the swayamsewaks, and he cannot be second to anyone within the family.

After Gandhi Was Gone

The subject of Gandhi's assassination is perilously tempting, yet ignoring it is equally constraining.

As a political journalist, one gains significant exposure to crooks—the dominant breed in politics. Often, they exploit journalists to climb the ladder. I have seen them standing at the gates of local newspapers, pleading with reporters to publish their statements, only to become central ministers the next day, refusing to even recognize those same reporters. These types exist in every political party, as the same leader can be in one party today and in another, with a completely opposing ideology, tomorrow. Not a day goes by without hearing praise for the Constitution that enables a lewd Bhojpuri singer or actor, a hardened criminal, a bank thief or a promoter of communal violence to sit in Parliament and preach to the nation. Some of them might even be descendants of those who conspired to kill Gandhi—or those who continue to kill him symbolically.

The 'teetotaller' politicians of Gandhi's dream, as outlined in the new constitution of the Congress Party, never materialized. Instead, Mahatma was struck down the day after he proposed the dissolution of the Congress.

Gandhi is among the most ridiculed figures in the world. A popular saying in North India goes: '*Mazboori ka naam* Mahatma Gandhi (Helplessness, thy name is Mahatma Gandhi).'

Well-received fictions, blockbuster Bollywood and Hollywood movies alike, mock Gandhi. Beyond ridiculing Gandhi, we have also vandalized his statues ever since they were erected. People insult him by painting his idols in their political colours.

For instance, on the morning of 1 August 1918, the villagers of Dhaka–Ghanshyampur, under Banda police station in Shahjahanpur district, awoke to find that unidentified individuals had painted a twenty-year-old white marble statue of Gandhi in saffron. Such incidents were rampant in the Vidarbha area, prompting the government to create a special police unit to prevent them.

Golwalkar was in Madras the day Gandhi was assassinated and, during a meeting, declared that they would 'frustrate all the attacks on the Sangh' as their work was 'not dependent on anybody … It will not be over because someone looks down at us.'[124]

He was arrested on 2 February, charged with being part of the conspiracy that led to Gandhi's death, and the RSS was banned two days later.

The enduring bitterness between the RSS and political leaders was evident in a series of letters exchanged between Syama Prasad Mookerjee and Shaikh Abdullah, the prime minister of Jammu and Kashmir, in the early 1950s.

Abdullah believed that the RSS, after its ban, had re-emerged under the guise of the Praja Parishad, raising concerns about its activities in the state.

In a letter to Mookerjee dated 4 February 1953, Abdullah expressed these concerns directly, 'We can't ignore the activities of the Praja Parishad, which you justify, are meanwhile working as dangerous influence against the unity and integrity of the state.'[125]

Abdullah's fears were rooted in the leadership of the Praja Parishad. Its president, Pandit Premnath Dogra, was a known RSS leader, while its general secretary, Balraj Madhok, had previously served as a sangh pracharak in Jammu and Kashmir.

Golwalkar was granted bail on 6 August and met Patel a month later, seeking to lift the ban on the Sangh. The home minister suggested merging the Sangh with the Congress, but Golwalkar rejected the offer. He was arrested again in Delhi on 13 November.

Golwalkar believed that Nehru's actions against Sangh workers after Gandhi's assassination set the RSS back by twenty years. Sangh members often reiterate this to express their anger towards Nehru.

On 9 December, the Sangh organized a protest (Satyagraha) with the slogan, '*Sangh ke khilaf arop siddh karo ya pratibandh hatao* (Prove the charges against the RSS or lift the ban).'

Nehru agreed to lift the ban on the condition that the RSS adopt a formal constitution, primarily because they lacked a defined membership roll.

The draft of the RSS constitution was sent to Patel in June 1949, and the ban was lifted on 11 July. Golwalkar was released the following day.

Half a century later, Rajabhai Nene and Modi wrote, 'It was known to all that the ban was wrong and vindictive. The government itself had mentioned about the cabinet meeting of 9 November [1947] in its notification of ban on the Sangh on 4 February 1948.'[126] They further claimed that the government had been planning to ban the RSS months before Gandhi was assassinated.

To this day, the RSS does not maintain a formal membership roll, allowing it to easily dissociate from its members. Meanwhile, its political arm, the BJP, now offers membership through missed phone calls.

The Jawaharlal government had little specific evidence against the RSS or Golwalkar, other than the fact that the organization was emerging as a socio-political opposition that could potentially align with a non-Congress group.

Interestingly, Nehru, in a speech in Amritsar the day before Gandhi's assassination, mentioned the Sangh negatively, but not the Hindu Mahasabha, likely because Mookerjee was in his cabinet, and Nehru didn't want to destabilize his position.

What remains puzzling is why Ashutosh Lahiri, the president of the Delhi branch of the Mahasabha, was never interrogated in connection with Gandhi's assassination. His office had been a hub of activity in the months leading up to the murder at Birla House.

Lahiri had been imprisoned in the Andaman Jail from 1915 to 1921 for conspiring against the government. During his time there, he met both Savarkar and Bhai Paramanand. After his release, he was transferred to Alipore prison for a year before being fully released. Soon afterward, he relocated to Delhi.

Lahiri was known to Jawaharlal. A delegation led by Lahiri had met the prime minister soon after independence, demanding certain privileges for Hindu refugees. Nehru argued that East Pakistan was a separate entity and that he wouldn't interfere. Lahiri had also advocated for the creation of a special army to protect Hindus in East Pakistan. Although Nehru didn't act on his demands, he also showed no interest in taking action against Lahiri.

Historians typically avoid criticizing Nehru, but during a conversation with me at his residence in Aligarh on 11 April 2024, Irfan Habib, professor emeritus at Aligarh Muslim University, remarked with a laugh, 'I don't know why Nehru was in a hurry to close Gandhi's murder case.' This doubt will exist until some classified documents related to the incident are declassified.

The background for the Kapur Commission on Gandhi's assassination was established on 12 November 1964, just three days before Godse's fifteenth death anniversary. A special meeting was convened at Udyan Mangal Karyalaya in Shaniwar Peth, Poona, called Satyavinayak Puja.

Gajanan Vishwanath Ketkar, the grandson (daughter's son) of Tilak, arrived in a wet dhoti and changed into one of Godse's, which was kept in the building. He told the gathering that he knew Gandhi's murder had been planned in advance. Quoting Godse, he stated, 'Gandhiji wants to live for 125 years. I will see how he does so.'[127]

As people began to follow newspaper reports, many started believing that Ketkar was aware of Godse's plan. A mob attacked him near Jain Mandir in Poona on 22 November, placing a garland of shoes around his neck.

He fled to Madras after an arrest warrant was issued against him and later surrendered there, but he retracted his statement. However, he maintained that he and Balukaka Kanitkar had decided to communicate the information to the government, sending it to BG Kher and Morarji Desai, the premier (chief minister) and home minister of Bombay. They discussed that a police reporter had been present at the scene and would report to the government, but Balukaka reminded Ketkar that police reporters were often lazy and wouldn't follow up.

Later, Ketkar told the commission that Godse had approached him in October 1947, asking for an article for his publication. 'I then tackled him and asked him if he was going to commit the murder of M Gandhi himself. He said it was correct that he was going to do that,' Ketkar revealed to the commission.

Justice Palekar Naik of the Bombay High Court heard Ketkar's bail plea. Ketkar claimed he had been struggling for the release of Gopal and Vishnu Ramakrishna Karkare since 1957. He presented a printed invitation card issued by one M.G. Ghaisas in court. It read:

> Shri Gopalrao Godse, brother of the patriot late Nathuram Godse, Shri Vishnupant Karkare and Shri Madanlal Pahwa have been released from jail. Out of joy for the said release, we, a circle of friends, are going to perform the mahapuja of Shri Satyavinayak. We propose to call the aforesaid three people for offering congratulations to them. You are, therefore, requested to remain present along with your circle.

Ketkar claimed in court that he had given advance notice of Godse's plan to Kher by registered letter.[128] Ketkar was released after eight months, having tendered an apology in which he promised not to attend such functions or praise Gandhi's assassin and the Mahasabha.

Backpedalling, denying, disowning, and offering apologies are all political instruments. We witnessed this after the tragic burning of Graham Stuart Stains, an Australian missionary, and his two sons, Philip and Timothy, in Orissa on 23 January 1999.

The RSS has often been uncertain about whether it aligns with Gandhi and Gandhism or stands opposed to them. Golwalkar, in his writings, seems eager to recount the Mahatma's reaction when he visited an RSS camp in Wardha in 1934. He noted that Gandhi was amazed to see members of every caste working together in the camp, performing all tasks equally. Golwalkar writes:

> This experience had left such a deep impression on Gandhiji's mind that he recounted it years later in his address to the swayamsewaks at Bhangi Colony, Delhi, in September 1947. He had then said that he was very much impressed with the discipline, the complete absence of untouchability and the rigorous simplicity among the swayamsewaks.[129]

Why, then, was the RSS so eager to gain approval from Gandhi? Later, Rajendra Singh, alias Rajju Bhaiya, the then sarsanghchalak of the Sangh, explained in an interview with *Outlook* on 19 January 1998: 'Godse was motivated by [the idea of] Akhand Bharat [undivided India]. His intention was good but he used a wrong method for a right goal.'

Koenraad Elst also remarked, 'They have exhausted themselves in denials and condemnations of the [Mahatma's] murder.'[130]

Repudiating literature is as easy as dismissing a minor incident. Bhagwat said at a meeting with Muslims in Vigyan Bhawan, Delhi, on 20 September 2018, that the *Bunch of Thoughts* by Golwalkar is 'not eternal'. He added, 'We have published a book titled *Vision and Mission: Guruji,* which contains his [Golwalkar's] eternal thoughts. We have removed all those thoughts that may have emerged in certain circumstances, and included those that are eternal.'

An RSS spokesperson said on 9 March 2006, in Nagpur, that Golwalkar's book, *We or Our Nationhood Defined*, published in 1939, is 'neither representing the views of Guruji [Golwalkar] nor of the RSS.'

It is not that Gandhi never changed or contradicted himself. On many occasions, he stated in his speeches that his view could evolve over time on certain issues. He openly acknowledged his personal evolution and insisted that his latest statements should be considered his final views on any issue. What was Gandhi's self-realization and evolution, became abnegation for his detractors. These critics disregarded the fact that it was through the power of self-realization that Gandhi 'challenged the might of the British Empire and won freedom for his people'.[131]

Gandhi succeeded because he implemented every idea within himself first. The relevance of his legacy is yet to be judged holistically, but we are already beginning to forget him. This forgetfulness becomes deliberate when someone is vying for his space.

To facilitate this, many leaders confine Mahatma within a framework of 'cultural Indianness' to create a parallel. For instance, Om Birla, the speaker of the lower house, wrote in an article for *Antim Jan*, 'An amazing personality has come to us to remind our identity. I am talking about our prime minister Narendra Modi.'[132]

2

Vinayak Damodar Savarkar

The Chest

Whether you like him or not, Savarkar was a man of indomitable spirit. He possessed the resilience to survive even in the most adverse conditions. This strength was partly due to his meticulous care of his health. Savarkar himself often wrote about his well-maintained muscular body in his jail diary.

Most of the letters he sent to his youngest brother, Narayan Savarkar, from Port Blair prison included updates on his health, along with advice to maintain good physical condition. In one such letter, written eighteen months after his incarceration, Savarkar remarked, 'I never had a serious illness and have managed to keep my weight just what it was when I came here … My mind has so quickly adapted itself to the change in circumstances.'

In a letter dated 15 December 1912, he also described his daily routine and the secret to his good health:

> While my hand and feet are automatically doing the given task [prison work from 5 a.m. to 10 a.m.], my spirit avoiding all detection, is out for a morning trip and across seas and oceans, over hills and dales, it roams sipping only pleasant things, and things noble, like a bee amongst the flowers.

This power of imagination, to transcend the immediate reality, remained with Savarkar throughout his life. A similar quality was embraced by Narendra Modi, who, like Savarkar, demonstrated a remarkable spirit. It was evident when Modi echoed Savarkar's fantasy during a public meeting in Gorakhpur, saying, 'I am Modi; I climb stairs while running.'[1]

Though we have not seen him running upstairs, we have seen Modi performing gym exercises and yoga in front of cameras.

In his book, *Jyotipunj*, Modi reflects on his first mentor in the RSS, Sangh Yogi Vakil Laxmanrao Inamdar. According to the translator's note:

> Those who came in contact with Sangh Yogi Vakil Laxmanrao Inamdar believed that he had some extraordinary spiritual power. Regular exercise, dhyana, reading of Gita and weekly fasting were its secret. Same is the secret of impressive personality and fitness of our Modiji. He also does regular dhyana and pranayama etc.

Thirteen years prior, health-conscious Modi began to showcase his fitness regimen. I first witnessed his bravado in 2003, during the assembly elections in Chhattisgarh. At the time, the state's chief minister, Ajit Jogi, had gained notoriety for his misrule. Surrounded by a large number of non-performing officers and ministers, Jogi's reputation only worsened. His opponents and the public accused his son, Amit, of amplifying his father's notoriety, using state power to intimidate them.

During his tenure, intelligence officers kept a watchful eye on every reporter from national newspapers and their stories. Jogi was friendly with his allies among journalists and often provided them with 'Maina', a government-owned chopper, to visit the forests. His senior officers would host liquor, Kadaknath chicken, music parties, and more for the journalists. The helicopter was named after the mynah, the state bird, and tragically crashed in 2007 in the Balaghat district of Madhya Pradesh. Four people, including two pilots, died. Some believed the Naxalites brought it down, while others attributed the crash to a technical snag.

The notorious Vidya Charan Shukla and his elder brother Shyama Charan Shukla had been attempting to replace Jogi as chief minister since 2000, when Chhattisgarh was carved out of Madhya Pradesh. Shyama had served as chief minister of Madhya Pradesh three times in the past, while Vidya was the information and broadcasting minister in the undemocratic government of Indira Gandhi during the mid-1970s. The 'brusque' Vidya, known as the 'excellent hatchet', was a henchman of Sanjay, Indira's youngest son.[2]

Indira had obtained the Shukla brothers' consent before enacting the Wildlife (Protection) Act, 1972, which banned shikar (hunting) of tigers and lions. Vidya proudly told me during a meeting in Raipur in 2002 that they used to run a venery company for wealthy European and American visitors, including Hollywood actors. His shooters would assist the hunters in killing the big cats. The hunter would then pose with one of his legs and the butt of his rifle resting on the slain animal to showcase his bravery.

Vidya joined the BJP at the end of 2003, bringing the upper-caste vote to the Hindutva party.

In his campaign against Jogi, Modi would ask the crowd, 'Do you think a man with a 32 inches chest can fight someone with 48 inches?' In a section of society, a masculine chest symbolizes courage. Although Chhattisgarh is a women-dominated tribal state, the people embraced Modi's virile and brute comparison.

In the 2014 Lok Sabha elections, Modi proclaimed in his distinctly orthoepic manner that his chest measured 56 inches. He claimed that the then Samajwadi Party president, Mulayam Singh Yadav, had a chest measurement of only 36 inches, and therefore, the socialist leader was not a match for a Hindutva leader. At that time, Akhilesh Yadav, Mulayam's son, was the chief minister of Uttar Pradesh. When the BJP won seventy-one out of eighty parliamentary seats in the heartland state, credit was given to Modi.

Overall, the BJP performed well across the country under Modi's leadership. His publicity managers presented him as the perfect blend of development and Hindutva.

Modi's right-wing populism was such that his publicists claimed he had influenced Donald Trump's re-election campaign, particularly when Trump adopted a nativist and anti-Muslim stance. They heralded this as a sign of the rapid Indianization of the US.

Before that, Trump had controversially suggested injecting disinfectant into the body to kill the coronavirus.[3] Many in India believed he was inspired by an experiment conducted in India. In Uttar Pradesh, specifically in Bareilly—home to a significant Sunni Muslim population—the local government doused hundreds of migrants, returning home from Delhi, with a sodium hypochlorite solution, commonly used to fumigate swimming pools. Local officers argued they were effectively sanitizing the migrants against COVID-19.[4]

Modi's followers embraced the theory of Indianization, yet the situation in India remained more complex. During his tour of the riot-torn district of Muzaffarnagar in 2014, graphic author Joe Sacco asked one of the young daughters of Momim Jolla, a devout Muslim, about her ultimate ambition. The girl replied, 'I want to see America.' Then, she asked Joe unexpectedly, 'Will you take me to your country?' I was accompanying Joe at the time and heard this without surprise. What this homely girl, who never ventured out of her street without a veil, expressed reflects the desire of the majority of Indian youth—whether educated or uneducated, Hindu or Muslim—over the past several decades.

Years later, when Modi claimed in public speeches that he had created 80 million jobs between 2020 and 2024, economist and Nobel laureate Amartya Sen challenged the narrative. In a speech in July 2024, Sen said:

> The education system was not at all developed significantly. The main reason behind Indian's unemployment is the neglect in education and healthcare ... The [Indian] government is now worried about the problem of unemployment. This is an admission that the problem persists. Why didn't countries like Europe, Japan and China face this problem?

Sen's remarks came amid a report by the Centre for Monitoring Indian Economy, a private body, which revealed that India's unemployment rate had risen from 7 per cent in May 2024 to 9.2 per cent in June 2024.[5]

As I reflected on the state of affairs, I couldn't help but think of Savarkar, whose chest measured only 36 inches. With Modi's chest shrinking due to age, I wondered how Savarkar would have reacted upon realizing that India had still not become the Hindutva nation he envisioned—despite his so-called staunchest followers now ruling the country.

Running a secret movement for India's freedom from British rule, Savarkar frequently travelled to Paris for health reasons. However, as a habitual revolutionary in his own right, he continued his work from Paris, which included smuggling weapons to India for an armed rebellion or to assassinate an English officer. While returning from Paris to England, he was arrested at London railway station on 13 March 1910 for waging war against the King Emperor of India and was subsequently put in Brixton Jail. Although he held a passport to stay in England, his frequent visits to Paris were illegal. The government was particularly vigilant following Savarkar's arrest due to rumours that his colleagues were planning his escape.

In London, he was tried for 'abetting murder in India by supplying firearms from England' and for 'sedition'. Since the effect of his offences was felt in India, Sir Rufus Isaacs (later Lord Reading) and Sidney Rowlatt (who later became known for the Rowlatt Act, which empowered the British police to arrest any person without trial) argued in the case titled *Emperor vs Vinayak Damodar Savarkar*, leading the court to order the government to send him back to India for further trial.

His journey to India began on 1 July aboard the SS *Morea*. Savarkar was comfortable on board; he wore European attire and mingled with fellow passengers. On 8 July, as the ship anchored at Marseilles harbour, he entered the bathroom at 7 a.m. The Scotland Yard officer had instructed an Indian policeman to keep a watch on Savarkar, but he managed to bolt the door and escape before it could be broken down. A quartermaster and the steward of the *Morea* spotted Savarkar as he plunged into the ocean and swam toward the wharf. The revolutionary, who stood 5 feet 2 inches tall, crossed the water and ran to the customs barrier, shouting to be taken before a magistrate, as he needed asylum. The gendarmes, however, refused to listen and brought him back to the ship, handing him over to the British police. He was apprehended and transported to India under the Fugitive Offenders Act, 1881. The *Morea* reached Bombay with Savarkar on 22 July.

L'Humanite, a newspaper owned by Jean Jaures, the mayor of Marseilles, labelled the incident an 'abominable violation of the rights of asylum'. The publication reminded that England 'felt very proud ... she gave asylum to Mazzini during his fight with Austria and also to Kossuth, the Hungarian patriot'.[6]

Dubbing him as 'the great Hindu political leader'[7], Jayakar wrote, 'Savarkar, who is 36 inched round the chest, succeeded in getting through a 12-inch circular porthole, after scraping his body very severely in the process.'[8]

The bench of the Bombay High Court that heard Savarkar's case consisted of Chief Justice Bansil Scott, N. Chandavarkar, and John Heaton. They sentenced him to fifty years in prison. He was lodged in Bombay's Dongri Jail, where a constable presented him with a badge indicating his year of punishment as 1910 and his release date as 1960.[9]

From there, he was transferred to Thane Jail. According to his own accounts, a hawaladar would stare at twenty-seven-year-old Savarkar while he bathed. Leering at him, the hawaladar would ridicule Savarkar, telling his subordinate constables to,

> See the body of elder brother! It is like a piece of gold. See the muscles of his arms, his broad chest! It is confirmed that you used to wrestle ... See, you should have spent your youth in a foreign country, mixing with the local beauty. This tenderness

> of yours and this hardship ... what tempted you to wear these iron shackles?[10]

A boastful Savarkar lamented being turned into a subject of entertainment, calling himself 'a lion caged for exhibition'.[11]

The war over the size of chests dominated the 2014 parliamentary election campaign. Every leader was forced to address it. The media was equally fascinated by this 'chest race', and questions about Modi's challenge became mandatory in interviews with Opposition leaders. Unable to remain silent for long, Mulayam responded to Modi's wisecrack and reminded him of his speeches during the 2002 communal riots in Gujarat:

> Modi Saheb! You talk about a 56-inch chest but you were behind the massacre in Gujarat as the chief minister of the state. You tried to stop me from visiting Muslim localities during the riots, warning that I would be killed there. I feared nothing. I have a very strong chest, and I went to those areas in Ahmedabad ... A Muslim woman took me inside a room and showed me the injuries on her body by removing her clothes. And now your leaders are apologizing to the community. The Muslims know who their true friend is. Modi Saheb! You kill Muslims and then apologize to them. But this community is with me in their hearts.

Some of the BJP nominees in the election had apologized to Muslim voters while campaigning in areas of Uttar Pradesh where the minority population was decisive.

Since Modi had simultaneously built his election campaign around the Gujarat model of development wrapped in

Hindutva, Mulayam stated that he wanted to remind the BJP leader that the dirtiest rivers flowed in Gujarat. He added:

> There are 37 per cent women and 50 per cent children suffering from malnutrition in your state. There are 89 per cent men and 90 per cent women working in the unorganized sector in Gujarat. You talk about 56-inch chest, yet you commit atrocities against the Muslim sisters of Gujarat. You must not leave Uttar Pradesh without addressing these issues.

Mulayam, a former wrestler-turned politician was hesitant to flaunt his chest with the same pugnacious pride that Modi displayed with his '*chhappan* inches'.

Ultimately, Modi won and became the prime minister. In February 2015, he attended the wedding ceremony of Mulayam's grandnephew, Tej Pratap Yadav, in Saifai, their ancestral village in Uttar Pradesh's Etawah district.

Modi and Mulayam embraced each other on a giant stage in Saifai, as if they were brothers who had lost their way in a fair as toddlers and were now reunited. The two opposite political figures seemed to merge together. This bond became even more apparent during the 2019 parliamentary elections when Mulayam, a member of Parliament, blessed Modi, saying, 'I wish you become the prime minister again. You have been doing all my work whenever I approach you.'[12]

The majority of the offices of the RSS and its various wings were established in Uttar Pradesh on land provided by Mulayam during his three terms as chief minister. He openly confessed to having given several acres of land to Nana Deshmukh to expand his ashram in Chitrakoot.

Mulayam had a knack for supporting Savarkar at every stage. Had the Hindutva leader been alive, he likely would have continued to be a friend to both Muslims and secular parties alike. Always considered a great friend of the left-wing parties, Mulayam didn't hesitate to send Sanjay Dalmia and Sacchidananda Hari Sakshi, two close associates of the RSS, to the Rajya Sabha from his Samajwadi Party in 1994 and 2000, respectively. Sanjay is the son of Vishnu Hari Dalmia, a former Vishwa Hindu Parishad president and admirer of the Hindu Mahasabha leaders of the past. Sakshi is currently a BJP MP and has, for the past two decades, been known for his admiration of Savarkar and Godse. He calls Godse a 'patriot and a nationalist' and often demands the Bharat Ratna for him.

Govindacharya, a former RSS ideologue, did not mince words at an ABVP meeting in Allahabad in 1998, 'We are like centipedes. We have a hundred legs. We will continue moving toward our target even if some of our legs are broken.'

It is evident that there are overlapping members in the Mahasabha and the RSS, just as the Indian National Congress and the Mahasabha had a joint platform and allowed dual membership for many decades during the freedom struggle.

The Meaning of Aga Khan

It is hard to imagine how Savarkar would have reacted to Modi bestowing the Padma Vibhushan on Shah Karim Al Husseini Aga Khan IV, the successor of Sultan Mohammed Shah Aga Khan III, in 2015. After all, the family was the force behind the creation of Pakistan.

Initially, Mahatma Gandhi declared that Pakistan would be formed 'on my dead body', but, later in life, he agreed to its formation, recognizing that the two communities couldn't exist in peace and harmony.

Savarkar never accepted the creation of Pakistan. Yet, in his final days, he claimed his life's mission was complete, and at the age of eighty-two, he was too frail to take up a new cause. He stopped eating, drinking, or taking medicine at his home in Bombay, renouncing his body on 26 February 1966, after twenty-five days of atmaarpan (dedication of the soul).

Some people fulfil their life's mission without others fully understanding what it was. Savarkar's critics might argue his mission culminated in Gandhi's assassination, while his supporters would say it was the unification of Hindus.

In a way, Savarkar's mission was truly accomplished forty-eight years after his death when the BJP won a majority in the Parliament for the first time, and Modi became the prime minister.

But are Hindus truly united when they award the Padma Vibhushan to Aga Khan IV, the successor of someone who was at the heart of the idea of Pakistan? How would Savarkar have reacted to one of the nation's highest awards being presented to Aga Khan IV? Perhaps he would have rebuked Modi.

Frustrated with Congress's politics, where public opinion was often disregarded, the nation turned to Modi with such hope that during his initial years as the prime minister, the common man rarely initiated any public debate. Just a year into his leadership, Modi honoured the grandson of Aga Khan III, and nobody questioned him.

If people do not take the time to understand figures like Gandhi or Savarkar, how will they ever understand the Aga Khans, who led an unchanging sect—a branch of Shia Islam—from a distant land? Aga Khan IV holds British, Portuguese, French, and several other citizenships, but not

Indian. Queen Elizabeth II granted Aga Khan IV the title of 'His Highness' nine years after Gandhi's assassination.

Aga Khan III presided over numerous meetings in England and India before Independence, during which the concept of a Muslim league and the idea of two nations were conceived. In 1897, the year of Queen Victoria's Diamond Jubilee, he attended three meetings in India. In one such assembly, representing the Muslims of Western India, the idea of a separate land for Muslims was first hinted at.

Agha Khan III's close relationship with Lord Minto played a significant role in securing special electorates for Muslims in the imperial council and in all provinces except Punjab. He led the Shimla Deputation of thirty-five influential Muslims to the viceroy, Gilbert Elliot, the fourth earl of Minto, advocating for special legislative representation for Muslims. Eventually, a separate Muslim electorate was granted through the Morley-Minto reforms in 1909.

Aga Khan III also supported the partition of Bengal in 1905 and served as the president of the All India Muslim League from 1907 to 1913. The league was formed on 30 December 1906 in Dhaka, during a meeting of affluent Muslim leaders close to Lord Minto. Khwaja Salimullah, the nawab of Dhaka, led the meeting with Aga Khan III by his side.

Like a politician, Aga Khan III did not hide his role in the creation of Pakistan. However, he emphasized that Nehru and Patel were the only Congress leaders approaching Gandhi's stature. He noted that 'the strength of nationalist sentiment grew steadily throughout these years' and also 'the consciousness among the Muslims that they must work out their own destiny' and strengthen themselves 'steadily'.[13]

The 1928 Congress session in Calcutta, which promoted self-government, was not acceptable to the Muslim leaders.

Aga Khan III felt that the Congress was 'underrating—indeed, ignoring—Muslim claims to be considered a nation within a nation'.[14]

That same year, at the Muslim League meeting in Calcutta, Jinnah was authorized to press for five amendments to the (Motilal) Nehru Report at the All India Convention. When the Congress rejected the demand for one-third of the seats to be reserved for Muslims, a disillusioned Jinnah left Calcutta for Delhi to attend the All Party Muslim Conference. Under the chairmanship of Aga Khan III, the conference passed Jinnah's fourteen-point demands.

Aga Khan III noted that he was convinced the assembly was 'one of the most important in the long series of such assemblies … It was a vast gathering representative of all shades of Muslim opinion.' He proudly wrote, 'I can claim to be the parent of its most important and lasting political decisions.'[15]

The Aga Khan Development Network has been active for many years, but it was the Modi government that awarded Aga Khan III's successor one of the highest civil honours. The process for conferring such awards begins months in advance, meaning Modi had this in mind either before or within a few months of taking office as the prime minister of India.

In a similar vein, Sir Moneckji Byramji Dadabhoy, a Parsi lawyer and critic of both Mahatma and the Indian National Congress, showed affection for the imam in 1924. Dadabhoy, an industrialist and member of the Council of State, moved a resolution on 5 February advocating for a Nobel Peace Prize for Muhammad Shah for his efforts to 'maintain peace between Turkey and the Western Power'. It comes as no surprise, as politicians often show extraordinary affection for the wealthy.

Perhaps Savarkar would have opposed Modi's decision. Maybe he would have remained silent on honouring the wealthy religious leader or even strengthened the romance of Hindutva by allying with a closed-door Islamic sect.

Interestingly, between 1939 and 1943, Savarkar allied his Hindu Mahasabha with the Muslim League and Muslim leaders in Sindh, the Northwest Frontier Province, and Bengal.

It is not my intention to prove that Savarkar, the forerunner of Hindutva, was an opportunist and courted the Muslims for power. Even Gandhi's Congress aligned with both the Muslims and the Mahasabha, before and after Independence. At times, they didn't seem so unequal.

At the Kanpur session of the Mahasabha in 1942, Savarkar justified his collaboration with the Muslim league as 'compromises' and claimed 'responsibility [for] joining hands with the League upon invitation in Sind'.[16]

In Bengal, during the Mahasabha's twenty-fourth session, Savarkar noted that the coalition government, 'under the leadership of Fazlul Huq and Mahasabha leader Dr Syama Prasad Mookerjee, worked successfully for a year or so'.[17]

Mookerjee was the finance minister in Fazlul Haq's ministry in Bengal in 1941-42. The Mahasabha collaborated with the Muslim League in Sindh under Ghulam Hussain Hidayatullah and in the Northwest Frontier Province (NWFP) under Sardar Aurangzeb Khan.

It is no secret that, a few years earlier, Savarkar supported Mookerjee's demand for a separate Hindu province in Bengal, which suggested he was not averse to the idea of a separate Muslim Bengal either.

At the Mahasabha's twenty-second Madura Conference in 1940, Savarkar explained that their past actions were primarily aimed at opposing the Congress Party. He reaffirmed that he would continue to form similar alliances in the future.

The Congress never missed an opportunity to foster hatred towards Savarkarites, yet in 2019, they had no qualms about allying with the Shiv Sena—a party that follows and venerates Savarkar and Godse. Bal Keshav Thackeray, also known as Balasaheb, founded the Shiv Sena, and his son Uddhav Thackeray became the chief minister of Maharashtra with the Congress's support. The Thackerays have long been advocating for Savarkar to be awarded the Bharat Ratna.

Inspired by Savarkar's discourse on armed rebellion, Dhingra shot Wyllie dead at Jahangir Hall, Imperial Institute, in South Kensington, London. Savarkar had often stated in his speeches after his release from the Andaman Islands that he had gone to London not only to study but also to learn how to manufacture bombs and initiate a revolution in his own fashion.

Every evening, while sitting by the fire at London's India House, Savarkar and other inmates would pledge:

> There would be Hindi (in India) as a national language,
> Devanagari as a national script,
> There would be one God, one nation, one language,
> One caste, one human, one hope.[18]

Some ridiculed them for making such pledges, but many others were energized by their commitment.

In a speech to students in Dadar on 18 November 1953, Savarkar said, 'My indirect purpose of going to England was to learn to make bomb so that we use it against the British.'[19]

Aga Khan III, the chairperson of the meeting, denounced the act as 'violent' and 'shameful', calling for it to be 'condemned unanimously'. Savarkar, however, stood to protest against any condemnation of Dhingra's act. He opposed the resolution, shouting that the decision was 'not unanimous'.[20]

Many revolutionaries of that time lived at London's 'India House', run by Shyamji Krishna Varma. The house provided a space for political discourse, cultural activities, and the distribution of nationalist literature. In December 1905, Shyamji announced a one-time scholarship of Rs 6,000 for six Indians to reside there, travel, and raise awareness of India's struggle for freedom. S.R. Rana of Maharashtra wrote to Shyamji, offering to sponsor three additional Indians and naming the scholarship after Rana Pratap, Shivaji, and a Muslim king.[21]

Savarkar received Shivaji scholarship on Tilak's recommendation. He went to England, enrolled in a law course at London University, and founded the Free India Society alongside Dhingra, Paramanand, and Lala Hardayal Mathur. They lived together in India House until Wyllie's murder, after which police began conducting raids.

Until then, Savarkar was relatively unknown to British spies and the Indian revolutionary world. He was assaulted by a Eurasian youth at Jahangir Hall and briefly detained before being released due to a lack of evidence. This was the first and only time he was seen protesting in support of a friend. We might also consider it the second time if we take into account his childhood act of raising a group to support the Chapekar brothers.

Along with Aga Khan III, figures like Surendranath Banerjee, Bipin Chandra Pal, Mancherji Bhavnagri, Dinshaw Petit, Fazalbhai Karim, and Shreemant Ganesh Krishna

Khaparde, also known as Dada Saheb, were present. One of Dhingra's brothers was also there and was attacked by the British attendees. Pal condemned the murder as well.

Gandhi wrote, 'One of the accepted and "time-honoured" methods to attain the end is that of violence. The assassination of Sir Curzon Wylie was an illustration of that method in its worst and most detestable form.'[22]

All of Savarkar's meetings with Gandhi had come to nothing, as Gandhi had not accepted even a fraction of Savarkar's ideas. Nevertheless, Savarkar remained resistant to any criticism.

There were a few individuals who earned Savarkar's admiration in his writings, including Tilak, Shivrampant Paranjape, and Moonje. However, Savarkar also admired Khaparde, who supported Aga Khan III in condemning the murder of Wyllie. Khaparde had travelled to London to pressure the British government to release Tilak, who had been sentenced to six years of rigorous imprisonment for sedition by the Bombay court in 1908.[23]

Khaparde, a Deshastha Brahmin, had worked closely with Tilak to disrupt the Surat Conference of the Congress in 1907, when a permanent rift between the moderates and extremists was formed. Tilak failed to assert his dominance over the party. '... [In] later years he [Khaparde] became as mild as a dove and too moderate even for the Moderates'.[24]

Nehru recalled an incident in 1918 when they were invited as guests of Rash Behari Ghosh. In casual conversation, Khaparde mentioned that Gokhale was a British agent who spied on him in London, and he described Tilak as 'a saint'.

Rash Behari Ghosh, a prominent lawyer, retorted, 'I hate saints, I want to have nothing to do with them.'[25]

Mandyam Prativadi Thirumalacharya (M.P.T. Acharya) and Varahaneri Venkatesa Subramanian Aiyar, both members of India House tried to protect Savarkar from being attacked by the aggressive Eurasian at Jahangir Hall. Acharya, an Aiyangar Brahmin from Madras, was involved in left-leaning nationalist movements during the First World War. He co-founded the Communist Party of India (CPI) in Tashkent, Soviet Union, in October 1920, but was suspended from the organization after three months when he opposed M.N. Roy's decision to bar followers of other revolutionary groups from joining. Later, Acharya turned to anarchist movements.

After Savarkar's arrest in 1910, Acharya went to Paris and connected with socialists there. Whether with Hindutva or socialism, this freedom fighter and journalist opposed Gandhi's non-violence but never endorsed militarism in the Savarkarian sense. He served as proof that Savarkar didn't harbour hatred for leftists or anarchists in the way his followers would later.

Acharya's foreign colleagues described him as 'incorruptible' and 'the most prominent figure among Indian libertarians'. He was also opposed to the Bolshevik regime in Russia. In 1922, he met and married Magda Nachman, a Russian artist.

Ideologically, Acharya was a stark contrast to Savarkar, who was the most organized among the revolutionaries. Acharya observed that he and others were 'anarchists, because we do not want authoritarianism outside or inside, because to us anti-Marxists, life and society must be, immanently, one indivisible whole, impossible of mechanical separation—as the Marxists inorganically think and believe'.[26]

Aiyar, a Tamil Brahmin from Trichinopoly (now Tiruchirapalli, Karur, Ariyalur, and Perambalur), believed in armed struggle. He also escaped to Paris after Savarkar's arrest. From there, he returned to Pondicherry the same year. His disciple, Vanchinatha Iyer, assassinated Robert Ashe, the district collector of Tirunelveli. After the First World War, Aiyar moved to Madras and became the editor of *Desabhaktan*, a newspaper. He is also known as the father of Tamil short stories.

Both Acharya and Aiyar were more talented individuals than Savarkar and had grander visions, but they were less calculative, less aggressive and less vocal than the Hindutva leader.

Savarkar took issue with Aga Khan's speeches but did not oppose everyone who condemned Dhingra's act. He was a revolutionary in his own way but was also a politician, no different from the politicians of the past or the present.

Aga Khan III never condemned the Jallianwala Bagh massacre, the most glaring wound inflicted by the Raj on India. In his memoir, he made it clear that he wouldn't do so. His role in the creation of Pakistan became evident when he wrote about the viceroy's acceptance of their demands, the foundation of the All-India Muslim League, and 'my election as its president marked for me the culmination of a period of concentrated political effort'.[27]

Perhaps some Indians hate Jinnah, but Aga Khan III compared him to the Prophet.[28]

Supercilious Savarkar

Savarkar's dominance within the Mahasabha had become questionable. This was why Mookerjee was unable to give an immediate opinion during the cabinet meeting following

Gandhi's death. On Gadgil's suggestion, he issued a statement 'a day or two later', stating that communal parties had no place in a democracy. Presumably, it must have been difficult for anyone associated with the Mahasabha or the RSS during those days. A large number of Hindutva workers were being attacked by Gandhi's angry supporters, who believed from the very first day that the Mahasabha was behind the assassination.

Nevertheless, many in Nehru's cabinet wanted to give the Mahasabha the benefit of the doubt. Patel and Gadgil believed that any government action against the Mahasabha would be seen as political vendetta and 'suggested that action should be taken only in the case of individuals and institutions against those we had irrefutable proof'.[29]

Savarkar had followers and disciples, but no colleagues or friends after his first release from prison. Besides Shivaji, Tilak was the only person whose influence remained significant for Savarkar. There were many reasons for this, but the most important was the consolidation of Hinduism.

Savarkar spoke out against untouchability, but his aim was to assimilate the 'untouchables' into Hinduism. However, he didn't reject the varna system. He argued:

> To regard our 70 million co-religionists as untouchable and worse than animals is an insult not only to humanity but also to the sanctity of our soul. It is my firm conviction this is why untouchability should be principally eradicated. Untouchability should go also because its eradication is in the interests of our Hindu society.[30]

Later, he wrote:

> [It] should not be forgotten that the practice of birth based caste division must have been responsible for the mighty consolidation and amazing stability of the Hindu society under certain circumstances and conditions.[31]

Savarkar also believed that Hinduism survived due to the strength of the upper castes. He wrote, 'There remained no trace of the Greeks, the Huns and the Sakas in Bharatwarsha because the arrows of the Kshatriyas and ritual fire of the Brahmins reduced them into ashes.'[32]

Savarkar failed to consider that the victims of untouchability, throughout history, have primarily blamed the varna system for their plight. Moreover, many of them have long harboured substantial contempt for Hinduism itself.

The freedom of the country was secondary for some. This laid the groundwork on which Savarkar built and expanded individually and ideologically.

Like most Chitpavans, Tilak believed that the reawakening movement in Maharashtra began with Chiplunkar's *Nibandhmala*. Chiplunkar, a government schoolteacher, started publishing the magazine in 1874 from Poona. However, he was transferred to Ratnagiri for writing against British rule.

Despite this setback, he continued publishing essays against the Raj and resigned from his job in 1879. A man of letters, Chiplunkar returned to Poona, where he met Agarkar and Tilak, and together they began working on their shared cause. With vaunting ambition, Chiplunkar was quoted as saying after completing the 30th edition of *Nibandhmala*:

'I am the Shivaji of the Marathi language, who had not his equal either to precede or succeed.'[33]

Tilak claimed that before *Nibandhmala*, supporters of the Hindu religion were only focused on protecting Indian culture. 'Chiplunkar didn't have the tendency of seeking protection or apology. He not only attacked foreigner Christian missionaries but also the indigenous social reformers.'[34]

Gandhi, arguably one of the most truthful leaders in human history, was fully aware of his social limitations. He begins his autobiography with, 'The Gandhis belong to the Bania caste and seem to have been originally grocers.'[35]

The significance of caste is also evident in Kelkar's narrative. He wrote about the origin of the Tilaks and emphasized caste supremacy early on. After noting that Tilak was born in Chikhalgaon in Dapoli Taluka, Ratnagiri district, Konkan, Kelkar elaborated on the spirit of caste. He mentioned that some who sought to insult the Chitpavans or portray them in a negative light would claim they were born from the 'pyre'. However, those who took pride in their birth within this holy caste believed that 'the Konkansthas are the God's chosen people' of 'pure heart' and they 'may rightly be compared to the Phoenix'.[36]

Gandhi's analytical understanding of his environment was extraordinary. This is the primary reason he didn't openly react to caste bias after the initial years following his return from South Africa. Instead, he quietly sought to reduce opposition from the 'greenish-brown eyes' by declaring Gokhale, one of them, as his guru. A particular caste group were his harsh critics, and so he found a guru from that very caste. I wouldn't say that this was a conscious strategy on Gandhi's part, but it certainly helped him gain followers within that community.

Nevertheless, little has changed to this day. The followers of Savarkar continue to abhor Gandhi. The constant blathering of Hindutva leaders against the unorthodox Gandhi is proof of this. Yet, this also occurs because they find him indispensable.

Before Gandhi entered Indian politics, the Congress carefully maintained the superiority complex of the upper classes. It would publish the names of its delegates at every annual session, with their caste listed in the next column.

One such list was from the twenty-fifth Congress session held in Allahabad. Sir William Wedderburn was Congress president, and Rash Behari Ghosh chaired the convention committee in 1910–11. Out of 636 delegates, about 245 had 'Brahmin' written next to their names.

The Congress never sought to break free from its caste shackles. After all, leaders like Motilal, Jawaharlal, and many others were Brahmins themselves and dominated the northern landscape. They knew the masses would remain loyal to the Congress through Gandhi, but their dilemma was whether to appease the upper castes. This predicament persists to this day.

Gandhi succeeded in drawing a thick curtain over caste dominance within the party because he wanted to prevent an open conflict between Brahmins from different regions, which could have crushed others caught in between.

Savarkar's awareness of his superior caste was evident in his observation that Sultan Pheroz Shah, the ruler of Tughlaq dynasty who ruled over Delhi from 1351 to 1388, 'hated the

Brahmins far more bitterly than other Hindus'. He attributed to the emperor, based on historian H.S. Williams' statement, the remark that 'Brahmins are the veritable keys to the strong fortress of the Hindu religion.' Savarkar also noted that the Brahmins organized 'a resistance movement against the Jizya tax, freshly imposed on Hindus'.[37]

However, this was not the complete truth as Hindus of all castes opposed the tax. Additionally, the Brahmins Savarkar referred to did not necessarily represent the Brahmins of Kashmir or Delhi or Uttar Pradesh.

Scientific Substratum

Science underwent a revolution in the 19th and the early 20th centuries, a period that coincided with the emergence of Hindutva proponents in India. The foundation of the New English School and the Deccan Education Society in Poona were key steps in this direction. Chiplunkar established two printing presses there: Aryabhushan Press and Chitrashala. Poona, in particular, showed great potential to lead the country in the growth of knowledge.

Baron Karl von Drais, a German civil servant, invented the Draisine, a proto-bicycle, in 1817. This design evolved into the modern bicycle over the next eighty years. The Orient Express began its service in 1883, connecting Paris and Istanbul, while the first Oxford English Dictionary was published in 1884. In 1887, Philip Diehl, a German American, invented the wall-mounted ceiling fan.

Indians also made modern initiatives but eventually stagnated in their outlook towards knowledge. The situation was conducive to growth, as wealthy figures like Motilal Nehru and Sapru from Allahabad, along with other Brahmin leaders of similar stature from various parts of the Indian subcontinent, were allies of the Raj. They witnessed the metal coating of the Grant Trunk Road.

The Red Hill Railroad was opened in Madras, and this development eventually led to the introduction of the first electric passenger train in India, which ran between Victoria Terminus and Kurla in 1925.

A medical college was opened in Calcutta, and an engineering college in Roorkee. The British established the universities of Calcutta, Madras, and Bombay. However, our leaders showed little interest in progressive education; instead, they often diverted the youths from it. Poona had the potential to spearhead a scientific revolution, but it was first curated as a league of higher order and later became a centre of reverse terrorism.

The British promoted science and education because they believed they would remain in India indefinitely. They did not foresee the two world wars that would weaken most great powers. Unfortunately, many influential indigenous minds, despite their sectarian and casteist tendencies, were largely indifferent to the idea of knowledge and development. The British, for their part, did not hinder the country from thinking in terms of progress. They established schools and colleges and allowed private industries to flourish. India has continued with the industrialization policies of the British even after Independence.

Chetty, the finance minister of India, said while presenting the first Union Budget:

> We cannot afford to lose the benefit of the long years of experience which private enterprises has gained in the building up of our industrial economy. I believe that the general pattern of our economy must be a mixed economy

> in which there is scope both for private enterprises and for State enterprises.[38]

We continue to hear similar sentiments during the presentation of the annual budget even today.

The war for independence was not very intense in Poona, which is why Viceroy Lord Ripon and Governor of Bombay Sir James Fergusson were made patrons of Fergusson College. The heroes of the time in Maharashtra were, in fact, the heroes of the Raj.

India undertook some scientific initiatives after Independence, establishing the first Indian Institute of Technology in Kharagpur in 1950, followed by other such institutes. The Bhilai Steel Plant and factories, including Bharat Heavy Electricals Limited, began to emerge in 1955 and thereafter. While these efforts aimed to improve the economy, the development of science was also a crucial aspect of these initiatives.

Gandhi wanted to return to the village but never opposed science or the development of theories through experiments. He was against the Western model of industrialization, as it was based on urban structures, whereas India was predominantly rural. He once urged the students of Rashtriya Pathshala in Khamgaon, Maharashtra, to consider upgrading the spinning wheel, believing in the importance of strengthening the rural economy. His expectation was justified, as Khamgaon had been a centre of cotton production and trade since the early 19th century.

Some contemporary thinkers in Indian universities believe that the majority of India is once again resisting knowledge and science while clinging to faith, which leads to directionlessness and self-destruction.

What the followers of absolute Hindutva are doing today reflects a temperament that moves away from science. Some allege that we are living in an age of disrespect for knowledge.

Savarkar didn't say much of substance about science, except in the context of bomb-making. If he ever spoke about science, it was always through the lens of religion.

Irritated by those who struggled to find common ground with Hindutva, Savarkar boasted of the Hindu religion's resilience during foreign rule:

> We cannot sit back and think that we will survive just because we survived in past. We have science in front of us now. We'll win as Hindus if we fought this war [to protect Hinduism] with patience, with the weapons of science against science.[39]

It remains unclear whether he was referring to technology, scientific knowledge, or rituals.

Savarkar was born in Bhagoor, in the Nasik district, about a decade before the plague devasted the country. The Chapekar brothers—Damodar Hari, Balkrishna Hari, and Vasudeo Hari—became heroes among the revolutionaries of the province after they shot at two plague officers, Walter Charles Rand and his escort, Lt Ayerst, on the Diamond Jubilee of Queen Victoria's coronation, leading to their arrest and subsequent death sentences. Savarkar and his group, Mitra Mela, took an activist stance, opposing the mourning session for Queen Victoria after her death.

After matriculation, he attended Fergusson College in Poona, where he formed the Savarkar Group. He published a paper called *Aryan* and also wrote for *Kaal*, edited by Paranjape, who introduced him to Tilak. However, he was expelled from Fergusson College for burning foreign clothes.

Later, Savarkar expanded the base of Mitra Mela and renamed it the Abhinav Bharat Society. He completed his BA from the University of Bombay.

Savarkar's characterization of the revolt of 1857 as the first war of India's independence, along with his ideology of Hindutva, established him as a prominent figure in his class. For him, Hindutva was beyond debate; it transcended knowledge and science.

Savarkar was a rebel of his own kind. Although he protested against Aga Khan III's speech following the murder of Wyllie, Bipin Chandra Pal, who was aligned with the Imam on a common issue, became Savarkar's host when India House closed. While Pal was occasionally in England, Savarkar and Acharya stayed with his son, Niranjan.

He wrote that 'Bipin Babu' cooked 'fish and flesh in the Bengali style … served them to me with great importunity and had added to his moral credit the meritorious act of polluting a strictly vegetarian Maharashtrian Brahmin like me'.[40]

Savarkar revelled in having meat, which was considered a crime among the Chitpavans. He and his friend eventually moved from there after a crowd stormed Pal's place.

Savarkar spoke against untouchability and advocated for Hindu unity, but he believed that untouchables could be 'cleansed'. While in prison, Savarkar clung to his deep

Brahmanical belief, and his approach to untouchables remained puritanical. He stated that the tel godam (oil mill) of Cellular jail 'proved very useful in bringing converted Muslims to purify and induct them back into the Hindu religion'. However, the Muslims would reject the converted Hindus, pushing them out of their queues upon seeing their new choti (hair knot).

Savarkar claimed to have helped untouchables, saying, 'I would call them [untouchables] to the godown on the pretext of some work. I would make them soap and take pure bath and make them wear new clothes and sit with me for meal.'[41]

However, Savarkar's account raises doubts. Barindra Kumar Ghosh, who also worked in the oil mill, mentioned the Hindutva leader's name only once in his jail diary. Ghosh noted that he and the Savarkar brothers were still in Andaman when many other prisoners had been sent back to their respective states. Barin worked in the oil mill but didn't mention Savarkar's purification rituals. Instead, he wrote, 'Bhai Paramanand, a former Professor of Dayanand College, had never joined any strike and was made a compounder in the hospital.'[42]

Barin and many other prisoners were assigned harsh work and often went on strikes, which led to even harsher punishments. Savarkar was not part of these protests.

Forgetting that Tilak was a desperate politician seeking to take over the Congress Party with the help of Hindutva would be a mistake if we are trying to understand the connection between the past and the present. The people of Poona called Tilak the 'Father of Hindutva' years before Savarkar's rise.

However, Tilak and Savarkar were two similar metals that couldn't form an alloy. Savarkar was released from jail four years after Tilak's death, finding the ground prepared for him.

Tilak was more of a politician than someone solely dedicated to the freedom of India, as evidenced by the Panchhaud Mission controversy. The Panchhaud Mission is a church located in the Guruvar Peth area of Poona. Gopalrao Joshi, a social worker, invited leaders to the church to discuss social issues. The next day, he anonymously published an article and pictures of the meeting in *Poona Vaibhav*, turning the Hindus' acceptance of tea and biscuits from the Christians a significant controversy. Upper-caste Hindus began ostracizing all those who were present in the church, including Tilak.

A committee was formed under two local residents, Venkat Shastri Nipanikar and Bindu Madhan Shastri, to resolve the issue. They approached the angry crowd and asked the church attendees to repent for their actions, but Tilak refused. Forty-six individuals were charged with losing their holiness. The allegations against nine of them were withdrawn for various reasons, while eight were cleared for not having tea during the meeting. Since they were physically present at the church, they were asked to donate as much as possible to the Brahmins. Sixteen people refused to appear before the commission but expressed their repentance on their own.

Tilak was among those who had taken tea. He claimed he did tapasya in Kashi to atone for the religious wrong he had committed, stressing that accepting tea and biscuits from the missionaries did not change his religion.

As a result, the upper-caste Hindus ostracized Tilak, refusing to attend the upnayan sanskar (thread ceremony) of his son, Vishwanath Balwant. They also boycotted the marriage ceremony of his eldest daughter, Ramabai. The affair occurred in October 1891.

Savarkar was more liberal in that he disagreed with the notion that accepting food from a Muslim would affect a Hindu's identity. He asserted that one's 'digestive system should be such that you remain a Hindu after having food from the hands of a Muslim, snacks from the hands of a Christian'.[43]

However, like Gandhi, Savarkar referred to the untouchables as 'bhangis'.[44] Gandhi might have used the term for clarity, Savarkar's usage stemmed from his limited vocabulary.

The Ganesha festival was well known in Maharashtra during the 1890s, but people celebrated it privately. Tilak recognized its political potential. Kelkar noted:

> People used to celebrate the Ganesh festival with great splendour and éclat even before the time of Tilak … The ingenuity of Tilak resided not in originating the festival but in giving it a collective aspect and utilizing it as a most efficacious means of creating national enthusiasm among the people.[45]

Gangadharrao Balkrishna Deshpande and Govindrao Yalgi, two Congressmen, first hosted the Ganesha festival as a public function in Belagavi (Belgaum, Karnataka) in 1905. The first idol of Ganesha was installed at Yalgi's house and opened to the public. They invited Tilak to attend, and a procession was held from the railway station to Zenda Chowk, where the idol was moved from Yalgi's house to accommodate larger crowds. Tilak, who was keen on religious symbolism to resonate with the public psyche, found this appealing and initiated a mass celebration in Poona and Bombay the following year. Zenda Chowk is now known as Madhyavarthi Sarvajanik Shri Ganapathi Utsav Mandal.

One might argue that freedom was the first step towards promoting science in India. But was religion a viable path to achieving freedom? Does religion ever foster a scientific temperament? There is no historical example to support this.

Savarkar often referred to his guru as 'the great Tilak'.[46] Later, 'Tilak started praising Savarkar when he was given a copy of the bomb manual', which Savarkar had secretly sent to India.[47]

With extremism as his method, Tilak advocated for 'swaraj' and Savarkar responded with a bomb. While Tilak's predecessors may have conveyed their ideas, Savarkar simplified them, though he lacked the popular eloquence of others.

Savarkar wrote, 'We want a Hindu nation because there is a nation of Hindus. First the river and then the bridge. Similarly, wish is first, nation is first and its analysis thereafter.'[48] For this vision, Savarkar's followers were armed with pistols and homemade bombs, tools he instructed them to use before engaging in the 'analysis' of their actions.

Savarkar and Hitler

We have often heard about the Hindutva brigade being accused of worshipping Hitler, one of the most despised dictators in modern history. This perception was shaped by the Congress and the left when people were still under the influence of Gandhi. They instilled fear that once the brigade's ideological followers gained power, they would alter the very fabric of the Constitution and the country.

This socio-political paranoia was deeply embedded within the intellectual class, to the extent that they overlooked the dictatorial tendencies of other political parties in India. The Mahasabha leaders of the past and the RSS remained ingrained in the public's mind as the harbingers of fascism. However, it's important to remember that when Nehru became the prime minister in the national government, the Mahasabha was his coalition partner.

Nehru and Indira favoured free thinkers, leftist intellectuals and historians of Hindi and English by granting them properties, prestigious positions, and important roles in premier institutions. Writings on Hindutva or critiques of the ruling dispensation were often suppressed from reaching the public.

People trusted the Congress because of Gandhi, and by extension, they trusted Nehru and the New Gandhis. However, as Gandhi's charisma began to fade, so did the public's trust in the Congress.

However, the actions of the prime ministers from the Nehru–New Gandhi family could also be compared to the oppressive methods of dictators. Banning the RSS after Gandhi's assassination may be debatable or even justifiable, but pressuring them to merge with the Congress was a form of coercion. Indira's imposition of the Emergency, Rajiv's handling of the Ram Temple or Shah Bano case and his desire to pass a bill restricting the press were not saintly acts.

While Indira Gandhi, as prime minister, imposed the internal Emergency, the real power lay with her son, Sanjay Gandhi. During this period, a large number of youths were forcibly sterilized, and all opponents and critics were imprisoned. One story from Allahabad recounts the arrest of writer and then head of the Hindi department at the University of Allahabad, Prof. Raghuvansh Sahay Verma. Physically challenged, he used his legs to help his hands move so he could write, requiring assistance to turn pages. Raghuvansh was accused of damaging railways tracks and cutting telephone wires. After his arrest, he was sent to Naini Jail. Upon hearing of this, some individuals informed Hindi poetess Mahadevi Verma, who knew Indira Gandhi personally. Mahadevi spoke to Indira over the phone, and Raghuvansh was released late that night. Ironically, he waited for dawn at the prison gate, near a heritage cell named after Jawaharlal Nehru, who had been held there during the freedom struggle.

While many memoirs have detailed the inhuman conditions of the Andaman Jail during British rule, the stories of torture during the Emergency in India's police stations and prisons remain to be told.

Despite this, Indira had the support of Hindi authors like Srikant Verma, a centrist poet, and Namvar Singh, a leftist literary critic. They, along with others, including Amrita Pritam, supported the Emergency. Some even wrote slogans and pamphlets for Indira.

Nehru allowed the idol of Rama to remain in the Babri Masjid and closed its gate. Later, when the district and sessions court in Faizabad ordered the gates of the Islamic shrine to be opened, Rajiv Gandhi, as prime minister, along with Congress's Vir Bahadur Singh, then chief minister of Uttar Pradesh, chose not to contest the judgement. They opened the gates for Hindus, hoping to win the majority votes, which instead shifted to the BJP.

Earlier, Rajiv, as prime minister, enacted a law in the Shah Bano case, denying Muslim women the right to alimony from former husbands after the utterance of 'triple talaq'. Shah Bano was married to Mohammad Ahmed Khan, a lawyer from Indore, and had five children when he expelled her from their matrimonial home in 1975. The sixty-two-year-old woman filed a case, and an Indore court ordered Khan to pay her Rs 500 per month. However, Khan invoked triple talaq, claiming he no longer needed to support her since she was no longer his wife. The case eventually reached the Supreme Court, which ruled in favour of Shah Bano's right to alimony, ordering Khan to pay maintenance. In response, the Rajiv government overturned the Supreme Court's decision.

Rajiv also attempted to control the press by introducing an anti-defamation law in 1988, which he withdrew two months later due to pressure from the public and the media. While the government claimed the law was aimed at curing scurrilous writing, the timing suggested that the then prime minister sought to suppress reports and opinions about the Bofors scandal. The bill included provisions for criminal action against the press for publishing controversial articles, with the burden of proof placed on the defendant. In other words, journalists would have to prove in court that their reporting was in the public interest.

Under Rajiv's leadership, India had signed a contract with the Swedish arms manufacturer AB Bofors to purchase advanced weaponry. However, reports in press alleged that AB Bofors had bribed several ruling party politicians and officials to secure the deal.

The Hindu Mahasabha, once the base organization of Hindutva, had almost vanished a few years after Independence, and the RSS took its place. However, at that time, its resources were too limited to effectively remind people of the Congress's darker side.

However, those who opposed Rajiv's defamation bill and were better positioned to protect the press ultimately showed a similar temperament. In 1999, a reporter posed an uncomfortable question to Brinda Karat, a leader of the Communist Party of India (Marxist) (CPI[M]), in Chitrakoot. Karat had come to participate in a protest against a man who had raped his daughter.

Instead of answering, she responded, 'Are you a Bajrang Dal member?' Bajrang Dal is the militant youth wing of the RSS.

In recent years, the CPI(M) government in Kerala has been more in the news for harassing journalists than for anything else. A provincial party functionary was recently quoted as saying, 'The media will face action for reporting against the government in the state and more cases will be filed if [it] continues to indulge in anti-government activities.'[49]

In a significant ruling, the Kerala High Court quashed criminal cases against two journalists, stating, 'The press can't be prosecuted for a sting operation conducted in good faith.'[50]

Efforts to curb the media have become an everyday issue in the state, which appears to be the last fortress of the left. While past villains remain, those who once opposed them are now transforming into the same villains in order to retain power.

In 2013, Rahul Gandhi gave a lecture on the RSS to some journalists at his party office in Lucknow. At the end, someone asked, 'Don't you think Modi is bigger than the RSS in the present situation?'

Rahul, with a sudden change in expression, replied, 'This is something I expect only from a Sangh sympathizer.' He didn't like the implication that Modi was dictating the RSS, as he had concluded that the RSS would rule the country from behind the scenes.

In 2000, I was in Nagpur, attending K.S. Sudarshan's first press conference as RSS sarsanghchalak. Sudarshan mentioned Samuel P. Huntington's book *The Clash of Civilizations*, and I asked him why he was viewing it through an Indian perspective. 'It seems you have read the book. Are you a leftist?' Sudarshan asked.

It has become a convention that if you seem unfriendly with Congress or the left, you are branded a Hindutva votary, and if you ask tough questions to the Hindutva brigade, you are labelled a leftist. There are leftists and Congressmen who would tear apart a Savarkar admirer if given the opportunity. Likewise, there are Savarkarians who would throw Congressmen into the Arabian Sea if they had the chance. We don't want to listen to Savarkar or Nathuram or Modi if we love Gandhi, Nehru, or Rahul. We are a people content with half-truths.

Amidst all this, there has been a consistent affinity between Hindutva forces and the fascist world since the time of Tilak. Hindutva's proximity to fascist ideology has historical roots. A researcher, A. Oak, quoted Kelkar at Tilak's sixteenth death anniversary in Poona, saying that if Tilak were alive, he would have 'favoured the Fascist rule in Germany and Italy and would have supported its transference to India'.[51] Oak explained that Kelkar believed 'politics was essentially kind of a war for him [Tilak], just as war was an extension of politics for Clausewitz'.[52]

Carl von Clausewitz, a Prussian military strategist, joined the Russian Army in 1812 to resist Napoleon. He was also the military tutor to Prussian prince, Friedrich Wilhelm, who eventually became king. Nazi Germany adopted Clausewitz's theory, and America's actions in Afghanistan and other

Islamic countries in recent decades have also followed this philosophy.

Clausewitz believed that war was 'a continuation of political intercourse, with a mixture of other means'.[53] He was a strong advocate of the militarization of society and the nation, a view that found great admirers among many Hindutva leaders. This is reflected in Savarkar's belief that 'the Devil can be fought by arch-devil only'.[54]

For Savarkar, the devil could be Britain, the Congress, the Muslims, or Gandhi—but never Hitler or Clausewitz. So mesmerized was he by the despot that he claimed India had received support 'from Hitler, the dictator of Germany and General Tojo, the military leader of the Japanese.' Savarkar stated that Germany and Japan had supported the 'revolutionary party from the very beginning' for 'violent agitation in Europe by the Abhinav Bharat Sanstha' and 'against the British by Netaji Subhas Chandra Bose in the Second World War'.[55]

Like most warmongers, Savarkar believed in militarization. He embraced what he called Chanakya's theory, which held that 'warlike spirit and armed strength were the very life-breath not only of the political but also of the civil life of a community'.[56]

Savarkar's senior, Moonje, founded the Central Military Education Society in 1935 and Bhonsle Military School in 1937 in Nasik, realizing his dream of militarizing the country.

Moonje was present alongside Hedgewar during the founding of the RSS in Nagpur, joined by Dani, Umakant Keshav Apte (alias Babasaheb Apte), M.S. Golwalkar, Balasaheb Deoras, Madhukar Rao Bhagwat, and Dadarao Paramarth. Also present were Savarkar's elder brother, Ganesh Damodar Savarkar (alias Babarao), L.V. Paranjpe, and B.B. Tholkar. It is unclear whether they were familiar with the world.

However, Savarkar was mistaken about Hitler. In a conversation with Otto Strasser on 21 May 1930, Hitler said:

> You have spoken in favour of the so-called Indian 'Freedom Movement', but it is clear that this is a rebellion of the lower Indian race against the superior [Hochwertige] English Nordic race. The Nordic race has a right to rule the world and we must take this racial right as the guiding star of our foreign policy.[57]

In another interview with the press in Berlin in December 1931, Hitler said it would be unwise for Germany 'to gloat over the prospect of the loss of India by the British Empire, which would be a misfortune for the rest of the world, including Germany'.

Nehru had a clearer understanding of Hitler, remarking that the dictator 'has pointedly declared himself in favour of British imperialist rule in India'.[58]

Although Hedgewar had differences with the Mahasabha and left it, the evolution of the RSS suggests that Savarkar's party essentially merged into the Sangh in principle after Gandhi's assassination. Today, Savarkar's Mahasabha survives within the RSS.

Many saw the RSS's formation as a contrast to the Mahasabha. Hedgewar was unhappy with the Mahasabha's involvement in electoral politics. However, dual membership between the two groups remained possible. Hedgewar couldn't stop the leaders of his organization from supporting the Democratic Swaraj Party, a local branch of the Swaraj Party.

On the seventeenth anniversary of Tilak's death, Savarkar joined both the Mahasabha and the Democratic Swaraj Party. He regarded Tilak's ultimate goal as the protection of Hindu Dharma, drawing inspiration from his vision and ideology.

Savarkar cited an article written by Tilak in *Chitramayajagat*, where the term 'Hindutva' was first used. Highlighting Tilak's 'deep erudition and insight', Savarkar observed that '[Tilak] had his eyes not on Hindutva as such but only on what was popularly called Hindu Dharma'.[59]

Further, Savarkar referenced a letter written by Tilak to Shyamji Krishna Varma in January 1896. In this letter, Tilak inquired, 'A Brahmin youth wishes to get military training. Is it possible for you to use your influence and get him recruited to army of the state?'[60]

This anecdote aligned with Savarkar's own advocacy for young Hindus to join the military, 'which his supporters described as an effort for Hindus to obtain military training'.[61]

However, Savarkar's legacy has been subject to critical scrutiny. The historian Dr Saroj Kumar Singh describes him as an 'extraordinary embodiment of utter mediocrity'. He further states, 'In the large corpus of his writings, there is barely anything to suggest a creative mind at work, as one searches in vain for any original idea.'[62]

Savarkar's theory of national protection was rooted in the belief that Hindus must take up arms. This, for him, was Hindutva. The RSS has never strayed from this sacred directive.

Six years younger than Savarkar, Hedgewar was born into a Deshasth Rigvedi Brahmin family in Nagpur. His mentor, Moonje, sent him to Poona for further studies after he was expelled from Neel City High School for singing 'Vande Mataram', a song from *Anandmath* by Bankim Chandra Chatterjee, which depicts a conflict between Hindus and Muslims.

Hedgewar later moved to Calcutta to pursue medical education. During this time, he was associated with the Hindustani Sewa Dal, which was later renamed the Congress Seva Dal, the volunteer wing of the Congress Party. However, he eventually parted ways with the organization and joined the Mahasabha.

Savarkar, on the other hand, displayed a sharper sense of political clarity compared to many of his Hindutva predecessors and contemporaries. This clarity was evident in his decision to never align with the Congress Party. From the outset, he remained a staunch critic of Gandhi's ideology and approach.

Bhagat Singh, Savarkar, and Others

There is an effort to glorify Savarkar at the expense of Gandhi and many genuine revolutionaries. Those involved in this ritual of glorification need to understand that they are diminishing the true contributions of the freedom fighter and champion of Hindutva.

On another level, some attempt to demonise Savarkar. They, too, may not realize that their criticism is actually enhancing the image of the Hindu revolutionary.

Perhaps Bhagat Singh, who in his twenties had no greater wish than to see India freed from all social and physical shackles, will be more widely revered in the future. He was, undeniably, one of the most respected freedom fighters, living on in the hearts of the people. No one dares to take Bhagat Singh's name in vain.

He and his comrades planned to kill James A. Scott, the superintendent of police in Lahore, for ordering a lathi charge during a protest against the Simon Commission. Lala Lajpat Rai sustained injuries in the incident and died seventeen days later. The revolutionaries sought to avenge Lalaji's death but mistakenly killed John Saunders instead.

The freedom fighters concluded that their voices were not reaching the right ears. When Bhagat Singh and Batukeshwar Dutt bombed the Central Assembly in Delhi to create 'a loud voice to make the deaf hear', they didn't flee. They wanted to be arrested to force the British to listen and leave India.[63]

Gandhi didn't turn the capital punishment of Bhagat Singh, Rajguru, and Sukhdev into a political issue. On 31 January 1931, in Allahabad, he stated that they 'shouldn't be hanged' or 'kept in prison', but added that this was his 'personal opinion' and that he couldn't 'make their release a condition'.[64]

When the revolutionaries were hanged, Gandhi was met with slogans like 'Gandhi Go Back', 'Down with Gandhism', and 'Long Live Bhagat Singh' on the first day of the six-day Karachi Session of the Congress. Gandhi attempted to distance himself from the issue by reiterating his warning against violence, saying 'With all the authority with which a father can speak to his children that the way of violence can only lead to perdition'.[65]

The differences between Gandhi and Bhagat Singh have always been an opportunity for the Hindutva brigade. This is why some Hindutva authors attempt to draw a connection between Bhagat Singh and Savarkar, but no genuine student of history can easily accept such claims. However, it is easy for non-students to sit and create a collage of the two revolutionaries.

There are books that claim Bhagat Singh and Savarkar admired each other. One such book is *Shodh Savarkarancha* in Marathi by Yashawant Dinkar Phadke, first published in 1984.

Phadke wrote books on Senapati Bapat, a freedom fighter from Parner. Bapat lived at London's India House while Savarkar was there and was an expert in bomb-making, though he embraced Gandhism in the late 1920s.

In addition to many books, Phadke also wrote about Chiplunkar, Tilak, Jedhe, Jyotirao Phule, and Ambedkar. It is intriguing that he authored eight books in English and forty in Marathi.

Phadke claimed that Bhagat Singh called Savarkar a 'braveheart', a 'fierce insurgent' and a 'fanatic anarchist' in articles published in the weekly *Matwala* on 15 and 22 November 1924.

Phadke also claimed that Bhagat Singh acquired Savarkar's *1857 ka Swatantrya Samar* in English and had it published. However, claims of Bhagat Singh's appreciation of Savarkar have emerged only in the past two to three decades, whereas the revolutionary's writings were accessible even before his execution.

Some Hindutva admirers have written extensively, portraying Savarkar as a figure deserving sympathy. One writer even claims that Bhagat Singh visited Ratnagiri specifically to obtain Savarkar's book on the 1857 First War of Independence. According to this account:

> The meeting was a secret; it was held at nine in the evening. Bhagat Singh touched his feet and discussed several things. Before leaving, he had the permission to reprint the book, which was considered the Gita of the revolutionaries.[66]

A Hindutva blogger also claimed that during Gandhi's visit to Ratnagiri, he praised the place, calling it a 'pilgrimage' as it was 'the birthplace of Tilak' and a 'refuge for Savarkar'. Allegedly, Gandhi said, 'Though we possessed a difference of opinion, yet it never means that our friendship [with Savarkar] has diminished a bit.'[67]

According to such narratives, both Gandhi and Bhagat Singh admired Savarkar. Interestingly, Savarkar once stated, 'The real hero is one who successfully sneaks out after attacking the crook enemy,' emphasizing that in that case, 'he is not a coward'.[68]

However, neither Gandhi nor Bhagat Singh ever showed any inclination to 'sneak out'. Gandhi faced the batons of British forces head-on during his protests, while Bhagat Singh and Batukeshwar Dutt remained in the Central Legislative Assembly after the bombing, boldly shouting slogans to proclaim their cause.

The day Manoj Sinha stated in Gwalior that Gandhi didn't study law, the *Organizer* —a mouthpiece of the RSS— published an article comparing Savarkar to Bhagat Singh. The article claimed that 'Bhagat has not written a word of criticism' against Savarkar and that the two revolutionaries could 'understand each other's hearts and minds very well'. It also quoted Bhagat Singh from the March 1926 issue of *Kirti* magazine, where he noted that the 'impact of the Swadeshi movement reached England as well and Mr Savarkar opened a house called "India House"'.

In a speech in Varanasi on 17 May 2014, Modi said that after becoming Gujarat's chief minister in 2001, he went to Geneva and 'carried Shyamji Krishna Varma's ashes back to India on my shoulder' after seventy-three years, adding that 'it was perhaps my destiny to fulfil his last wish'. The prime minister has yet to comment on the ongoing effort to help Savarkar claim India House from Varma, who founded it twelve decades ago and offered shelter to many, including Savarkar.

The *Organizer* further asserted that 'according to Gandhiji's follower Y.D. Phadke, Bhagat Singh drew inspiration from Savarkar's *1857 Ka Swatantrya Samar* but ignored Savarkar's *Hindupadapada Shahi*. However, it has now come to light that Bhagat Singh also drew inspiration from *Hindupadapada Shahi*.'[69] They didn't elaborate on where this 'light' came from.

Bhagat Singh refused to seek clemency, yet some writers have continually tried to prove that the revolutionary harboured no anger towards Savarkar.

In Bhagat Singh's final petition to the governor of Punjab in 1931, he stated that the struggle against the British would continue as long as a 'handful of parasites' exploited India and its resources. He argued that the fight would persist even if the government managed to win over 'the leaders of the upper strata of the Indian society through petty concessions and compromises'. He honoured the sacrifices of Jatin Das, Bhagwati Charan Verma, and Chandrashekhar Azad, declaring, 'We claim to be shot dead instead of to be hanged.'[70]

In contrast, Savarkar's 1913 appeal to the Home Member of the Government of India expressed regret over his earlier actions. He wrote that anyone with 'humanity at heart will blindly step on the thorny paths which in the excited and hopeless situation of India in 1906–07 … beguiled us from the path of peace and progress'. Savarkar promised that, if released, he would become 'the staunchest advocate of constitutional progress and loyalty to the English government' and was 'ready to serve the Government'.[71]

Though Bhagat Singh also wrote letters to the British government, he never sought their sympathy. In a letter to the inspector general of Punjab after being transferred from Delhi to Mianwala Jail in June 1929, he asked, 'How can I appoint my lawyer while I am here?' highlighting the difficulty of arranging legal representation due to travel constraints.[72]

When the counsel of Hari Kishan Talwar, who had failed in his attempt to assassinate Sir Geoffrey de Montmorency, the governor of Punjab, on 23 December, demanded an 'incredible fee' and argued in court that the revolutionary had no intention of killing the officer, Bhagat Singh became furious. From jail, he wrote urging his comrades to 'formulate definite ideas about the future policy regarding defence'. Although Bhagat Singh asked his friends to appeal to the high court in an effort to save Hari Kishan's life, he emphasized, 'After his arrest the political significance of the action should not be diminished.'[73]

As a matter of principle, Bhagat Singh believed Talwar should accept responsibility for the act with pride.

Savarkar's views on Muslims presented another significant obstacle that prevented any rapport between him and Bhagat Singh. Savarkar remarked:

> Our Muslim or Christian brethren were forced in past to adopt non-Hindu religion. This was the reason that they got the same ancestry of fatherland, language, culture, customs and history. Hindustan … can never be their sacred land. Their sacred land is far away in Arabsthan or Philistine.[74]

Blaming Savarkar or his admirers in this post-truth era would be a mistake. Even the Congress Party has often attempted to claim Bhagat Singh as its own. On 23 March 2023, the ninety-second anniversary of Bhagat Singh's execution, an online article from the Congress Party caught my attention.

The article asserted that Bhagat Singh had written in *Kirti* in 1928, urging the youth of Punjab to embrace Nehru's ideology. This suggests that even Nehru, according to the Congress, needed Bhagat Singh's legacy as a crutch to elevate his own standing.

Like the narrative linking Bhagat Singh to Savarkar, this too is a relatively modern claim. It exemplifies how individuals and political parties seek to associate themselves with the revolutionary, undeterred by the risk of being labelled as opportunistic or insincere.

However, Bhagat Singh neither needs Nehru nor Savarkar. He stands as the tallest figure among revolutionaries and freedom fighters, revered for his ideological clarity, decisive actions, and ultimate sacrifice.

We know that the Congress Party influenced historians whose books were prescribed in universities and for competitive examinations. They labelled Bhagat Singh and his accomplices as 'revolutionary terrorists'. Gradually, they downplayed

Bhagat Singh's contributions due to his undisputed stature, while making Savarkar a target of criticism.

The situation was different before Independence and the assassination of Gandhi. The Congress and Gandhi didn't support Bhagat Singh; instead, they offered assistance to Savarkar.

Gandhi often expressed sympathy for the Savarkar bothers due to their suffering in prison. It was only because of Gandhi's positive gesture towards the Savarkar brothers that Defence Minister Rajnath Singh could assert in a speech in New Delhi on 12 October 2021 that 'lies were spread about Savarkar repeatedly that he filed many petitions seeking his release from jails . . . It was Mahatma Gandhi who asked him to file the mercy petitions . . .'

Savarkar likely would have documented or acknowledged this if he had indeed acted on Gandhi's suggestion, but his views on Gandhi were crystal clear. He wrote about the practitioner of 'non-violent truth-assertion' and the 'non-cooperation movement, who later on came to be widely known as Mahatmaji', noting 'I happened to be closely acquainted in a friendly way when he had come to England' and that 'throughout our lives we came together and many times in conflict—in the political arena in India'.[75]

Savarkar remained critical of the 'chicken-hearted and pro-British' Congress leaders, who he believed were 'frightened of the Muslims and still very eager to have anyhow, by fair means or foul, whatever little political power they could grab' when the British left India in 1947.[76]

In 1963, Savarkar completed his *Six Glorious Epochs of Indian History* in Marathi, providing ample opportunity to confess if Rajnath Singh's claims were true. It is evident that the BJP leader's assertion was part of a half-baked agenda to align Savarkar more closely with Gandhi.

If Savarkar was portrayed negatively in the post-Independence era, merely polishing his image through unsubstantiated claims will not suffice. Such agenda-driven writings will only push Savarkar further into a dubious space. The claims about Gandhi's remarks in Ratnagiri and Bhagat Singh's 'feet-touching gesture' will not contribute positively to this story.

However, emphatically blaming Savarkar and declaring that he shouldn't be respected because he sought clemency holds little merit. It is a well-established fact that during his early years, Savarkar actively fought against the Raj.

Additionally, some revolutionaries sought clemency, while others received a 'general pardon' after the First World War. The process was similar for all, as they were required to submit a standard affidavit that they wouldn't engage in activities against the British Empire.

I cannot resist quoting a few sentences from Barin's memoir about Cellular Jail, covering the years 1909 to 1920.

While many writers have previously claimed that some prisoners submitted clemency petition to Sir Reginald Craddock during his visit to Cellular Jail in 1913, Barin didn't indicate that there was any discussion of mercy.

Barin himself exchanged a few bitter words with Craddock.[77] His maturity matched that of Bhagat Singh, except that he was not willing to face the gallows. The youngest brother of Aurobindo Ghosh, Barin was born three years before Savarkar. He returned to Calcutta, his ancestral town, from London in 1902 and began working alongside Aurobindo. The Bengal revolutionaries intensified their activities following the partition of Bengal in 1905, and in 1906, he launched *Jugantar*, a Bengali weekly.

Barin also established a camp in Maniktala, Muraripukur, in 1907 to recruit revolutionaries for armed rebellion, referring to it as an 'Ashram for Revolutionary Sanyasis'.

Things changed after Khudiram Bose and Prafulla Kumar Chaki's failed attempt to assassinate Magistrate Douglas Kingsford on 30 April 1908. Many revolutionaries were arrested as a result. Norton, a prosecution counsel at Alipore court, sought to build the case against Aurobindo and others based on the false testimony of Narendranath Goswami, a state approver.

The revolutionaries managed to send Kanailal Dutt and Satyendra Nath Bose to the jail's hospital, where Goswami was kept among English prisoners. Kanai shot Goswami dead with a revolver that had been smuggled into the jail. He stood tall and smiled before his hanging. An English officer present at the scene asked Barin, 'How many more like this do you have?'

Additional Session Judge Charles Porten Beachcroft acquitted Aurobindo for lack of evidence and sentenced Barin, Ullaskar Datta, Hem Chandra Das, Hrishikesh Kanjiwal, Indu Bhushan Roy, Bibhuti Bhushan Sarkar, and Abinash Chandra Bhattacharya to death. Their sentences were eventually commuted to life terms, and they were sent from Calcutta to Andaman Cellular Jail. Barin escaped after six years but was arrested again. Following his release under general amnesty in 1920, he worked as a journalist for several publications.

While recounting his transportation from Alipore Jail to Andaman and the food served on board the SS *Maharaja*, the ferry that carried Indians across the Black Waters, Barin indicated that religion was the last thing on his mind. When someone on the ship remarked that 'the Mussalmans cook rice' and they wouldn't receive any, fearing it would compromise their dharma, he responded, 'Who can destroy our caste? Our dharma is built in iron, come on let us have the *mlechha* [untouchables] rice … Are not the *mlechhas* men?'[78]

While Savarkar claimed in his memoirs that he converted Muslims to Hinduism in jail, Barin noted that Brahmins were forced to remove their sacred threads as soon as they entered the prison, yet nobody dared to touch the beards of Muslim or Sikh prisoners. 'The strangest thing was that not a single Brahmin raised any objection' when they were stripped of their sacred threads.[79]

Savarkar claimed that members of his organization 'outside in the upnivesh [Andaman]' continued to hold meetings 'from time to time and awaken the people, educate them by giving lectures on political issues'.[80]

However, there is no concrete evidence to substantiate this assertion. He appeared more comfortable in Cellular Jail than others, receiving 'confidential' news as soon as the jail authorities were informed. He claimed to have learned about the attack on Lord Hardinge in Delhi within hours and even teased the staff about it.[81] These are Savarkar's own accounts and cannot be independently verified.

Savarkar spent nine years and ten months in Cellular Jail. He was subsequently moved to Ratnagiri Jail on the grounds of ill health and shifted to Yeravda Jail after three years. He was released on 6 January 1924 but prohibited from engaging in any political activity. He remained the president of the Hindu Mahasabha for six consecutive terms after all restrictions were lifted in 1937. Although many individuals led the Mahasabha afterward, Savarkar remained its preeminent figure until his death. He lived through the inglorious activities of the Mahasabha and died when the organization was nearing its end.

Savarkar wrote about his frequent interactions with jail officials during his imprisonment in the Andaman Islands. When a rumour surfaced that Lala Hardayal had been arrested in America, Savarkar asked a jail worker to find out what had happened and was mistakenly informed that Lala would be brought to Bombay. Later, when an official asked him if he knew Lala, Savarkar replied, 'Yes, I have the honour of his friendship.'[82]

Savarkar was imprisoned in the Andaman jail on 4 July 1911. On 2 May 1921, he boarded a ship named Maharaja to be transferred to Ratnagiri jail, where he remained for roughly three years. His accounts of this 'jail-journey' were written retrospectively, seemingly with the intent of portraying himself as fearless and resolute. However, none of his fellow inmates have provided any corroborative accounts of an intrepid Savarkar during his incarceration.

While there were numerous writings on prominent freedom fighters by their contemporaries, what we know about Savarkar largely comes from his own accounts. It has only been in recent decades that authors from various political backgrounds have begun to either criticize or defend him in their writings.

Barin Ghosh, on the other hand, followed a different revolutionary path. He rejected notions of ritualistic purity by eating rice cooked by Muslims, offering a more direct approach to challenging untouchability.[83]

Barin's voice is as candid as Gandhi's in his autobiography or Bhagat Singh's in his writings. Bhagat Singh's perspective, however, was unique and vibrant; he focussed on larger ideological and collective concerns rather than personal glorification or individual narratives.

Sachindranath Sanyal was a revolutionary who was arrested and released multiple times, yet he never ceased his activities. After being released from Cellular Jail for the second time—thanks to an application from his mother, Ksheroda Vashini Devi—Sanyal became involved with the Hindustan Republic Army (Hindustan Socialist Republican Army). He was later sent to Kala Pani for the third time due to his role in the Kakori conspiracy.

Despite Savarkar enjoying good conversations with the jail officers, Sanyal revealed in his memoir that prisoners generally disliked interacting with the staff at Cellular Jail. He was admitted to the jail hospital in February 1920 when a warden informed him that the jailer had summoned him to his office. The jail officials would often call prisoners to misbehave with them. 'This made me burn in anger from tip to toe,' Sanyal wrote. Such encounters could lead to fights and 'at times, the prisoners used to die'. He continued:

> A fight may break out with the jailer if I go there, and if I tolerate the insult to avoid this fight then I will fall in the eyes of my friends ... I told the warder that I was unwell and couldn't go to the jailer's office ... The warder returned and said it was necessary.[84]

However, when he mustered the courage to go, the jailer told him, 'Cheer up man, you are released.' When Sanyal informed Upendranath about the release order, Upendranath congratulated him but didn't smile or react; he didn't even lift his head.[85]

Sanyal learned that Barin, Upendranath, and Hemchand would also be released alongside him. These revolutionaries had no desire to be admired by Gandhi. There was a growing discontent among them regarding Gandhi's actions, and this frustration reflected in Sanyal's words: 'Mahatma Gandhi started publishing that the coordination of the Indian revolutionary movement was not possible with the values of Ancient India.' he wrote.[86]

Perhaps it was a method of Gandhi to discredit the romantics. Values and religion are time-tested tools used to besmirch rival ideologies.

Savarkar Revived

Savarkar became more prominent than ever in 1998. Rightists, centrists, leftists, and editors alike discussed him, but his mention was incomplete without Godse.

At that time, Atal Bihari Vajpayee was the prime minister, and Sonia Gandhi had taken over as Congress president. Editors would assign reporters to cover stories on Savarkar and Godse.

As a student at the University of Allahabad, I often witnessed anti-Hindutva students chanting during nearly every protest procession on campus: 'Gandhi *ham sharminda hain, tere quatil jinda hain* (Gandhi, we are ashamed that your killers are still alive).' Such protests frequently ended in violence, with students throwing stones at the university administration or the police as their most fitting tribute to Gandhi.

For the first time, RSS-backed organizations began displaying a portrait of Savarkar at their meetings.

The Congress had a different approach in the past. Indira Gandhi didn't allow any controversy related to Savarkar to arise; she resolved such matters swiftly.

On 8 May 1980, Pandit Bakhle, the then secretary of the Swatantrayaveer Savarkar Rashtriya Smarak, Bombay, wrote to Prime Minister Indira Gandhi about their decision to build a Savarkar memorial in the city. In her reply, dated 20 May 1980, Indira acknowledged Savarkar's significant role in India's freedom struggle, stating, 'Veer Savarkar's daring defiance of the British Government has its own important place in the annals of our freedom movement. I wish success to the plans to celebrate the birth centenary of this remarkable son of India.'[87]

Her letter marked a resumption of Congress's gesture towards Savarkar, whom they neither loved nor hated before Gandhi's assassination. They treated him like any moderate revolutionary and responded cautiously to his legacy.

In 1921, Jamnadas Dwarkadas, a Congress icon from Bombay, forwarded a letter from the Hindutva leader to Sir William Henry Hoare Vincent, a member of the Legislative Council of India, appealing for the release of Vinayak and his elder brother, Babarao Damodar Savarkar, during the visit of the Prince of Wales to India. Babarao had been imprisoned in the Andaman Islands since 1910, and the brothers were expected to be transferred to the Bombay Presidency Jail in May 1921. However, instead of being moved to Bombay, they were taken to Alipore Jail. From there, Babarao was transferred first to Bijapur Prison and later to Sabarmati in January 1922. He was released on medical grounds after eight months due to his poor health.[88]

Savarkar, on the other hand, was transferred to the Bombay Presidency Jail and later to Ratnagiri.

Jamnadas wrote:

> I enclose herewith a letter from Dr N.D. Savarkar about whose brothers I have spoken to you. It seems they are not being properly treated and that on the whole they were better off in the Andaman than they are here. The brothers make a most fervent appeal that they should be released at any rate when the Prince Edward of the Wales visits India … they [Savarkar brothers] are now prepared to promise that they would work the reforms in which they believe, it would not be improper for me to suggest that the Government of India would be doing the right thing if they release the brothers at the time of the Prince's visit.

The typed letter of Jamnadas included handwritten parts, some of which were unreadable. 'I believe that they would be prepared to give any undertaking that the Government of India may require,' he added in the letter.[89]

Jamnadas wrote the letter for Savarkar while Gandhi was at the centre of Congress activities, opposing the visit of Prince Edward, who stayed in India for four months, including the second half of November 1921.

In 1924, the Bombay Legislative Council, an advisory body to the government, advocated for the removal of restrictions on Savarkar. Despite interruptions from the government bench in the House, Dr M.B. Velkar, a physician and follower of Tilak, continued to enumerate 'the rigors of Mr Savarkar's jail life'. He attempted to convince the House that the political situation had changed since Savarkar's conviction. 'Mr Surve brought an amendment to the effect that all the restrictions except those relating to political matters should be removed.'[90] The official report of the Bombay Legislative Council debates of 21 July 1924 indicates that the resolution was defeated. A.N. Surve, a member representing Bombay, had proposed the amendment.

M.B. Shivdasani, who represented Surat district, addressed the council, stating, 'He [Savarkar] may have been misguided. He did several things which the Indian nation would not and does not approve of. All the same, you cannot deny that he is a patriot, and no virtue is greater than that of being a patriot.'[91]

Similar debates continued in the council throughout July, but the government refused to relent.

However, there is no evidence that Gandhi asked Savarkar to write a mercy petition. Gandhi's solicitude towards Savarkar stemmed from courtesy towards a fellow countryman. In a letter to Narayan Savarkar, Gandhi once wrote:

> I shall try to do whatever I can for political prisoners. It has never happened that I kept quiet out of fear. Even regarding political prisoners, I would consider it improper to do anything for those who are in prison for crimes of murder. I shall not argue with the point. I shall of course do my utmost for Bhai Vinayak Savarkar.[92]

The second resolution of the Congress session in Kakinada, presided over by Maulana Mohamed Ali, stated, 'This Congress condemns the continued incarceration of Vinayak Damodar Savarkar and expresses its sympathy with Dr N.D. Savarkar and other members of his family.'

In another letter to Savarkar after the death of his brother, Gandhi wrote:

> Bhai Savarkar, I write this after reading the news of the death of your brother. I had done a little bit for his release and ever since I had been taking an interest in him. Where is the need to condole with you? We are ourselves in the jaws of death. I hope his family is all right. Yours, M.K. Gandhi.[93]

There are many more examples of the Congress siding with Savarkar, in stark contrast to the way he was treated after the rise of Sonia and Rahul in politics.

Savarkar's wife, Yamnabai, fondly known as Mai, was felicitated by the Hindu Mahila Sabha (the women's wing of the Mahasabha) in Poona in December 1950. The keynote address was delivered by Sushilabai Gokhale, an enlightened woman educated at Fergusson College and the wife of Anant Ramachandra Gokhale, who was associated with the Bharat Seva Samaj, founded by Nehru.

The past precedents didn't stop Rahul Gandhi from saying at a public meeting in Balapur, Akola, on 17 November 2022:

> Gandhi, Nehru, Patel all went to jail but they never signed any such letter to British despite being under pressure. Savarkar wilted under pressure … He told all those leaders to follow him by signing the letter, but they didn't buckle under the pressure.

Rahul's rhetoric against Savarkar lacks political punch. There was a significant difference between Cellular Jail and other prisons; Gandhi, Nehru, and Patel were never sent to the Andaman gaol because they had never killed or conspired to kill a British officer.

Nehru had privileges that Savarkar and many other freedom fighters lacked. In May 1920, he stayed at the Savoy Hotel in Mussoorie with his mother, Swarup Rani, and his wife, Kamala. One day, he was summoned by the authorities and asked to give an undertaking that he wouldn't contact the Afghan delegates, who were staying in the same hotel for war-related negotiations. He refused, leading to his internment order. Nehru returned to Allahabad. Motilal Nehru, knowing Sir Harcourt Butler, the then governor of the United Provinces, wrote to him about the situation. Butler replied that Nehru could have complied with the order without 'any injury to his dignity'. Motilal responded that they would move to Mussoorie if the health of the two women required it, 'order or no order'. As Motilal and Nehru left for Mussoorie, they 'received a telegram rescinding the order'. Later, the father and son met two members of the Afghan delegation at the hotel.[94]

Always in crisis regarding his comparative identity, Savarkar was no less forthcoming when he wrote his own biography, *Life of Barrister Savarkar*, under the pseudonym Chitragupta. In doing so, he made himself vulnerable, providing his critics with reason to question his authenticity. The book was first published by B.G. Paul and Co. in Madras in 1926, but Ravindra Vaman Ramdas, the publisher of the second edition for Veer Savarkar Prakashan in 1986, revealed the connection, stating at the launch that Chitragupta and Savarkar were one and the same. After his release from jail, Savarkar was under government observation and directed not to engage in political activity, which led him to write under pseudonyms. However, the government had no issue with *Life of Barrister Savarkar* and didn't ban it.

The creation of an aura of greatness around oneself is not unusual in certain political contexts worldwide. It was not only Savarkar who was affected by this syndrome; others mentioned in this book were similarly influenced. 'From the very beginning, the Fuhrer's faithful entourage realized the importance of the myth which was to be created around Hitler' and 'the elements of simple humanity to his existence were to be expelled'. 'The legend of his modesty and frugality was created, and a suggestion of his chastity was whispered.'[95] This was done to cleanse the image of an insane dictator who believed in mass killing. It is no surprise that such leaders, from any part of the world, would admire Hitler, and India is no exception.

Although all restrictions on Savarkar were officially lifted on 10 May 1937, the government remained wary of him. The internal security agency of the Government of India expressed concerns in a series of letters. One such letter from the Intelligence Bureau to the home department highlighted the Mahasabha's planned meetings in Delhi on 16 January and 19 January 1941 for 'direct action … on the Pakistan issue'. It stated that 'Savarkar was reported to be in favour of organizing a general boycott of British goods and defiance of the Arms Act.' The letter mentioned Ashutosh Lahiri as supportive of 'the boycott of British goods'.[96]

Assassin's Creed

The government discussed fears of communal violence across India if any punishment were handed to Savarkar in Gandhi's murder case. However, there was no hesitation in sending Godse and Apte to the gallows.

The strength—or perhaps the cowardice—of Nehru was evident in a communication dated 1 February 1949, marked as secret:

> [The] Government understands that the Judgment in Mahatma Gandhi Assassination Case will be delivered at 11:30 on Thursday, the 10th of this month. So far as it is possible to judge from the nature of the evidence recorded by the judge, I think it would be reasonable for us to proceed on the assumption that Mr Savarkar will be acquitted for want of legal proof.

H.V.R. Iyengar, an officer in the Government of India, wrote to Shankar Prasad, secretary to the home minister, noting that there might be 'some demonstrations either immediately after [Savarkar's] release or later in the day'. There may also be 'an attempt to hold a public meeting to celebrate his release'. He further added, 'I write this to inform you that in Government's view no demonstrations should be allowed and if permission is asked for to take a procession or to hold a public meeting, such permission should be refused.'[97] Although the government didn't seem eager to implicate Savarkar in Gandhi's assassination for mysterious reasons, it was nevertheless concerned about the outcome of his release.

Godse, Apte, Karkare, Badge, Shankar Kistayya, Gopal, Savarkar, and Parchure were arrested for their involvement in Gandhi's assassination or their alleged role in the conspiracy. They were brought from Bombay and Gwalior to Red Fort prison to stand trial before Judge Atma Charan.

The chargesheet in the *Crown versus Nathuram Vinayak Godse and Others* was submitted under various sections of the Indian Penal Code and the Indian Arms Act, 1878.

Karkare, a resident of Pune, owned a lodge in Ahmednagar. His involvement with the Mahasabha extended beyond

Maharashtra. In 1946–47, he visited Noakhali with ten youths to protect Hindus during the riots. This isn't unusual, as even today the Sangh sends its workers to various places for what is termed 'social work'.

Pahwa was already in jail for hurling a guncotton slab near Gandhi's prayer ground. He was a refugee from Pakpattan, Montgomery (modern-day Sahiwal district, Pakistan), where his family was killed in riots after Partition. An Intelligence Bureau report from Inspector A.S. Balkundi of Ahmednagar mentioned that Pahwa led a procession of refugees, shouting 'against the Muslims' and chanting '*Veer Savarkar Ki Jai*'.

Balkundi's letter was endorsed by officials in the Ministry of Home Affairs, including M.K. Sinha, the deputy director, but it was ignored. Sinha later told the Kapur Commission that they couldn't 'connect this Pahwa with Madanlal Kashmirilal'.[98]

Sinha's plea that he failed to recognize Pahwa as Madanlal Kashmirilal was accepted by the probe team without any further investigation.

Kashmirilal was Pahwa's father. After Pahwa's mother passed away, his father remarried. Pahwa ran away from home and worked in the British Indian Army from the age of seventeen to twenty.

Badge, a former petty knife seller, later opened 'Shastra Bhandar', an arms store in Poona. He was granted a pardon because he turned approver. Kistayya, his servant, assisted him and others in Delhi.

Parchure, a former wrestler and Ayurveda doctor from Gwalior, was allegedly the one who procured the automatic pistol used to kill Gandhi. Many referred to him as the 'Second Savarkar' due to his radical speeches and controversial actions against mosques in Gwalior. It is said he had an MBBS degree from Grant Medical College in Bombay but was dismissed from Jamsetjee Jejeebhoy Hospital in 1935 for insubordination. He abandoned Western medicine, studied Ayurveda, and began practising in Gwalior.

Gopal Godse, employed in the ordinance department, served during the Second World War before being posted at Kirkee Depot near Poona. The high court noted that on 14 January, Gopal applied for seven days of casual leave, citing agricultural works as the reason. Before Godse's final departure for Delhi, he made Gopal's wife, Sindhutai, the nominee in his life insurance policy. Godse also gave Gopal Rs 250 to purchase the revolver. Gopal then accompanied Karkare from Bombay to Delhi the next day.

A total of 149 witnesses testified, and the trial court sentenced Godse and Apte to death. Karkare, Pahwa, Gopal, Kistayya, and Parchure were sentenced to life imprisonment, while Savarkar was acquitted.

The appeal was heard in the high court of East Punjab in Shimla's Peterhoff, the viceregal residence, by a three-judge bench comprising justices Achhru Ram Sahgal, A.N. Bhandari, and G.D. Khosla. Justice Bhandari found insufficient evidence against Kistayya and Parchure, leading to their acquittal. He also recommended clemency for Gopal. In a separate order, Justice Achhru Ram similarly acquitted Kistayya and Parchure and expressed sympathy for Gopal and Madanlal due to their young age. However, Achhru Ram's recommendation to send Madanlal's case to the government for a reduced sentence was rejected by Justice Bhandari and Justice Khosla.

The charges against Kistayya were questionable, as no independent evidence was produced against him. But even today, a separate investigation is needed to understand why the prosecution failed to prove the charges against Parchure beyond reasonable doubt, leading to his acquittal.

Godse, Apte, Karkare, Pahwa, and Gopal appealed the high court's decision to the Privy Council. The government's counsel, D.N. Pritt, a king's counsel, had previously defended Bhagat Singh, Sukhdev, and Rajguru. No effort was made by the Privy Council to re-investigate the assassination case in order to identify any additional co-conspirators involved with Godse and Apte.

The Crown rejected their petition for special leave, and Governor-General Rajagopalachari denied the mercy petitions from Apte and Godse's parents. Both men were hanged in Ambala Jail. Karkare, Pahwa, and Gopal served life sentences.

Later, Atma Charan became the judicial commissioner of Ajmer and then a judge of the Allahabad High Court. Justices Bhandari and Achhru Ram were appointed chief justices of the Punjab High Court. C.K. Daphtary, the prosecution lawyer, went on to become advocate general of Bombay and later solicitor general. He retired as the attorney general of India.

Recently, much buzz surrounded a remark by Abhijit Gangopadhyaya, a former judge of the Calcutta High Court, when he revealed that he and the BJP had approached each other, expressing his willingness to contest in the parliamentary election. When asked to choose between Gandhi and Godse, he sought time to respond. This incident brought back memories of 2020, when Ranjan Gogoi, a retired chief justice of India, was nominated to the Upper House, leading some to call it a quid pro quo reward. However, this path was laid decades ago.

C.K. Daphtary once remarked on the appointment of A.N. Roy as chief justice of India, saying, 'The boy who wrote the best essay got the first prize.' Roy was appointed the chief justice of India by the Indira Gandhi government in 1973, superseding several senior judges, which led to Justice K.S. Hegde resigning in protest. Notably, Hegde had been elected as a Congress Rajya Sabha member in 1952, later serving as a member of Parliament from the Bangalore South constituency in 1977 on a Janata Party ticket, in between serving as a Supreme Court judge from 1967 to 1973.

Baharul Islam served in the Rajya Sabha from 1962 to 1972, after which he was appointed a judge of the Guwahati High Court. Following his retirement from the high court in 1980, he was appointed to the Supreme Court, and four years later, he returned to the Rajya Sabha. Mohammad Hidayatullah, after retiring as chief justice of India in 1979, went on to become vice president of India.

Savarkar led a mysterious life at his residence, Savarkar Sadan, in Bombay after his release from Yeravda Jail. Even before, he seldom aligned himself with any of his followers, except Dhingra. Savarkar was instinctively a leader, not a follower. While there is no public record of him personally taking up arms, it is well documented that he inspired many young men to bomb or shoot British officers.

Babarao Savarkar was sentenced to life imprisonment for promoting war against the government. Mohanlal Pandya, once a Gandhian, attempted to assassinate Viceroy Lord Minto by throwing a bomb, though the attempt failed. Pandya's transition from a Gandhian to a Savarkarian was seamless.

Among Savarkar's associates, the most daring was Anant Kanhere, who assassinated A.M.T. Jackson, the collector of Nasik, with a pistol allegedly sent to India from London by Savarkar through Chaturbhuj Ameen, a cook at India House. Jackson, a Sanskrit scholar, was considered a friend of Indians. Some of Savarkar's friends were unhappy with him due to Babarao's convictions, and Savarkar's first sentence of transportation for life came from this 'Nasik Conspiracy Case'.

Another theory suggests that a French woman smuggled some of the arms from London to the Nizam's Hyderabad. It included one of the pistols being used by Kanhere to murder Jackson.

Eighteen-year-old Kanhere came from a poor family in Aurangabad, where he studied at an arts school. His father was a pensioner. Savarkar's men selected him for the assassination, and he carried it out as Jackson was leaving a theatre after watching the Marathi play *Sharada*. After the killing, some bystanders stopped Kanhere from shooting himself. He was tried and eventually hanged.

Vasudev Balwant Gogate attempted to shoot Sir Ernest Hotson, the acting governor of Bombay, inside the library of Fergusson College in Poona. He had met Savarkar the day before committing the crime. Although Hotson survived the attack, Gogate was arrested and later released in 1937. After his release, Gogate transitioned to a career as a lawyer and embraced the practice of non-violence.

Wamanrao Chavan, a young man from Savarkar's group in Ratnagiri, also attempted an assassination, firing at a British officer at Dhobi Talao in Bombay.

However, he quickly distanced himself from those who, influenced by Savarkar's ideology, committed murder.

It was evident that Savarkar suffered from a holier-than-thou syndrome. He reacted negatively when asked to be photographed on the first day of the trial at the Red Fort, informing the court that he was not ready for it. Through his lawyer, L.B. Bhopatkar, Savarkar insisted on remaining seated in a chair rather than on the bench with the other accused, citing his ill health.

Photographs from the first day show him sitting in the third row of the dock, looking sternly serious, while the other accused, except Godse, appeared to be laughing. Savarkar, however, seemed detached and unconcerned.

The following day, he was given a space outside the dock, and cameramen were instructed not to photograph him. '[He] sat alone ... as though he felt the need to be protected by a bodyguard.'[99] He sat in a 'low chair', which was 'nearest to the court'. While the other accused interacted with each other in the courtroom, 'Savarkar sat there, sphinx like in silence, completely ignoring his co-accused in the dock.'[100]

P.L. Inamdar, the lawyer of Parchure, who met Savarkar in jail, noted that Godse was 'deeply hurt' by Savarkar's 'calculated, demonstrative non-association with him either in court or in the Red Fort jail ...'[101]

During his meeting in the Red Fort jail, Savarkar, described as a 'staunch RSS man' didn't ask a 'single question about the case against my clients, Dr Parchure and Gopal or about any of the other accused including Nathuram …'[102] He was not inclined to discuss matters with his colleagues, yet he relied on those who were awestruck by his ideas.

He lived a private life, continuing his activities in secret from the comfort of his home, meeting only select individuals on the second floor. Savarkar seemed aware that the time was ripe to cement his legacy and wrote feverishly to fulfil his ambition of being on the same pedestal as Mahatma Gandhi.

Some members of the Mahasabha believed that Nehru should have been eliminated as well, but Savarkar allegedly felt that only Gandhi stood between him and the realization of Hindutva in India.

During Gandhi's assassination trial, there was an attempt to mislead the case. The lawyers representing the conspirators and assassins tried to introduce unfounded claims that Godse and Apte had opposed Savarkar during the Mahasabha's 1946 convention in Barshi, Maharashtra, when the proposal to join Nehru's interim government was discussed. This was likely a diversion tactic to suggest that Savarkar had no involvement in Gandhi's killing.

Savarkar's War

It is important to note that Gandhi took a personal interest in temporarily recruiting youth for the Indian Army during the First World War. This approach was not dissimilar to Savarkar's idea of the militarization of society, which he derived from Tilak. Savarkar's followers accepted his belief in militarism without question.

While the Congress Party officially denied India's participation in the Second World War, Savarkar, during a meeting with Viceroy Linlithgow, stated:

> In the capacity of a revolutionary, I favour militarization of the country. I think that the country's interest lies in the fact that the borders are guarded by the Hindu military units and its internal security too is ensured by the Hindu units.[103]

Linlithgow wrote to the secretary of state for India after the meeting, stating that 'the essential thing for Hinduism and Great Britain was to be friends … The Hindu Mahasabha favoured an ambiguous undertaking of Dominion Status at the end of the war.'[104]

Savarkar made his position clear at the Jodhpur session of the Mahasabha in January 1955, saying:

> The boarders of India, its civilization and culture can never be safe till we don't do Hinduization of politics and militarization of Hindus in the country … I give them [Hindu youths] this direction only that they should join military in maximum number and acquire military education so that they contribute to their country's independence when the time comes for it.

However, Savarkar preferred to stay away from the battlefield personally.

In contrast, Nathuram believed in pursuing the conflict to its conclusion. In his ninety-three-page statement before the court at the Red Fort, he declared:

> I did not make any attempt to run away; in fact, I never entertained the idea of running away. I did not try to

> shoot myself. It was never my intention to do so, for it was my ardent desire to give vent to my thoughts in an open court.[105]

For Savarkar, the battlefield was a place to escape from. His vision of war was fundamentally a Hindu war; his struggle for freedom was one for Hindus, and his identity was tied to the representation of Hindu interests.

3

Jawaharlal Nehru

The Shades of Allahabad

Allahabad doesn't internalize; it doesn't introspect. It doesn't welcome anyone. Students from across North India come to study at the University of Allahabad, yet the city offers them no employment. A state university, named after Rajendra Singh, also known as Rajju Bhaiyya, the fourth sarsanghchalak of the RSS, has been established to ease the burden on the central university.

The city never discusses the future; it prefers to dwell on what you did—what you ate and whom you insulted the day before. Rumour is the lifeblood of the city, with residents spending hours gossiping about each other. Mirza Ghalib once wrote about Allahabad: '*Hazar az fitan-e-Ilahabad* (God, save me from the snitchers of Allahabad).'

The system cultivates felons and swiftly eliminates them when they overstep their bounds, only to hand the reins to someone else.

According to a survey, Allahabad produces a truckload of crude bombs daily. Over a hundred youths have lost limbs while assembling these bombs, locally known as tamaatar (tomato). They often explode during assembly, killing or disabling their makers.

The dream of the youth here is to become corrupt provincial officers, serving criminals or politicians. Those who fail often turn to practising law or resort to crime.

It is also common in Allahabad, since pre-Independence, for authors and politicians to pay an organization or informal group to hold a function in their honour. One of my professors in the English department, a dark, bulky devout Brahmin once asked me—a postgraduate student—to establish a literary award and confer it on him. He went ahead and did so when I refused.

I lived in Allahabad for almost a decade, just behind Anand Bhawan. Every day, I passed by this abode of the Nehrus and the New Gandhis—first as a student at the University of Allahabad, and later as a journalist. I constantly heard stories about the opulence of the Nehrus and their habits, so distant from common life. Often, I would visit Anand Bhawan to see and understand the kind of life Motilal and his son Jawaharlal led.

There were occasions in the pre-Independence era when British forces occupied the old building, but the servants stood their ground, reminding the soldiers that they were intruders. My friends and I used to say that the history of the gardeners, sweepers, and servants of Anand Bhawan should have been written instead of the Nehrus's.

The bungalow originally belonged to Justice Mahmud, who sold it to Raja Paramanand, a judge from Shahjahanpur. Motilal bought it from him in 1899 and named it Anand Bhawan. A mansion was constructed there in 1928 when the Nehrus decided to dedicate the old bungalow to the nation. The old building was then renamed Swaraj Bhawan.

After Motilal's death, Anand Bhawan was transferred to a trust (later named the Jawaharlal Nehru Memorial Fund) associated with the Congress. The trustees were Jawaharlal, Seth Jamnalal Bajaj, B.C. Roy, and Dr Mukhtar Ahmed Ansari—the grandfather of Mukhtar Ansari, a convicted mafia-politician from eastern UP, who died in prison under allegedly mysterious circumstances.

In the last three decades, mafias, builders, and politicians have completely overshadowed everything in Allahabad.

Jawaharlal was born in this city of rumourmongers, and he lived every bit of its affluence. One rumour claimed he was born in Meerganj, the city's red-light area at the time. Later, I discovered that his father's first house was near Meerganj. The habit of believing rumours stayed with Jawaharlal throughout his life. He would keep his ears open for gossip circulating in Allahabad and often spread it with enthusiasm.

Jawaharlal's family was considered close friends of Harivansh Rai Bachchan. In 1941, Bachchan was appointed as a junior lecturer at the university. After eleven years, he sought partial financial assistance from Jawaharlal's government to pursue further studies abroad. To secure this, he met Humayun Kabir, the education secretary, Maulana Azad, the education minister, and Rajendra Prasad, the President of India. Despite his poem 'Madhushala' already being popular, he was rejected by all of them. On the advice of his wife, Teji, he finally approached Jawaharlal, who asked one of his officers to look into the matter, and the grant was eventually approved.

However, the assistance intended for Bachchan was delayed when rumours spread in Allahabad that the poet and Teji were about to separate due to his alleged affair with a

Muslim woman. It was also claimed that Teji, who was living in Allahabad with their two sons, Amitabh and Ajitabh, was in great distress. These rumours, which were aimed at undermining the government's support for Bachchan's studies at Cambridge, eventually reached Jawaharlal's ears. In the 1990s, Hindi story writer Markandeya told me that the rumour had been intentionally spread to harm Bachchan, and as a result, the aid was temporarily withheld.

In 1953, while receiving an honorary doctorate from Cambridge University alongside German novelist Thomas Mann, Jawaharlal met with Bachchan for a brief two-minute conversation. During the meeting, the Indian prime minister asked the poet, 'Are you still here? I suppose you didn't plan such a long stay. I have heard an unlikely story about you.'

Bachchan knew what Jawaharlal was referring to and replied, 'The truth will come out with time.' He recounted this story in his autobiography, *Kya Bhulun Kya Yaad Karun*.

Jawaharlal had written the foreword for 'The House of Wine', an English translation of 'Madhushala' by Marjorie Boulton, an Oxford student, with assistance from Ram Swaroop Vyas. However, after their interaction at Cambridge, Bachchan never sought the prime minister's help. Despite this, the two families remained close.

After returning from Cambridge, Bachchan taught at the university for a year before securing a position as officer on special duty in the foreign ministry. A bungalow was allotted to him on New Delhi's Willingdon Crescent, about 200 yards from the prime minister's house.

Bachchan wanted to leave Allahabad because the city's intellectual and political elite had rejected him as a poet of substance. I have heard stories of how Brahmin youths would hide 'Madhushala' under their pillows to avoid the wrath of their parents. Despite Allahabad's reputation for late-night drinking sessions, some residents viewed the poems as 'immoral'.

The Bachchans' connection with Indira Gandhi, and Amitabh's friendship with her eldest son, the then prime minister Rajiv Gandhi, has been retold so often that people have lost interest in it. However, after Rajiv's assassination, Indira's daughter-in-law Sonia and her son Rahul cold-shouldered the Bachchans, as they did with many friends. The present Nehrus (the New Gandhis) have no taste for rumours—or for truth.

Chilean poet Pablo Neruda was insulted upon his arrival in Bombay in 1950 when French physicist Joliot Curie had sent him to India with a letter for C.V. Raman and Jawaharlal Nehru. The poet-diplomat recounted this strange encounter with the customs officer at the airport in his *Memoirs*.

The customs inspectors thoroughly checked his belongings for two hours, sealing them, including identification papers, and then allowed him to go to a hotel without anything.

He states:

> My luggage didn't amount to much, only a medium-size suitcase with my clothes, and a small leather bag containing my toilet articles. But my trousers, my shirts, my shoes were lifted out and checked over by five pairs of eyes. Pockets and seams were explored with meticulous attention. In Rome I had wrapped my shoes, so as not to soil my clothes, in a wrinkled newspaper I had found in my hotel room. I believe it was the *Osservatore Romano.* They spread the page on a table, held it up to the light, folded it as carefully as if it

> were a secret document, and finally put it aside with some of my papers. My shoes were also studied inside and out, like unique samples of fabulous fossils.

His luggage was eventually sent back to his hotel, but he later discovered everyone in India whose addresses were written in his diary had been interrogated.[1]

In his memoirs, Neruda also vividly describes his meeting with the first prime minister.

Neruda met Jawaharlal in the latter's office. The prime minister rose from his chair and shook the emissary's hand 'without any trace of a welcoming smile'. The poet recognized him, noting that he had been 'photographed so often that it's not worth the describing'. He further added that Jawaharlal's '[dark], cold eyes looked at me without feeling'.

Neruda recalled meeting Motilal and his son thirty years earlier at a rally for independence. He reminded Jawaharlal of this, 'but it produced no change in his face'. 'He replied in monosyllables to everything I said, scrutinizing me with his steady, cold eyes,' Neruda remembered. He further added:

> He finished, put the letter back into its envelope, and looked at me without a word. It suddenly struck me that my presence provoked an involuntary dislike in him. It also crossed my mind that this man with a bilious complexion must be going through a bad physical, political, or emotional experience. There was something high and mighty about him, something stiff, as if he were accustomed to giving orders but lacked the strength of a leader.[2]

In 1955, Neruda was a member of the Lenin Peace Prize committee in Moscow during an international assembly.

Some Indian delegates proposed the name of India's prime minister. 'The shadow of a smile crossed my face, but none of the others on the jury understood it, and I voted affirmatively,' Neruda reflected.[3]

That same year, the prime minister was awarded the Bharat Ratna. In his speech during the decoration ceremony of Jawaharlal Nehru, Rajendra Prasad, the President of India, stated:

> [His] lifelong services to our nation are written in letters of gold on every page of our recent history ... I have felt that I can do no better than conferring on him the award of Bharat Ratna which is the highest award of honour that we have ... I am taking this step on my own initiative and without any recommendation or advice from my prime minister.

There were arguments suggesting that Jawaharlal was in Austria when he was nominated for the award and had no influence over the decision. However, it is widely understood that, in the Indian democratic system, the President is often seen as aligned with the prime minister.

Jawaharlal's government reciprocated by awarding the Bharat Ratna to Rajendra Babu soon after he retired as President. Indira accepted this honour on behalf of her government. Residents of Jiradei, Prasad's village in Siwan district, recall that he had three sons: Mrityunjay, Dhananjay and Janardan. Mrityunjay, persuaded by Jayprakash Narayan to enter politics after the Emergency, became an MP from Siwan as a nominee of the Janata Party but later distanced himself from politics. The villagers remember Mrityunjay as a saint, while they characterize Dhananjay as his opposite.

Prasad himself remained neutral on all matters, except when it came to the prime minister.

Born and brought up in this area, I spent many summers of my childhood playing in the deserted campus of Rajendra Babu. I often overheard the elders of the area complaining to each other, saying that, unlike Jawaharlal, he did nothing for himself, his family, or the place.

As an outsider, Neruda was unaware of the reason behind Jawaharlal's inconsistent behaviour, which might have been a reflection of the political developments at the time. In 1950, Purushottam Das Tandon, as Congress president, nominated a working committee to address various issues, including the position of the prime minister. Jawaharlal, a member of this committee, resigned and announced that he would also step down as the prime minister.

That was a strategic decision. Congress members under Pant in Uttar Pradesh and Gopi Krishna Vijayvargiya in Madhya Pradesh turned rebellious and declared their support for him. Tandon was ultimately forced to resign, and Jawaharlal reclaimed the presidency of the Congress Party. He had previously led the party twice. Four years later, he relinquished the position to Uchharangrai Navalshankar Dhebar, a close confidant, who had served as chief minister of Saurashtra for over six years. Dhebar held the party's top post until February 1959, when Indira was poised to take over. This trend continues even today, with the Nehru–New Gandhi family determining who will be the president of the Congress.

Lal Bahadur Shastri's government established the Jawaharlal Nehru Award for International Understanding, while the Indira Gandhi Peace Prize was instituted by Rajiv's government. The Congress government awarded the Bharat Ratna and this prize to Rajiv posthumously. The New Gandhis opened the door to receiving awards from their own government.

Modi has a strong precedent for ignoring those who question why he seeks honours, awards, recognitions, or membership in the global club of the statesmen. He frequently compares himself to Jawaharlal to position himself as a true leader while simultaneously blaming Nehru for every problem in the country, aiming to prevent any resurgence of the Congress Party.

When Modi received CERAWeek Global Energy and Environment Leadership Award in March 2021 during a virtual programme, he referenced it in several public meetings thereafter, claiming that this honour was an honour for India. However, his grand aspirations were overshadowed by reports in the international media of dead bodies floating on the Ganges in Allahabad during the COVID-19 pandemic.

Jawaharlal was the only son of his parents, Motilal and Swarup Rani. His great-grandfather, Lachchminarain Nehru, and grandfather, Ganga Dhar Nehru, held positions as 'vakil' and 'kotwal', respectively, in the Mughal government. However, the family was uprooted from Delhi during the 1857 revolt and relocated to Agra, where Motilal was born.

His eldest uncle, Bansi Dhar Nehru, worked in the judicial department of the Raj, while his second uncle, Nand Lal, served as diwan in Rajputana before becoming a lawyer in Agra.

In his autobiography, Jawaharlal described his father was initially 'a nationalist in a vague sense of the word, but he admired Englishmen and their ways'. The family led a 'Westernized' lifestyle.[4]

As a child, Jawaharlal often observed his father enjoying whisky, red wine, and claret with Englishmen, where he first encountered Tej Bahadur Sapru, a member of the Allahabad Bar. Later, Sapru, a Kashmiri Brahmin, attempted to outwit Motilal and Jawaharlal.

Sapru was a proponent of gradual change throughout his socio-political career and was opposed to the Congress's civil disobedience and non-cooperation movements from the outset.[5]

Sapru also harboured some contempt for Jawaharlal, apparently because he despised socialist and communist ideas. According to Bose:

> The truth is that there was no political similarity between Sapru and Nehru. It appears that their personal relationship was tense from 1933 to 1939. Sapru thought that he and Jayakar were no match [for] Nehru. Nehru looked casteist … Sapru was ready to accept a lot from British socialism but he was an opponent of communism.[6]

Despite the hurdles placed before them by Sapru and Jayakar, the Nehrus managed to navigate them with determination.

It must have been a difficult task, but Motilal was a man of strong willpower. When most leaders would have succumbed to caste pressures, he refused to undergo any purification rituals after the Kashmiri Brahmin community declared him an outcaste for crossing the sea to visit Europe.

When I visited Anand Bhawan and saw Motilal's pictures and belongings, I was reminded of Prithviraj Kapoor as Akbar in K. Asif's *Mughal-e-Azam*. The sense of elitism may have led Motilal to disregard the sentiments of his community.

Gandhi also faced ostracism for studying abroad. Upon his return as a barrister, his eldest brother took him to Nasik for a holy bath in the Godavari. They then returned home to Rajkot, where his brother organized a caste dinner in his honour.

Crossing the ocean was a non-issue for fifteen-year-old Jawaharlal when he travelled to join Harrow. After two years, he gained admission to Trinity College, Cambridge, where he studied chemistry, geology and botany until the age of twenty. He read Garibaldi in school and delved into the works of Nietzsche and Bernard Shaw in college. In 1907–08, he began contemplating a career in politics and identified himself as a Tilakite or an extremist.

Jawaharlal and Savarkar

Savarkar lived in London from 1906 to 1910, during which Jawaharlal was also there. Although he heard about Varma and India House, he 'never met him or visited the house'. Later, he recounted, 'Long afterwards, in 1926, I saw Shyamji in Geneva … he regarded almost every Indian who came near him as a spy sent by the British Government.'[7]

The founder of India House viewed Jawaharlal with suspicion; however, this impression is solely based on Jawaharlal's assertion that Varma looked at every Indian with doubt.

If Jawaharlal didn't express any interest in meeting Savarkar in London, then Savarkar didn't attempt to meet him either. This was a deliberate choice, especially given that Savarkar was meeting everyone else in an effort to expand his Hindutva constituency.

Savarkar was more egoistic than the son of the successful barrister from Allahabad. It was not in his nature to approach someone whose ancestors had served the Mughals.

Savarkar was connected to Gandhi in London, albeit as a critic. Gandhi was already known among Indians in London due to his struggles in South Africa. Although Jawaharlal took a keen interest in India's political developments, he didn't feel inclined to connect with Gandhi at that time; this only happened later when Motilal recognized it as a promising opportunity.

The prodigal son, Jawaharlal, left Cambridge after earning his degree in 1910, joined the Inner Temple that same year to study law, and returned to India in 1912 as a barrister. At that time, Motilal was fifty-one years old. Jawaharlal returned to India with a clear resolution to enter politics, as he had no desire to be a bureaucrat or a revolutionary.

On the other hand, Savarkar's return home was not a happy one. Even though he had become a celebrated figure among Maharashtrian Brahmins and some fellow coreligionists due to his protests in London and the Marseilles episode, his long incarceration thereafter tarnished his political prospects.

The situation was more favourable for Jawaharlal. Although Motilal entered politics relatively late, he launched himself perfectly into the Swaraj Party after Gandhi called off his Non-Cooperation Movement.

Jawaharlal attended the Bankipore Congress session in 1912, where he observed no political unrest among its members. He first met Gandhi after four years in Lucknow and soon became his disciple. Both Motilal and Jawaharlal admired Tilak, but they eventually drifted away from his ideas due to the influence of seniors like Rash Behari Ghosh, who disapproved of Tilak's philosophy

The sequence of events suggests that they were grappling with their political identities and found Gandhi a more appealing option after he founded the Satyagraha Sabha in 1919 in response to the Rowlatt Act (Criminal Emergency Power).

That year, Gandhi visited Allahabad at Motilal's invitation and stayed with them. During this visit, Motilal shared Jawaharlal's extreme ideas with Gandhi, who advised him to embrace non-aggressive actions. This interaction set the stage for Gandhi to adopt Jawaharlal as his successor. While Motilal occasionally diverged from Gandhi's views, he ensured that his son remained closely connected to Gandhi.

As expected, Jawaharlal rose quickly in the Congress ranks, becoming its secretary in 1919. By 1923, he had gained enough confidence to publicly express his opposition to the Mahasabha, particularly criticizing the Hindutva ideology. He aggressively condemned the outfit during a 1933 convention at the Banaras Hindu University, and continued to do so in subsequent years.

In *The Discovery of India,* written between 1942 and 1944, Jawaharlal linked the Hindutva ideology to what he called a 'lynching mentality', reflecting on the dangerous consequences of such ideologies.

> Savarkar wrote *The History of the War of Indian Independence* some thirty years ago, but his book was promptly banned and is banned still. Some frank and honourable English historians have occasionally lifted the veil and allowed us a glimpse of the race mania and lynching mentality which prevailed on an enormous scale.[8]

Although Savarkar's book was proscribed, it was not entirely unavailable. Jawaharlal formed his view based on secondary information.

He also noted in the book that the league didn't perform well in the 1937 elections, and the Mahasabha failed completely. He asserted that these groups had no genuine interest in India's independence, writing:

> There was a fundamental difference between the outlook of the Congress and that of the religious-communal organizations. Of the latter the chief were the Moslem League and its Hindu counterpart, the Hindu Mahasabha. These communal organizations, while in theory standing for India's independence, were more interested in claiming protection and special privileges for their respective groups.[9]

Despite his criticism, Jawaharlal, mindful of Tilak's stature, referred to him as 'the real symbol of the new age' in opposition to the partition of Bengal and claimed that the Muslim League and the Hindu Mahasabha were equally unreasonable.

The All India Muslim League diminished significantly after partition, as most of its leaders migrated to Pakistan, leaving behind a small fragment known as the Indian Union Muslim League, which has a base in Kerala and some support in Tamil Nadu. Hindutva persisted in ideological form within the RSS, and the BJP gained a majority after sixty-seven years of independence.

The plan Tilak had envisioned during the 1907 Surat session of the Congress was realized 107 years later when Modi kissed the steps of the Parliament. However, Tilak's mission to take over the Congress remained incomplete, echoing in Modi's call for a 'Congress-free Bharat' to his supporters.

Veer Savarkar or Veer Jawahar

Some critics of Savarkar argue that he began using the prefix 'Veer' (brave) on his own. Some attribute it to Vaishampayan, a Marathi poet, while others claim it was Veer Vamanrao Joshi who called him 'Swatantrya Veer' in 1924. Sadashiv Ranade also wrote a biography titled *Swatantryaveer Vinayakrao Savarkar Yanche Charitra* in Marathi, published in the same year.

If Savarkar did not adopt the prefix himself, it may have been bestowed upon him due to the bravery he demonstrated by risking his life in France. Additionally, his long incarceration in Cellular Jail could have contributed to this honorific.

The Publication Division of the Government of India released *Yah Gatha Veer Jawahar Ki* (This Story of Veer Jawahar), a Hindi biography by Kanhaiyalal Mishra 'Prabhakar', initially published in the 1970s. The first chapter titled, '*Ek Heeron Jadi Jindagi*' ('A Diamond Studded Life'), describes how Jawaharlal's life was a blend of precious stones.

We all know the patriotic song '*Mere Desh Ki Dharti*' ('The Land of My Country') from Manoj Kumar's 1967 Hindi film *Upkar*. In this song by Gulshan Kumar Mehta, the phrase 'Veer Jawahar' is prominently featured.

Legendary Hindi poet and author Nirala (1899–1961) was critical of the prefix Veer and ridiculed the first prime minister in one of his poems titled '*Kale Kale Badal Chhae*' ('The Dark Cloud Covered the Sky').

One of the lines in Nirala's poem reads:

Mehngai ki baadh badh aai, gaanth ki chooti garhi kamaai,
Bhukhe nange khade sharmae, na aaye Veer Jawaharlal.

(The flood of inflation is rising, the savings are gone; the hungry and naked are shyly standing there, but Veer Jawaharlal doesn't come).

This poem appears in several collections by Nirala, including *Bela* and *Nirala Sanchaita.*

If India had two Veers, it is clear that Savarkar was the first.

This epithet gained significant traction during the Modi government's 2022 scheme, Agnipath, when four-year recruits in the Indian forces were named 'Agni-Veer'. We know who the 'Veer' of the RSS–BJP government is. In 2024, there were claims that the scheme was introduced against the wishes of senior army officers, suggesting that the ghost of Moonje has resurfaced. Moonje, a mentor to Hedgewar, is often regarded as one of the first to advocate for mandatory military training for every Indian, as discussed in the previous chapters.

Jallianwala Bagh Scam

Their quislings, turncoats and traitors all
Come laden with gossip and tales to narrate.
'Revel', 'robbers', 'scoundrel' and more—
Names used against us to aggravate.
Frame sour heroes with guilt and treason,
Damage they wreak on our nation great![10]

Punjabi poet Nanak Singh was present at Jallianwala Bagh on Vaisakhi Day when Brigadier General Reginald Dyer ordered his troops to fire upon the crowd gathered to protest the Rowlatt Act. Nanak remained unconscious beneath a pile of corpses and emerged hours later. His collection of poems about the massacre was published a year later and promptly banned by the British government.

The lines above refer to Indians who were pleased with the enactment of the Rowlatt Act, which empowered the British police to arrest individuals and detain them without trial.

Approximately 400 residents of Amritsar were killed, and 1,200 were left wounded after 1,650 rounds of firing. The officers considered bombarding Amritsar but feared that any damage to the Golden Temple would galvanize the entire Punjab.

The massacre at Jallianwala Bagh created a situation for the first major scandal in the Congress, and perhaps in the country. As life began to normalize in Punjab, the Congress decided to conduct relief work and initiate an inquiry into the killings.

Two committees were formed for relief efforts and to conduct the inquiry. Malaviya and Shraddhanand were assigned to lead the relief work for the victims, while Motilal and C.R. Das took the responsibility for the probe.

A sub-committee was formed for the inquiry, with Jayakar at the helm. Summoned by the party leadership, he arrived in Lahore on 12 December 1919 to join Malaviya and other leaders in beginning the work. Gandhi stayed in an old building belonging to Rambhuj Dutt Choudhary, while Motilal rented a house where Jawaharlal also stayed.

As the report was completed under Gandhi's supervision over the next six months, Jayakar was tasked with publishing its copies. There was a public fund of Rs 5 lakh for this work, managed by Jehangir Bomanji Petit, from which Jayakar withdrew Rs 50,000. He travelled from Bombay to Lahore with the printed report to discuss it with senior party members, and then met them again at Sewa Ashram in Nagwa, Banaras.

Gandhi expressed doubts about the allegations made against British officers and asked Jayakar if there was evidence to substantiate the claim that Jallianwala Bagh had been turned into a pen by the British force. Jayakar, along with Motilal and Das, believed that 'Dyer had laid a trap to drive the people into the Jallianwala enclosure with the view of giving them condign punishment ... Gandhi violently differed from our view.'[11] Following this, another sub-committee was appointed by the Congress in Banaras. Gokaran Nath Misra, the joint general secretary of the Congress, informed Jayakar via letter that he was to draft a petition to the Parliament regarding the massacre. Jayakar, however, refused to participate.

Five years later, news surfaced in a section of the Bombay press alleging that the funds withdrawn by Jayakar had been misappropriated. Jayakar defended himself, stating that he had distributed Rs 4,385 to support students from poor backgrounds between 1920 and 1925, whose careers were at risk due to Congress's activities.

Gandhi likely would not have approved of this approach. While addressing students in Ahmedabad on 15 November 1920, he advised medical students who had paid their fees from their own resources to refrain from participating in the Non-Cooperation Movement. For those who had received scholarships and were contracted to serve the government for a specific period, Gandhi suggested that they should not make any hasty decisions. He said, 'I can't give them [the medical students] money, which is collected from the people [to raise a movement].'[12]

Jayakar later sent a cheque for the remaining balance of Rs 1,240 to the party, explaining that the rest of the funds had been spent on preparing the report.

Despite this, he received a letter from Jawaharlal, then the secretary of the AICC, requesting him to pay the outstanding amount in his name. Jayakar 'discovered that the AICC desired to have this amount for the purpose of meeting the expenses of the election propaganda of the Swaraj Party'.[13]

Jayakar held regular meetings with Gandhi and corresponded frequently with him about the report. Jawaharlal wanted Jayakar to stay in Allahabad and oversee the publication of the Jallianwala Bagh report, but this never came to fruition. The two continued exchanging letters about the fund mismanagement controversy and made conflicting statements in the press until the matter subsided in 1930.

Later, Jayakar attempted to distance himself from the past by collecting Rs 16,000 from the sale of stage show tickets, which he deposited with Congress treasurer Jamnalal Bajaj. He also contributed Rs 25,000 to Gandhi for the promotion of khadi.

In 1951, Saifuddin Kitchlew was appointed a life trustee of the Jallianwala Bagh National Memorial Trust, alongside Jawaharlal and Maulana Abul Kalam Azad.

It was ironic that while the Jallianwala Bagh fund had become a point of contention in India, some British citizens were deeply disturbed by the massacre. Politicians Robert Williams, Robert Smillie, and George Lansbury wrote in *Daily Herald* that the incompetence of certain officers had 'brought these peaceful law-abiding people to the verge of open undisguised revolution'. They emphasized that 'Indians ask [for] the same rights, the same duties, the same recognition as Serbia, Poland and other small European peoples', urging their fellow Britons to protest 'against the bombing and shooting of unarmed men and women'.

Kim A. Wagner, in his 2019 book *Jallianwala Bagh: An Empire of Fear and the Making of the Amritsar Massacre*, claimed that the British newspaper *Morning Post* came to Dyer's defence and launched the 'General Dyer Fund', raising about £26,000, which included a £10 contribution from *The Jungle Book* author, Rudyard Kipling. Kipling, born in Bombay, lived in Allahabad during 1888–89, working for the *Pioneer* newspaper. A worn-out plaque at the old Belvedere House complex, across the University of Allahabad, still commemorates his association with the city.

The Story of Vande Mataram

'Vande Mataram' has become more of a political tool than a national song. Composed by Bankim Chandra Chattopadhyay in 1876, it was incorporated into his novel *Anandamath* six years later.

By the late 1920s, a faction within the Congress, closely aligned with Savarkar's ideology, adopted *Anandamath* as an unofficial Magna Carta for Hindutva. In 1937, Jawaharlal read an English translation of *Anandamath* to understand the controversy surrounding the song 'Vande Mataram'.

In a response to Subhas Chandra Bose, who had expressed concern about the opposition to the song and sought clarity on the Congress's stance, Jawaharlal wrote:

> I have somehow got an English translation of *Anandamath* and reading these days to get acquainted with the background of this song. It certainly appears that its background can provoke the Muslims … I can't understand it without a dictionary.[14]

The reasons behind Muslim opposition to the song remain a matter of debate. However, it is widely believed to stem from Bankim Chandra's overt animosity towards Muslims in *Anandamath*, particularly the 'insulting epithets' he uses to describe them. Furthermore, the song's idolatry and its association with Hindu deities, especially in *Anandamath*, are not acceptable to many Muslims.[15]

As one author noted that 'the Mother in "Vande Mataram" has, it is said, too much likeness to a Hindu goddess' and it is a 'champion of revival of Hinduism'.[16]

Jawaharlal blamed communal forces for exploiting 'Vande Mataram' and expressed a desire to discuss the issue with Rabindranath Tagore in Calcutta on 25 October.[17] Tagore's opinion was crucial, as he had first sung the song at the 1896 Calcutta session of the Indian National Congress. The Congress working committee officially adopted the song at the end of October 1937, amid the Hindu Mahasabha's 'Vande Mataram Day' programmes in Poona and Bombay.

What Bankim Chandra invoked in his novel to promote regional Hindu nationalism, Savarkar later advanced in his historical writings. Even though Savarkar's *The Indian War of Independence* was banned, it reflects Bankim's influence.

He quoted the Marathi poet-saint Ramdas:

'Dharmasathi marawen, Maroni awadhyas marawen.
Maritan maritan dhyawen, Rajya apulen.'

He translated the couplet as, 'Die for your Dharma; kill the enemies of your Dharma...' Savarkar emphasized that while some Muslim rulers opposed Britishers in 1857, the majority of landlords who participated in the First War of Independence were Hindus.[18]

Jawaharlal did not have an issue with 'Vande Mataram' itself, as it did not undermine his political standing, but he opposed Savarkar and his 'unmodern' ideas. Nehru described the 1857 uprising as a 'revolt' in which the Sikhs, Gurkhas and many Indians sided with the British, attributing this to the absence of a modern sense of nationalism at the time.

Jawaharlal had the chance to deprive Hindutva of 'Vande Mataram' and prevent its use against other communities, particularly minority institutions, but he didn't do so. The first prime minister was neither naïve nor short-sighted; he must have been aware of how the song was being misused even during his time.

Anandamath didn't suit the Congress politically, as it depicted the Hindu struggle against a Muslim ruler. However, it was also an opportunity for Jawaharlal to assert himself within the Brahmanical order of Maharashtra.

Instead, the song became further ammunition for Hindutva forces. Any Hindutva politician seeking to make a political comeback often starts by misusing 'Vande Mataram'. The euphoria surrounding the song continues to grow, and it remains a tool for Hindutva in its mission to undermine the Congress.

Jawaharlal missed out on taking credit for the song's acceptance, or perhaps it was a political miscalculation. The Congress appears to have conceded that 'Vande Mataram' is not theirs anymore.

In November 1998, the BJP-led central government made singing 'Vande Mataram' mandatory in primary schools. In July 2017, the Madras High Court instructed schools, colleges and institutions to organize the singing of the song at least once a week. By October 2022, the Maharashtra government had asked its employees to greet each other with

'Vande Mataram' instead of 'Hello' when starting phone conversations. A month later, the Delhi High Court observed that the national anthem 'Jana Gan Mann', written by Tagore, and 'Vande Mataram' held equal status.

It is not over yet. While waiting for someone at an RSS office in Lucknow in May 2023, I overhead a functionary telling his colleague to urge the state government to make the recital of 'Vande Mataram' mandatory at Darul Uloom Deoband.

Members of the RSS, VHP, and BJP often chant 'Hindustan *me rehna hai to* Vande Mataram *kehna hai* (You have to chant Vande Mataram if you want to live in India).' Whenever a right-wing leader stirs up this issue, the Congress routinely steps forward to oppose it. But doesn't the Congress remember that, back in 1937, the song was unacceptable to Muslims because Islam does not allow the worship of the motherland? Mohammad Ali Jinnah had strongly opposed it at the time.

Jinnah wrote in an article that Muslims across India rejected 'Vande Mataram' and 'any expurgated edition of the anti-Muslim song' as a national anthem. He reiterated this in his presidential address at the special session of the All-India Muslim League in Calcutta, adding that the Indian National Congress had imposed 'Vande Mataram' on the legislatures. This happened even though the Congress had dropped certain parts of the song from the original version before declaring its acceptance.

In January 1939, Mahatma Gandhi's draft for the Constituent Assembly, marked 'Strictly Confidential: Not for Publication', stated:

> As to the singing of the long-established national song, Vande Mataram, the Congress, anticipating objections, has

> retained as national song only those stanzas to which no objection could be taken on religious and other grounds. But except at purely Congress gatherings, it should be left open to individuals whether they will stand up when the stanzas are sung. In the present state of things, in Local Board and Assembly meetings, which their members are obliged to attend, the singing of Vande Mataram should be discontinued.[19]

Gandhi further noted, 'I will not risk a single quarrel over singing Vande Mataram at a mixed gathering. It will never suffer from disuse.'

Jawaharlal didn't publicly react to this, but his close associates—Rajagopalachari, Patel and Pant—disagreed with the proposal. They wanted to proceed with the full song. In fact, both Patel and Prasad had ended their speeches as Congress presidents in 1931 and 1934, respectively, with the song.

The Constituent Assembly of India adopted 'Vande Mataram' as the national song when Jawaharlal was prime minister. However, with Bakr-Id approaching, Jawaharlal cautioned that any public statements on cow slaughter, playing music in front of mosques, or taking out processions past them—contrary to tradition—should be avoided. Jawaharlal remarked, launching yet another contentious issue concerning the cow:

> There was a common view [in the Congress] that the legal rights of cow-slaughter and playing songs or taking out processions in front of mosques should be accepted and practical shape should be given to it, provided the tradition is definitely not against it.[20]

This may explain why Tagore believed that 'Jawaharlal was a truer representative of modern India than Gandhiji.' Tagore commented, 'Jawaharlal was by taste, training, and everything else an Englishman, but he had an Indian heart. On the other hand, he personally claimed to be a true representative of the Indian people.'[21]

Venkata Rao's remark in Golwalkar's *Bunch of Thoughts* suggests that the RSS held partially a similar view of Jawaharlal, that is, of him being an Englishman. He noted that Mahatma had chosen a successor who didn't align with his vision of man, nation, or God: 'The Nehru Mind is made mostly abroad and in spite of his [The] Discovery of India, Sri Nehru never succeeded in catching the spirit of Indian culture at its best.'[22]

Jawaharlal: The PM

M. Chelapathi Rau unknowingly left an intriguing comparison between Jawaharlal Nehru and Narendra Modi. The first prime minister never barred any questions during his press conferences:

> Sometimes the questions were irritating, at other times even insulting, but he enjoyed the exchanges ... He knew the faces, not always the names, but he seemed to know what was behind a question or who was behind a question.[23]

In contrast, Modi has shown a reluctance to hold press conferences. His interaction with the media is primarily limited to election-time publicity. However, it would be unfair to place all the blame on him; journalistic suppression is a wider political problem not limited to his leadership alone. Over the years, dozens of reporters have been arrested and even killed in Congress-ruled states for writing against the government. While the party in power may change, the treatment of the press remains largely the same.

The misuse or exploitation of journalism was always a point of concern for Savarkar. He blamed the press for neglecting national issues during the riots following the Partition in 1947, accusing it of aiding Jawaharlal in the process. Savarkar contended that Gandhian leaders and newspapers were silent about the failures of Jawaharlal's first government in protecting the lives, property, and honour of the people. He attributed this silence to the Congress's 'crafty design to capture Moslem votes in the joint electorates'. He wrote:

> Pandit Nehru, their megaphone, has recently been addressing a number of meetings, wherein instead of assuring and enlightening the people as to how his government is going to forestall and frustrate the covert machinations and pervert challenges of the Moslems to conquer and convert the whole of Hindustan into a Pakistan, he has been indulging into furious denunciations against the demand of a Hindu state.

Savarkar referred to Jawaharlal as a 'Carpet Knight' and claimed the Hindu sanghatanists had fought against the British while Gandhi was 'still in his clothes and the Pandit was not yet born'.[24]

In an effort to eliminate opposition and diminish the influence of leaders who could rival his stature, Jawaharlal consistently sought to bring the Mahasabha into the Congress fold. However, Mookerjee, the president of the Mahasabha, lacked the freedom to make decisions. Despite this, Mookerjee attempted to persuade Savarkar to moderate his stance on the Mahasabha, advocating for the inclusion of Muslim members.

Savarkar rejected the idea of following a constitutional approach and turned down Mookerjee's suggestion to grant equal rights to all religions by allowing non-Hindus to join the Mahasabha. Influenced by the prime minister, Mookerjee eventually departed from the Mahasabha in 1950 and launched the Bharatiya Jan Sangh (BJS) in Delhi on 21 October 1951.

On the other hand, Kripalani—who served as the general secretary of the Congress for twelve years, beginning 1928, and was elected its president in 1946—found himself powerless against Jawaharlal and left the party in 1951 to form Kisan Mazdoor Praja Party.

The BJS fielded 93 candidates for 489 parliamentary seats in 1952 and won 3, in what was independent India's first general election. It also fielded 425 candidates for 3,283 assembly seats across the country, winning 35. As the new party struggled in the elections, it merged with the Kisan Mazdoor Praja Party and the Socialist Party to form the Praja Socialist Party, which saw partial success in Kerala in 1954.

In that same year, Pottam Thanu Pillai, who had previously been in the Congress and served as the first prime minister of independent Travancore in 1948, joined forces with Mookerjee. Pillai became the chief minister of Travancore–Cochin with Congress's support, while Jawaharlal was both the prime minister and president of the Congress Party. Pillai later returned to the Congress and became the governor of Punjab.

Jawaharlal didn't tolerate even minor rivals. As Nana Deshmukh noted, 'The policy of luring into power by encouraging for defection started in the Congress during Sri Nehru's time.'[25]

The precedent of exercising absolute power set by Jawaharlal continues to be followed by others. Today, we see news channels universally praising politicians. Back in the 1980s and earlier, short films about Jawaharlal and Indira were mandatory screenings at the beginning and during intermissions in cinema halls, often leaving audiences exhausted.

It seems like a tradition among today's politicians to boast about their accomplishments, even when the work has never been done. There have been cases where their advertisements featured foreign bridges or towers, passing them off as their own achievements in India.

The works undertaken by Jawaharlal as the prime minister are something we studied extensively in our schoolbooks, especially in chapters on the Five-Year Plans. These plans were developed in collaboration with Russia, Germany, and the UK. However, there were also some exaggeration regarding government achievements, which irritated Shivadhar Pandey, a retired English teacher from the University of Allahabad and editor of *Chetna*, a small magazine that published his poem in the 1950s:

Congress *ka dekho khel*
Boi sui ki upji rail.
(See the game of the Congress. They sow a needle, and a rail is produced.)

Jawaharlal inherited a certain stubbornness from his father, Motilal. During the debate on the Steel Protection Bill in the Central Legislature under British rule, Motilal had planned a trip to Bombay. Although the Tatas were usually his hosts, he initially intended to stay with his friend, Pratap Pandit. However, a well-meaning friend, unaware of the change in plans, sent Motilal a telegram advising against staying with the Tatas to avoid controversy. In response, Motilal chose to stay with the Tatas, showing his resolve.[26]

This incident took place in the 1920s, when, following the recommendation of the Central Legislature, the government provided financial assistance to Tata Steel.

As discussed in previous chapters, Jawaharlal's rise to prominence involved sidelining his potential rivals, such as Narendra Dev and Kripalani. An exchange of letters between Subhas Chandra Bose and Jawaharlal sheds light on how Bose felt Jawaharlal had aided Sardar Patel in targeting him when he was re-elected as Congress president for a second term.

On 28 March 1939, shortly before resigning, Bose wrote to Jawaharlal:

> I have already asked you if you considered it fair on the part of Sardar Patel to declare that my re-election would be harmful to the country's cause. You never said a word that he should withdraw such a remark, thereby indirectly supporting his allegation.[27]

Jawaharlal replied, 'If Vallabhbhai is convinced that India's good requires Gandhiji's leadership, and that your re-election might deprive India of this leadership, then he can well think and say so.'[28]

Bose resigned after Gandhi showed complete non-cooperation and refused to suggest members for the Congress Working Committee.

Jawaharlal's dogged determination surfaced again in 1955, when, despite multiple warnings about the harmful effects of the Hirakund Hydro-Irrigation Project on the Mahanadi River in Odisha, he pressed ahead with the plan. Over one lakh residents were displaced as a result. However, the state government under Naveen Patnaik now provides leasehold land to the displaced families. In December 2023, 1,749 affected families were allocated land leases.

Many researchers call the Hirakund project a 'failed' initiative, blaming it for economic disintegration, deprivation, identity crisis, and instability among the oustees.[29]

Before and After Jawaharlal

Jawaharlal died of a heart attack in May 1964, and within five months, Gopal, Karkare, and Pahwa were released. Whether this was a mere coincidence remains unclear. Even if we consider it a coincidence, the fact remains that the Shastri government ignored a suggestion from Vasantrao Phulsing Naik's government in Maharashtra to oppose their release in court. Naik repeatedly made public that he had appealed to the Centre against the court's decision, but the Shastri government never explained why it didn't challenge the Habeas Corpus petition of Gandhi's murder conspirators.

Shastri's politics of ethics is frequently discussed in everyday Indian life. As railway minister, he took moral responsibility for the death of 112 passengers in a train accident in Mahbubnagar, Andhra Pradesh, and offered his resignation, which the prime minister initially refused. However, after another accident three months later in Ariyalur, Tamil Nadu, his resignation was accepted.

This topic was revisited in greater detail following a revelation by Ketkar, made six months after Jawaharlal's death and over sixteen years after Gandhi's assassination.

In November 1964, Bhupesh Gupta, a barrister-at-law from University College London and an MP from Bengal representing the left, raised a crucial question in the Parliament: 'What was the Bombay Government doing at that time [when Gandhi was killed]? We would like to know whether the Bombay Government, the Central Government and the Central Intelligence had any inkling or indication with regard to such things'[30]

It seemed that Jawaharlal had time for rumourmongers but little interest in investigating the facts surrounding the plans to assassinate Gandhi, which were already in the public domain. Despite many signs pointing to a conspiracy, the government appeared to have ignored them.

Did Jawaharlal not know that someone carrying a knife had rushed towards Gandhi at Dilkhush Bungalow in Panchgani? The *Times of India* reported on 23 July 1944 that some RSS members caused trouble there. On 22 June 1944, fifteen Hindu Mahasabha activists, led by Apte, had shown black flags to Gandhi in Panchgani.

While Gopal denied in 1966 that Godse was present in Panchgani, he confirmed that Apte and his team had been there to organize a demonstration. Sushila Nayyar, Gandhi's physician, claimed that Godse and others were at Sevagram in 1946. Volunteers at the ashram had found one of them carrying a knife, though they showed no immediate intention to attack Gandhi.

Ketkar's revelation prompted the government to order a fresh inquiry, first under Gopal Swarup Pathak, and later reconstituted under Justice Kapur when Pathak became a central minister. The Kapur Commission's findings once again compelled the nation to re-examine the events surrounding Gandhi's murder. The commission noted that Gandhi's protection was inadequate, and the inquiry that followed was far from the expected standard of honesty.

Jawaharlal's actions suggested that, while he opposed the Mahasabha and the RSS as political rivals, he was reluctant to fully pursue the assassination case, possibly because it exposed a failure of his own government.

The anti-Hindutva factions did not perceive any lack of sensitivity from Jawaharlal regarding Gandhi's murder or the subsequent mishandling of the investigation. Yet, his critics never saw his stance as a favour to them.

Addressing a rally in Ghazipur on the 127th birth anniversary of Jawaharlal, Prime Minister Modi took the opportunity to critique India's first prime minister. He claimed to be addressing the work that Jawaharlal had neglected.

Modi paid tribute to Jawaharlal, stating:

> In 1962, Lok Sabha member from Ghazipur, Viswanathji had told Panditji [Nehru] in the Parliament with tears in his eyes that although you became prime minister after your election from UP, there was acute poverty in the eastern part of the state. People collect grains of wheat from cow dung

and wash it to make it edible. This speech was given by the then Ghazipur MP Viswanath Prasadji before Pandit Nehru.

He further claimed that a report on poverty in eastern UP was commissioned by the H.N. Patel Committee at Jawaharlal's direction, but it never surfaced.

Modi said sarcastically:

> *Panditji chale gae* [Panditji passed away]. Many prime ministers came thereafter. I am ninth prime minister from UP ... that report remained locked in a box. I have purposefully chosen the date of 14 November to visit this place. The country should know on the occasion of the birth anniversary of Panditji about those who misled the country . . . Panditji, wherever is your soul ... You left behind a thick file in 1962 on the aspirations of poor people ... maybe the leaders of your party and your family cursed me and made false allegations against me ... But I am completing your job.

At the same time, despite the distaste for Jawaharlal in some quarters, Modi has always attempted to emulate him—and therein lies the success of India's first prime minister.

At Naraur Primary School in Varanasi, 200 students were tutored to address Modi as 'Kaka Modi'. On his sixty-eighth birthday, they wished him well. A class five student echoed to the press, 'Modi *Kaka aye the aaj* school me. *Hamko bahut achcha lag raha hai. Bole kheloge to khiloge* [Modi Kaka visited our school today. I liked it. He said if you play, you will grow].'

Jawaharlal's government used to organize similar programmes where children affectionately called him '*Chacha* Nehru'. In North India, terms like 'chacha' or 'kaka' are commonly used to refer to an uncle, and one can hope to immortalize oneself by entering the minds of children.

Jawaharlal took a concrete step in this direction in 1956 by founding the National Bal Bhawan, a supplementary school system designed to nurture creativity in children. Until 1989, when Rajiv was prime minister, Jawaharlal's birthday on 14 November was celebrated as Bal Diwas (Children's Day) in all government schools. On the day, children would chant, 'Chacha Nehru amar rahen.'

Bal Bhawans across the country still mark the day, albeit on a smaller scale, and the slogan-shouting has since faded. Perhaps the Congress will revive this tradition if it returns to power. However, it remains unclear whether Jawaharlal's critics have any similar plans for Modi.

4
Nathuram Godse

The Rise

Some of my friends questioned why I included a separate chapter on Nathuram Godse. They argued that the assassin of the Father of the Nation was not a civilized character, with many branding him as merely a button man. They stressed that Godse should be overlooked by history.

It was his and his master's grandiosity that captured my interest. Those who truly believe in Gandhi cannot hate Godse, even if he was consumed by venom. Gandhi's efforts to unite himself with the macrocosm are enough to suggest that, had he survived the bullets, he would have embraced Godse. Manilal and Ramdas Gandhi, two of Gandhi's four sons, even appealed for the commutation of Godse's death sentence, but the government refused.

The notion that his anger led him to kill Gandhi reflects an asinine mindset, yet this doesn't prevent some from admiring him. I sat with Godse worshipper Yati Narasinghanand Saraswati at the Dasna Devi Temple in Ghaziabad, just 40 km from New Delhi, in mid-2014. I was there with Joe Sacco for an interview. Whenever asked how much time he envisioned for converting India into a Hindu nation—the dream birthed by Savarkar and Godse—Yati would take a deep breath and stare into the void.

We had lunch together and then sat idly, curious to understand the life of someone willing to immerse himself and his followers in communal frenzy to punish members of another religion. In 2013, he was arrested for his involvement in the Muzaffarnagar riots, where over 50 people were killed, and 50,000 families were displaced.

A gym-fit youth in his early twenties approached, touched Yati's feet as he sat on a chair, and then stood beside him. After about thirty minutes, Yati asked, 'Do you want something?'

The youth replied, 'No.'

'Where do you live? Whose son are you?'

'I'm from the nearby village … I want you to assign me something. I am Shuklaji's son.'

'Are you Panditji's son? What can you do for me?'

'Anything.'

'Anything? Sure?'

'Yes.'

Yati turned to his armed bodyguard and said, 'Take this child's details and contact number.'

The youth, clearly enamoured by Yati's persona, seemed ready to do anything for Yati's vision of a 'Muslim-free' India.

Interestingly, Savarkar used to address Godse as 'Pandit'.[1]

Yati was arrested again in January 2022 in the religious town of Haridwar for calling for genocide against Muslims, urging every Hindu to take up arms. He was released on bail after a few weeks.

The seer supports temples dedicated to Godse, and there are at least three such makeshift shrines in western UP. These temples operate when the political climate is favourable and close when the situation turns adverse.

I later discovered that the youth was a school dropout from a well-off religious family of storytellers. He had no job and no desire to work. After hearing and seeing Yati, he found a godly figure in him—Yati was his medium to reach the divine. I didn't follow up on what job the godman assigned to the youth.

Yati wouldn't acknowledge that the devotion the youth felt for him, or that Godse felt for Savarkar, was similar to the love many Indians once had for Gandhi.

'India never loved Gandhi,' Yati said spontaneously. 'Deluded and avaricious Hindus and Muslims showed their love for him. Gandhi may be honest in his mission but nobody cared for this then or now. People stood by whoever promised them freedom from the Raj.'

After dropping out of school following a failed matriculation examination, Godse became involved in the textile business and also dabbled in tailoring. Eventually, he moved to Ratnagiri with his father, wherc he met Savarkar. Godse's first significant assignment was to protest against the Jizya tax in Hyderabad.

Known as Tatyarao among his close circle, Savarkar had mastered the art of identifying his blind followers. The name 'Tatya' has several meanings in Marathi, including Lord Shiva.

Savarkar founded the Hindu Rashtra Dal with Godse and Apte six years after their protest in Hyderabad, building on the foundation of the Rashtra Dal established two years earlier. They launched the newspaper *Agrani* with an initial loan of Rs 15,000 from Savarkar, with Godse as its editor and Apte as the manager. Unlike Godse, Apte was a science graduate and a schoolteacher in Ahmednagar.

The newspaper job helped Godse and Apte gain recognition in the local circles of Poona and Bombay two to three years before Gandhi's assassination. The provincial government had reports indicating that they were dangerous for the country.

Following a bomb explosion in Poona on 26 June 1947, B.G. Kher, the prime minister of Bombay Province before becoming the first chief minister of the Bombay state in independent India, inquired whether the editor of *Agrani* had been arrested. Morarji, Bombay's home minister, was aware of Godse's 'subversive activities'. N.R. Athawale, secretary of the Poona city Hindu Mahasabha, and Apte were arrested in connection with the incident. Athawale confessed that a manager of *Agrani* had provided him with the bomb. In response to the arrests, the Mahasabha observed a 'Black Day' in Poona, framing it as a 'Linguistic Movement'. Clearly, India's independence or future was not their priority, Hindutva was more important to them.

Agrani closed after running for three years due to failure to pay its security deposit, after which they re-launched it as *Hindu Rashtra*, featuring a picture of Savarkar on the masthead.

During the hearings of Gandhi's assassination case, Atma Charan noted that the Delhi police didn't investigate the bomb-throwing incident involving Pahwa. The judge also stated that G.C. Jain, a professor at Ruia College in Bombay, had informed Morarji about the conspiracy.

Jawaharlal, known for his curiosity, was aware of the court proceedings. However, his police mishandled the investigation, while he focused on seeking greater stability to rule. Historical records suggest that he needed Patel's support in the given situation.

Motilal's letter to Gandhi on 11 July 1928, provides insight into this. He believed that Patel, with his immense public service, could not be sidelined. However, he felt his son should be preferred. 'I am clear that the hero of the hour is Vallabhbhai, and the least we can do to appreciate his public service is to offer him the crown,' wrote Motilal, then the president of the Congress Party, who wanted his son to succeed him. He continued, 'Failing him [Patel], I think that under all circumstances, Jawaharlal would be the next best choice ... Our race is fast dying out and the struggle will sooner or later have to be continued by men of Jawahar's type.'[2]

Jawaharlal became the Congress president the following year.

As prime minister, Jawaharlal knew he had to maintain Patel's support to balance any internal opposition.

The Kapur Commission uncovered a statement from Patel made just a few days after Gandhi's murder: 'Jawaharlaljee wrote a letter to me two or three days after returning from Rajghat [after cremating Gandhi] ... that "gone is gone" and we should work together forgetting the past.' A more conciliatory Patel had celebrated his 72nd birthday in October 1947 and was receptive to Jawaharlal's idea.

Identifying a Godse appreciator in India was a tricky task in the past, as they were usually too shy to reveal themselves. However, after Hindutva gained political power in the late 1990s, such individuals began to emerge from the shadows, proudly admiring Godse. They openly claimed that he saved India by killing Gandhi. This increasing adulation of Godse may represent another step toward repudiating Gandhi, and they appear to be in a hurry.

Isolated pro-Godse remarks were also heard in the 1940s, but such expressions didn't bother Jawaharlal or subsequent Congress governments. In recent years, the sentiments have taken on political significance. In June 2023, Giriraj Singh, a Union minister in the Modi government, stated that 'Godse was a worthy son of soil'. Suddenly, many leaders echoed this sentiment in various languages.

It is not without precedent that such remarks don't trouble Rahul Gandhi now. Jawaharlal didn't waste his time on matters he deemed futile; his priority was to maintain power. As Patel became ill, Jawaharlal quickly sidelined Jayaprakash Narayan (J.P.), who many considered the true heir to the home minister. Some people close to Jawaharlal alleged that J.P. was a force behind the Mahasabha and the RSS, claiming he didn't deserve the position. When Patel suffered a heart attack and passed away in 1950, the prime minister appointed Rajagopalachari to his chair.

The distaste for J.P. was evident, as he stated in a speech in Patna on 15 February 1948 that Gandhi would have been alive if prominent Congress ministers hadn't patronized and attended RSS rallies.[3] Those patrons were clearly Jawaharlal's cabinet colleagues.

Much later, Nana Deshmukh boasted that the majority of J.P.'s followers during his Sampoorna Kranti (Total Revolution) to remove Indira from power were members of the ABVP.[4] J.P.'s surviving followers dispute this claim but acknowledge that he didn't prevent anyone from joining his movement. The rightist student wing associated itself with him to gain legitimacy.

Before 1998, editors would scold reporters for giving 'unnecessary' attention to RSS and VHP leaders, resulting in many stories being spiked. Suddenly, that year, newspapers began demanding copies related to Savarkar, Godse, and other Hindutva leaders. These leaders started to assert themselves, mounting pressure on newspapers to grant them a prominent space in news and opinion sections. Publishing a vicious statement from a VHP or BJP leader daily became mandatory.

The VHP began looking beyond India to implant the ideas of Savarkar and Godse into the minds of non-resident Indians. They established international wings of the organization and spent considerable time in America and European countries to promote Hindutva.

Dilip Padgaonkar, then managing editor of the *Times of India*, sent a general note to all offices, including my branch in Allahabad, stating that people were fed up with political news, interviews, speeches, and statements from politicians. This served as valuable guidance for a learner like me. Consequently, I stopped covering public speeches and statements made by politicians.

However, this turned out to be a fleeting lesson. Shortly after becoming HRD minister, Murli Manohar Joshi sent me a message through one of his secretaries, requesting a full-page interview in the Allahabad edition of the newspaper. I ignored the message and instead wrote several reports on how unpopular Joshi was in his constituency, despite the fact that he would likely win the parliamentary election with the active support of the RSS.

Soon after, a BJP national vice president approached me, saying, 'Please stop writing against Joshiji. In return, I can arrange a job for you at the BBC.'

I spent the whole day contemplating how to respond to him. In the evening, I called him at his hotel and said, 'I don't want to go to the BBC. I can oblige you by halting my reports against Joshi if you arrange a fifteen-minute interview with Prime Minister Vajpayee, who is coming here tomorrow.'

The leader promised me to try and took me to the airport the next day. I waited for the opportunity, but later he told me he had tried, but Vajpayee didn't have time. I can't be sure if he was avoiding me.

After a month, I received a call from my editor informing me that Joshi had met with one of the newspaper's directors. He claimed that a reporter was campaigning against him and misusing the paper. The editor suggested that I either conduct an interview with Joshi or be prepared to quit. I called Joshi's secretary, who had previously met with me, and asked him to prepare twenty questions and answers from Joshi's side and provide them to me. The secretary replied that I would receive the questions and answers from Joshi in two days. With no other option, I agreed to meet Joshi at his residence.

'*Ab aya hai unt pahad ke neeche* [You are finally humbled],' Joshi said while sitting on a cane chair. He pulled up his dhoti so I could see his feet, perhaps inviting me to touch them. I touched his feet, took the papers from his hand and was about to leave when he said, 'You can ask me more questions.'

As a reporter, it was tempting, even though I was on edge. He led me into a small room, sat on his bed, and offered me a stool about six feet away. While inspecting his fingernails, he said, 'Ask.'

'People are not happy with you in Allahabad because you are not accessible to them and have not done anything for the city. What will you say to the voters when you seek their support?'

Joshi stood up furiously and charged towards me. I dashed for the door to escape his wrath.

I couldn't sleep the whole night, fearing I might lose my job. There was also the anxiety that Joshi could send the police to arrest me for something he might fabricate against me.

The next day, I met with an RSS leader and requested his help. He told me to relax.

It was under this RSS leader's poll management that BJP workers campaigned for Joshi in the 1996, 1998, and 1999 Lok Sabha elections in Allahabad. However, the Sangh leader distanced himself from the poll campaigns in 2004, a few months after the death of Rajju Bhaiyya, and Joshi lost his influence in the area.

Since then, I have always advised new journalists not to miss the speeches, statements, or interviews of senior politicians. More importantly, any event or statement regarding Savarkar or Godse guarantees space in a newspaper. As a result, many individuals and organizations have started to speak up on behalf of these figures, knowing that their words will attract attention. Some of these voices continue to surface, occasionally offering support for Godse when they sense that public interest in them is waning.

The film industry also seems to be responding positively to these figures in recent years. This has led to the emergence of titles such as *Gandhi Godse: Ek Yudh* (*Gandhi Godse: A War*), *I Killed Bapu*, and *Godse*.

Godse's Growing Constituency

Robert Musil, the Austrian writer, famously wrote in his unfinished novel, *The Man Without Qualities*, 'For only fools, fanatics, and mental cases can endure living at the highest pitch of the soul; a sane person must be content with acknowledging that life would not be worth living without a spark of that mysterious fire.'

Written in the 1930s, Musil's words seem as if they are still in the process of evolving, their meaning resonating across time.

For nearly five decades, no one openly supported the insanity of Gandhi's killers. However, there were many who tried to help those serving life sentences for the crime.

Some leaders, eager to see Gopal released before he completed his sentence, pushed for changes in the law. In 1953, the government of Bombay made efforts to amend the law for his release.

Gopal wrote numerous letters to the home ministry, seeking release on furlough through higher classification and clemency. Records from the National Archives of India show he wrote in February 1952, January 1953, and March 1953.

His letter dated 13 March caught the attention of the Union home ministry, but his request was denied. It was noted that his 'release would be highly prejudicial to public peace'.

Gulzar Singh, undersecretary to the ministry of home affairs, responded to the government of Bombay, highlighting that Gopal had been classified as a B-Class prisoner while in Ambala. However, upon his transfer to a jail in Bombay, he was mistakenly upgraded to a Class I prisoner. At that time, Bombay had three primary prisoner classifications—Class I,

Class II, and Class III—each with further subdivisions; A,B, and C.

Gopal's prisoner status was elevated soon after the amendment of the Prisoners Act, 1894. Rajendra Prasad, as President, gave his assent to the Prisoners (Bombay Amendment) Bill, 1953.

Singh noted that the amendment granted the inspector general of prisons the power to release prisoners 'subject to the rules . . . made by the Government of Bombay' for 'prisoners on furlough when they satisfy certain conditions'.

Prior to the amendment, this authority rested with the state government under Section 401 of the CrPC, 1898, with certain limitations. The Prisoners (Bombay Amendment) Act, 1953, empowered jail authorities to release prisoners on furlough, regardless of whether they had been convicted in other states.

Singh's letter stated:

> This position, if correct, would be unfortunate. It is necessary to state that Article 72 (1) of the Constitution conferred power on the President to grant pardon, reprieves, respites or remission of punishments or to suspend, remit or commute the sentence of any person convicted of any offence against the laws relating to a matter to which the executive power of the Union extends, whereas Article 161 of the Constitution has conferred power upon the governor to grant pardon, etc. or suspend the sentence of any person convicted of any offence against the laws relating to matters to which the executive power of the State extends . . . The Inspector General will have no power to release on furlough the prisoners convicted of offences against the laws relating to matters in the Union list or the prisoners convicted by court of other states ... Subject to advice of the Ministry of Law, we may ask the Government of Bombay to make a rule that the Inspector

> General of prisons must consult the appropriate Government before releasing a prisoner on furlough.[5]

The decision to upgrade Gopal's prisoner status was later reversed. Initially, he had been classified as a 'B' category prisoner, as indicated in his warrant from 1948. However, after a controversy in 1953, the Bombay administration downgraded him to a 'C' category prisoner.

Gopal later wrote, 'The Maharashtra government victimised me by depriving me of my rights.'[6] Although different provinces had varying rules, Gopal, as a disciplined prisoner, sought privileges such as access to newspapers, food of his choice, and the freedom to meet people in jail—requests which were denied. His supporters, however, continued to push for his release.

In 1958, Raja Mahendra Pratap Singh, former president of the provisional Government of India, voiced his concern for Gopal. In the Lok Sabha, he asked 'whether is it a fact that Shri Godse was to be released in November 1957' and 'whether it is fact that his old father and mother died of shock, hearing the news that Shri Godse was not to be released till 1965?'

R.N. De, undersecretary to the Government of India, replied in the negative on 29 July 1958, while Mangli Prasad, undersecretary in the Ministry of Home Affairs, clarified on 13 August that Gopal's father had passed away from a cerebral haemorrhage on 3 March 1958, at the age of 83, and his mother had died of senile debility on 7 May 1957, at the age of 76.[7]

Numerous applications and questions were submitted to the home ministry and raised in the house, though not all those advocating for Gopal were admirers of Hindutva. In

1964, Shakuntala Paranjpye, a London university-educated writer and social worker, who was also a nominated member of the Upper House, raised the issue of Gopal's release in Parliament. Shakuntala was the daughter of Raghunath Purushottam Paranjpye, the principal of Poona's Fergusson College. Her father had fined Savarkar for holding a bonfire of foreign goods and faced the wrath of Tilak, who wrote several articles against him in *Kesari* in 1905.

Despite the twenty-two letters sent by Gopal and the support of various leaders, no action was taken during Jawaharlal Nehru's tenure. 'The government replied that keeping in jail or releasing someone is its prerogative.'[8]

The Raja Mahendra Pratap Singh State University, which opened in Aligarh in 2024, serves as a small gesture by the BJP government towards recognizing the freedom fighter's legacy. In 1991, the Chandrashekhar government awarded Shakuntala Paranjpye the Padma Bhushan.

After Savarkar's departure, Gopal's sole wish was to elevate his brother as a martyr. He wrote books, penned articles, and delivered lectures across the country. This became his last purpose in life.

Gopal and his wife, Sindhu, served the Hindu Mahasabha in various capacities. He worked for the group in Delhi and travelled extensively throughout India. He often reiterated that newspapers like *Agrani* and *Hindu Rashtra* were published to unite Hindus, but he deliberately avoided quoting the venomous attacks they made on Gandhi.

During these travels, Gopal found followers who gradually started to worship Godse. Godse himself possessed no inherent qualities to draw people to him. It was Savarkar's influence that charmed him, a result of Godse's own personal existential crisis. Since Savarkar had trusted Godse, other followers gathered around him, united by a mission that only Savarkar fully understood.

Savarkar maintained complete control over the activities of the Mahasabha and was fully aware of everything the organization was doing across India.

The Kapur Commission referenced an abstract from an intelligence report, noting that a Mahasabha procession took place in Delhi on 25 January in connection with Arya Samaj anniversary. In his speech, Swami Dharmanand, an Arya Samaj leader, claimed that Gandhi's fast had spoilt 'the show' aimed at removing Muslims from Delhi. Clearly, they had been planning something nefarious.

On 27 January, V.G. Deshpande, Digvijaynath, and Prof. Ram Singh, leaders of the Mahasabha, criticized Gandhi at an unauthorized meeting in Delhi, branding him 'anti-national' and 'pro-Muslim'. Digvijaynath urged the gathering to 'turn over Mahatma Gandhi and other anti-Hindu elements to Pakistan'. Although they were arrested after Gandhi's murder, the police could not find any evidence against them.

In an effort to consolidate its influence in the United Province, the Mahasabha sent 500 volunteers from Maharashtra to organize a protest against the partition of India on 3 July 1947, observing Black Day across the country. On 25 August, the Mahasabha held a meeting at Tilak Smarak Mandir in Poona to prepare for a Satyagraha in Uttar Pradesh on 3 December. Present at the meeting were Ketkar, Karkare, Apte, and Godse.

In 1921, Gandhi introduced Raghav Das to the masses at a meeting in Barhaj, and he later became known as the 'Gandhi of Purvanchal' (Gandhi of eastern Uttar Pradesh). He was tasked with organizing the non-cooperation movement in the Gorakhpur region. On 4 February 1922, a large number of protesters gathered in Chauri Chaura, east Uttar Pradesh. The following day, the same crowd clashed violently with the British forces at the local police station, prompting Gandhi to withdraw the movement. The British police arrested Digvijaynath for inciting the mob. The non-cooperation fiasco was orchestrated in eastern UP, and the mahant of the Gorakhnath temple, located barely 30 km from the site of the violence, emerged as the most active Hindutva leader in the region.

The *Leader* newspaper reported on 12 February that over 400 protesters were dressed in saffron robes. It is widely known that Raghav Das gradually distanced from Gandhism under the influence of Digvijaynath.

Patel was a skilled administrator and a sensitive politician, who navigated between Gandhi's guidance and Jawaharlal's actions while trying to assert his own individuality. Yet, Patel was ideologically aligned with Savarkar's views, which may explain why the BJP portrays him as a victim of Jawaharlal, claiming he deserved more recognition than what the Congress offered him.

In 2018, Modi unveiled the 'Statue of Unity', as a tribute to Patel. However, the 182-metre statue of India's first home minister, located in Kevadiya, Gujarat, is also a symbol of the Congress's failure to uphold its heroes.

Jawaharlal had his own distinctive style of leadership, often working with a sense of political insecurity. Yet, Gandhi recognized Patel's potential, which is why he became the home minister and deputy prime minister. Eventually, the Congress allowed the BJP to appropriate Patel's legacy.

A *Hindustan Times* report from 7 January 1948 quotes Patel in Lucknow:

> The Mohemmadans don't condemn Pakistan for its activities in Kashmir ... RSS should give up the use of force and the Congressmen shouldn't deal with the RSS with ordinances because RSS was not working with a selfish motive and the Congress should win them over. The Hindu Mahasabha could merge with the Congress.

Jawaharlal wrote to Patel, saying 'gone is gone', after Gandhi's death. However, Patel had already recognized the necessity of working in harmony with the prime minister. This understanding drove Patel to align his actions and rhetoric with Jawaharlal's efforts to bring Hindutva under the Congress umbrella, leaving no stone unturned in the pursuit.

Gandhi undertook a hunger strike to pressure the government into paying the agreed amount to Pakistan and to halt the atrocities against Muslims in Delhi. After two days, India paid the amount owed to Pakistan. The total was set at Rs 75 crore, of which Rs 20 crore had already been disbursed.

Gandhi ended his hunger strike on 18 January, after receiving assurances that the government would celebrate the *urs* of Sufi Saint Qutubuddin Bakhtiyar Kaki and that the houses of Muslims seized by Hindus would be vacated.

Maniben Patel, daughter of Patel, testified before the Kapur Commission, creating the impression that the home minister was opposed to transferring funds to Pakistan. While it may be accurate that he was reluctant to give anything to Pakistan, this was not a policy decision; he was simply unwilling to oppose the all-powerful Jawaharlal.

Kher was not alive in 1964 to respond to the commission, and Morarji changed his statement frequently. Jamshed Dorab Nagarvala, deputy commissioner of the special branch of the Bombay police, claimed he informed the then home minister of Bombay that Gandhi could be kidnapped. He attempted to vaguely link this tip-off to other information suggesting that a Sikh intended to meet the then speaker of the UP Assembly, Purushottam Das Tandon, with dubious motives concerning Gandhi.

Morarji, seemingly insensitive to the inputs received before and after, testified before the commission that the 'cause of the murder was the Hindu Mahasabha'. Later, Indira appointed him as her deputy prime minister in 1967, three years after she defeated him as a candidate for prime minister. He eventually became prime minister in the Janata Party government in 1977.

American journalist Seymour M. Hersh, in his book *The Price of Power: Kissinger in the Nixon White House*, claimed that Morarji acted as an American mole (paid informer) between 1967 and 1969. Morarji dismissed this allegation as 'totally baseless' but ultimately lost a libel suit against Hersh in a Chicago court.

The commission also discovered that a doctor from Alwar sent a leaflet to Jugal Kishore, warning of a conspiracy to kill Gandhi in Alwar and Bharatpur. Kishore replied to the doctor, stating that he would present the leaflet to Gandhi and Jawaharlal, but he didn't confirm this before the commission.

A few days before Gandhi's murder, an unidentified fifty-year-old man met Purshottam Trikamdas, a barrister, on the suggestion of Jayaprakash Narayan. The man warned Trikamdas that Gandhi's life was in danger and that 'arms were being procured'.

Morarji described this unidentified man as 'dotty'. It was later revealed that he was associated with Congress Radio, an underground radio station that operated first from Bombay and then from Nasik during the Quit India Movement.

The Kapur Commission quoted N.M. Kamte, the then inspector general of police, who vaguely attributed factors behind Gandhi's assassination to the 'Hindu Rashtra Dal [being] led by Chitpavan Brahmins'.

Gopal mentioned in *Gandhi Vadh aur Main* that Govind Malaviya, the son of Pandit Malaviya, informed Goswami Sri Krishna Jivanji Dada Maharaj, a religious leader and Congressman from Hyderabad, that Apte planned to bomb the Constituent Assembly in Delhi after the formation of Pakistan.

Parchure was notorious for inciting trouble near mosques in Gwalior. His speech on 2 December 1947, at Tilak Samarak Mandir in Poona, was extensively discussed during the trial for Mahatma's assassination. Investigators quoted him as saying, 'Gandhiji failed his duty as the Father of the Nation. He has proved to be the Father of Pakistan.' The government remained in deep slumber when such statements were made.

Despite numerous intelligence inputs, the police in Delhi allowed activities at the Mahasabha office and near Birla House to continue without interruption in the second half of January. The only action they took was to arrest Pahwa after he threw a bomb near Gandhi.

Security was enhanced, but Gandhi's refusal to allow searches of every visitor became a major excuse for the government to deflect blame after his assassination.

In his confessional statement, Godse blamed Mookerjee for turning the Mahasabha into a 'handmaid' of the Congress Party, deeming it 'incapable' of countering Gandhi's anti-Hindu activities.

Savarkar distanced himself from the Mahasabha before Gandhi's assassination, reportedly due to ill health at that time. Mookerjee took over as head of the Mahasabha in 1945. Why Savarkar didn't make Godse its president is a question that admirers of Godse often ask even today.

Gadgil opposed any action against the Mahasabha, arguing that it 'would be subject to the charge of political animus'.[9] However, he later contradicted himself, stating that the ban on the RSS was lawful and based on 'available information and investigation'. A close examination of the social dynamics in Maharashtra sheds light on Gadgil's mindset.

G.D. Khosla, one of the judges who heard Godse's case in the high court, was appointed to oversee relief and rehabilitation for the migrants arriving in Delhi in 1947. He met Gandhi at Birla House four days before the assassination.

Khosla remarked sarcastically:

> Bapu was completely, utterly right, just as he had been right in insisting that we fulfil our promise to pay Pakistan 550 million rupees, even though the money would almost certainly be spent to procure arms for use against India.[10]

This clearly reflects his feelings about both Gandhi and Godse.

In the last phase of his life, Gopal states, 'The Hindus are as much disillusioned politically as they are devoted in the orbit of religion', adding, 'I proceed in the last stage of life with the hope that the next generation will take leadership.'[11]

He was seventy-six years old at that time. However, I wonder what he thought when Vajpayee, a swayamsewak, became the prime minister.

Nonetheless, Godse would likely have been unhappy to see what his guru Savarkar's disciples were doing after 2014.

Yati Narasinghanand claims that politicians win elections by praising Savarkar and Godse but switch to worshiping Gandhi once they gain power. 'Because you will get good things of life; you will be worshipped; people will make you a mahatma; your photo would appear on the currency notes; your name would be recommended for Nobel Prize', he asserts.

He made strong remarks against Modi's slogan of '*Sabka saath, sabka vikas* (Cooperation of all, growth of all)', expressing disappointment that the BJP government had not taken substantial actions to undermine Muslims in India since 2014, which fell short of his expectations.

Savarkar's assertion remains largely true—educated individuals tend not to join their ranks. The seer's anger is rooted in ignorance. Modi's slogan is a political replica of

Gandhi's spiritual principle of Sarvodaya. However, we know the limits of a political catchphrase, which can be abandoned soon after its launch.

While the Citizenship Amendment Act was enacted and the special status of Jammu and Kashmir was revoked, Yati Narasinghanand's wish to see Muslims suffer didn't come to fruition. The sadhu began to speak out against the Central government but fell silent after a Union minster visited his ashram a few times. If Godse was alive, he would likely have been frustrated not only with the government but also with his self-styled disciples. After all, Godse didn't know a middle path; he believed in annihilation.

G.V. Behere, a Marathi writer, exhibited inconsistency in his views while writing the preface of *Gandhi Vadh aur Main.* He stated, 'It was an immature effort following a faulty path ... This was the reason Gandhiji could be eliminated but Gandhism remained the same—in the increasing order.' In the very next paragraph, Behere wrote, 'Today Gandhi's ideology is breathing its last, soaked in blood at the gate of Lahore.'[12] Behere acknowledges that killing Gandhi didn't achieve its intended purpose. However, he remains silent on any proposed future course of action.

Gopal claimed in the book that Patel, Desai, Nagarwala, and many other leaders and officers were aware, after the bomb blast at Birla House, that something significant was about to occur. He suggested that, as Atma Charan also realized, the incident might have been averted if police officers from Poona and Ahmednagar had been included in the security detail. However, he also noted that preventing such an incident is challenging if someone is determined to sacrifice their life.

Godse harboured a deep hatred for Gandhi even after the assassination, declaring in his high court statement that he had 'removed one who was a curse to India, a force of evil, and who had, during thirty years of . . . harebrained policy, brought nothing but misery and unhappiness'. He added that he didn't think 'the Nehru government will understand me, but I have little doubt that history will give me justice'.[13]

Hindutva's Lust for More

Modi won the parliamentary elections for the first time due to a strong campaign by Hindutva groups, which propagated the idea that Muslims would soon take over India. They spread misinformation through various media, claiming that Feroze, a Muslim from Gujarat, was Rahul Gandhi's grandfather, implying that Rahul supported the Muslim community.

Later, Sangeet Som, a BJP MLA from Sardhana in Meerut district and an accused in the 2013 Muzaffarnagar riots, was heard saying in a purported video, 'We are going to fight a war in (2017) Assembly elections. It would be between India and Pakistan. And it would be the victory of Pakistan if any other party won. If the BJP won, it would be India's win over Pakistan.'[14]

As expected, Som denied the statement after a few days, but by then, the message had already reached the masses, who were eager to believe it.

This was not an isolated statement from a Godse admirer; similar remarks were publicized across the country. Such sentiments were prevalent even before Gandhi's assassination. The Kapur Commission mentions an article published in *Hindu Rashtra*, which stated:

> The motherland was vivisected, the vultures tore pieces of flesh [from her], the chastity of Hindu women was violated on the open streets, everything was lost and the big guns of the Congress eunuchs watching the rape committed on their own wives have begun to growl at you.

Hukum Singh, a BJP MP from Kairana in western UP, took Som's venom a step further. In June 2016, he stirred controversy in the Parliament by presenting two lists of 409 Hindus who purportedly fled Kairana 'in fear of the criminals of the minority community'. The lists were eventually discredited when it was found that some families he listed were still living in the town. However, Singh had succeeded in dividing the people of the area along communal lines. The BJP won the 2017 state elections, and Mahant Adityanath of Gorakhnath Temple became the chief minister of Uttar Pradesh.

Hukum changed the texture of Kairana forever, nearly erasing its cultural history that had been shaped by the Muslim community. One of its proud residents, Muzaffar Razmi, wrote one of the most quoted Urdu couplets in Kairana in 1974:

Yah jabr bhi dekha hai tareekh ki nazron ne.
Lamhon ne khattah kee thee, sadiyon ne saza paai.
(This compeller was also seen through the prism of time.
Centuries were punished for a momentary mistake.)

Hukum was a product of the Congress Party and became an MLA the same year Razmi penned this milestone couplet. Interestingly, Razmi and Hukum attended Kisan Inter College together in Kairana, which is a tehsil and town in Shamli district.

While Hukum pursued further education at the University of Allahabad and later entered politics, Razmi became a government employee.

Ten years after Razmi wrote his celebrated couplet, the renowned Hindi writer Kamleshwar recited it during the commentary of Indira Gandhi's funeral procession on All India Radio. Inder Kumar Gujral read the poem after taking oath as prime minister in 1997. In 2010, former prime minister Manmohan Singh released Razmi's poetry collection titled *Lamhon ki Khattah* and asked the poet what could be done for him. A Sufi by nature, Razmi simply smiled in response.

After winning elections as a Congress nominee and later as a member of the Janata Party (Secular), Hukum joined the BJP in 1996, transforming from a Gandhian to a Savarkarite and admirer of Godse. When BJP leaders inquired about his reward for fostering a supportive environment for the party, he requested a portfolio for himself and an important position for his daughter within the party.

Historically, Hindutva leaders have fought for a Hindutva government, arguing that Gandhism was eroding Hinduism. Godse believed he was halting this erosion of his religious India by assassinating Gandhi. However, what he ultimately created were figures like Soms and Hukums.

Godse and the Barrister

Godse was arguably one of the most disciplined disciples of Savarkar. There is no evidence that he ever questioned his master before or after the assassination of Gandhi. Despite not denying his crime, Godse hoped Savarkar would support him, but this expectation went unfulfilled.

When Savarkar met Godse in prison on 27 May, he sought to understand what confessions had been made to the police and in court. 'He asked each one of us what the police and the court had made us to reveal. He told us after listening to us what evidence they could collect against us on the basis of our statements. He clarified to us all the probabilities.'[15]

There was ongoing communication between Savarkar and Godse in the Red Fort jail, where Godse was encouraged to make a confessional statement. He wished for Savarkar to write part of this statement, but he didn't receive a favourable response. Savarkar learned through his lawyers that Godse would accept responsibility for the crime, and he consented, indicating that Godse should proceed.

At times, Godse attempted to draft his statement in Marathi, which someone would then translate into English. It remains unclear how much of the final statement was authentically his own. 'Savarkarji would say, "I don't need to write for you. You show me whatever you write, I will suggest changes if needed."'[16]

The emotional statement delivered by Godse at the Punjab High Court, Shimla, is now part of the public domain and has, at times, been glorified. A careful reading of it suggests that he might not have killed Gandhi if he had not been a Brahmin. He began his statement with the declaration: 'Born in a devotional Brahmin family, I instinctively came to revere Hindu religion, Hindu history and Hindu culture.'

Godse also claimed to have worked for 'the eradication of untouchability and the caste system'. However, in Indian society, fighting against the caste system requires declassing oneself. Trust cannot be built with the underprivileged classes if someone constantly reminds them of their own upper-caste identity. Even Savarkar, who spoke of reform, engaged in rituals to 'purify' the untouchables, reflecting the notion that they required purification.

In contrast, Gandhi lived as one of the marginalized, sitting and working with the 'Bhangis', shedding his caste identity to fight for their rights. Godse, however, referred to Gandhi as the 'Father of Pakistan' and ended his statement with the hope that 'honest writers of history will weigh my act and find the true value thereof someday in the future'. This was a lofty expectation, particularly after he had taken justice into his own hands through bullets.

Interestingly, P.L. Inamdar, the counsel for Parchure, later revealed that Godse's statement was penned by Jamnadas Mehta, raising questions about its originality and authenticity.

A barrister at law, Mehta was loyal to Savarkar and handled legal issues related to the Hindu Mahasabha. He was initially part of the Indian National Congress and later joined the Democratic Swaraj Party (DSP). When the Congress refused to form a government in Bombay in 1937, the DSP supported the minority government of Dhamjishah Cooper, and Mehta became the finance minister. He extended his support solely on the condition that all restrictions would be lifted from Savarkar, a demand the British government accepted.

We don't need any special skill to understand the rest, especially when we see that Jawaharlal was eager to conclude the case and that Godse's statement, reportedly written by a supporter of Savarkar, included the line: 'I don't desire any mercy to be shown to me, nor do I wish that anyone else should beg for mercy on my behalf.'

Blinded first by an intense hatred for Gandhi, Godse's perspective became so warped that he failed to distinguish between a killer and a martyr. His actions and words opened every door to his own death. Both Godse and his accomplice, Apte, reached the noose sooner than anyone might have expected.

5

Narendra Modi

The Genesis and After

Abid Surti, in the preface of his book *Gujarati ki Lokapriya Kahaniyan* (The Popular Stories of Gujarati), writes, 'The Gujarati stories of today pass through life's thorny path via a diminutive, tender line like the edge of a razor.'[1]

In 2004, during the parliamentary elections, I travelled from Bombay to Bhusawal to interview Medha Patkar, a social worker. While seeking further details, I made my way to Nandurbar, a tribal district, to meet some local RSS leaders. As there was no cybercafé in the town, someone suggested I go to the nearest station in Surat. Once there, I found a café in front of the Surat railway station and decided to settle in to file my reports.

I noticed a young man nearby, dressed in soiled white trousers and a cream shirt, talking on a payphone. While sitting in a cubicle, filing my copies, I couldn't help but overhear his conversation. He was speaking to a woman in English, using an American accent, and frequently addressing her as 'darling'. The boy expressed his desire to do business in America and tried to convince her that she wouldn't be comfortable in 'Indian weather, atmosphere and narrowness'.

I asked the café owner about the young man. He told me the man came from a poor Gujarati family and had dropped out of school. Recently, he had enrolled in an American English-speaking course. The woman on the other end of the call was a forty-five-year-old manager at a firm in Washington, and the two had fallen in love while chatting on social media. She wanted to marry him and settle in India, but he wanted to live with her in America.

'So, what do you think will happen?' I asked the café owner.

'He is a Gujarati boy. I can tell you, he is going to become a successful businessman in America within the next ten years. The lady agreed today to send him an air ticket to Washington.'

Many years later, during one of my train journeys from Vapi in Gujarat to New Delhi, I asked a fellow traveller—a senior Gujarati executive of a private firm—what he thought about Modi.

'I am closely acquainted with Modi's village,' he said. 'The villagers say he is someone who doesn't listen to anybody. Once he decides to do something, he won't change his mind. It is all about determination and a complete disregard for what others think. He thinks like a knife.' He added, 'However, it is difficult to decipher Modi, as he has led a secretive life for many years.'

Like the figure from Surat, Modi knows exactly what he wants—a quality far less common than one might expect in a leader. Added to this is his spirit, which fosters a relentless killer instinct within him.

In the late 1990s, Murli Manohar Joshi equated himself with Atal Bihari Vajpayee and Lal Krishna Advani, the two most prominent leaders of the BJS and later, the BJP. He would often stress that he was their equal, referring to them as a 'Trimurti', which literary means 'the three idols'.

Rajju Bhaiyya, the supreme swayamsewak from 1994 to 2000, was an earnest man. He had significantly shaped Joshi's career, first as his physics teacher at the university, and later as his mentor within the RSS. However, Joshi's arrogance was well known in Allahabad. Few escaped his wrath. Many professors at the University of Allahabad, along with prominent leftist Hindi writers, would secretly touch his feet in private. Their wives would discreetly meet Joshi's wife, seeking promotions and awards for their husbands.

Rajju Bhaiyya passed away in 2003, and Joshi lost the Allahabad parliamentary seat in the election the following year. He moved to Varanasi, where he secured a win in 2009. Yet, afflicted by hubris, Joshi didn't hesitate to speak against Vajpayee or Advani. At that time, leaders like Modi were of little significance to him.

I waited with curiosity for Joshi's reaction when Modi announced his decision to contest from Varanasi. Joshi initially declared that he wouldn't let Modi enter his turf. But suddenly, he retreated and left Varanasi. I don't know what transpired between them, but the message to the heartland was clear—if Modi could cage Joshi, he could do anything.

Modi had been declared the BJP's prime ministerial candidate months before the general elections and was actively campaigning in Varanasi. Some teachers from Banaras Hindu University, recognizable by the sandalwood paste on their foreheads, would gather at a particular tea stall at Assi Ghat along the Ganges. They spent two to three hours there each day before heading to their classes, passionately discussing the candidates and their electoral prospects. One of the older professors would launch into an abusive tirade whenever he heard anyone speak against Modi. 'Modi is a particle of Lord Shiva, and I will kill you if you say one more word against the god,' he shouted. 'Kashi meant religion and now Kashi also means Modi. Accept it, whether willingly or unwillingly,' he declared. The area around Vishwanath Temple and the banks of the Ganges has been known as Kashi since ancient times.

Occasionally, a young unemployed leftist would join the group, drawing extra attention from the crowd. He seemed to take pleasure in irritating the old professor.

'From mythological identity to political existentialism, from a city of learning, physical enlightenment and the burning of bodies to ideological hatred, Banaras is passing through a strange time. The city, said to rest on Lord Shiva's trident, has slipped into a different mode. Instead of debating creation and destruction, spiritual light and liberation from the cycle of birth and death, the conversations at over thousand tea stalls in this town of more than 20,000 temples have shifted to a man projected by the BJP as the next prime minister.' The youth looked directly into the professor's eyes as he rubbed khaini (tobacco), continuing, 'My dear professor! You are not ready to lift your head out of your cockroach mentality and see the truth.'

Everyone there burst into laughter. The old man took a pinch of the rubbed tobacco from the youth's palm, placed it under his lower lips and retreated with a promise to return the next morning with a response.

As the results were declared and Modi won, a hoarding went up near Babatpur airport in Varanasi, proclaiming: '*Achche din aa gaye* (The good days have come).'

The next morning, the leftist youth asked the old professor, 'Tell me, professor, whose good days have come?'

'Modi and his friends' good days have come. My good days have also started because my neta is going to become PM. And the bad days of Gandhi and Rahul Gandhi have begun,' replied the old man.

The youth raised his hands above his head, joined his palms together, and cackled, 'I salute your determination, professor, because you have got one leg in the grave and the other on the chest of Varanasi. Your god must bless himself and you for 200 years because a large section of this country has resolved to go back to the Dark Ages.'

Longing for more after gaining the unconditional support of religion-sensitive Hindus and a large section of the country's affluent community, Modi intensified the myths surrounding him. Seeking additional support, he made his temple prayers a prime-time spectacle for news channels. The idea was to present himself as a showman, creating a sense of positivity among the people. He went into a cave in Kedarnath to observe penance and later meditated in Kanyakumari, all with cameramen in tow, broadcasting him around the clock. He suggested that every moment of a politician's life is a form of electioneering.

Freed from religious restraint, he began comparing himself to Gandhi and Nehru, crafting his speeches to claim he was directly under the command of Lord Shiva.

During the 2014 elections, Modi's team coined the slogan '*Har Har* Modi', a play on the sacred chant of '*Har Har* Mahadev' that echoes in the revered Kashi Vishwanath Temple. While a small section of residents saw it as an insult to the god, the majority accepted it, as they had already embraced him as a divine particle or a godsend messenger for the development of Hindus. As expected, in 2024, Modi declared himself a godsend. This left some Hindus wondering—if one man is godsend, then who are the rest of us? According to Hinduism, being born as a human is itself a decision of the divine.

Modi claimed that he left his home in Vadnagar, where he was born into a Modh Ghanchi family, and wandered in the hills of Uttarakhand. Modh Ghanchis are traditionally oil pressers. There are also Muslim Ghanchis, who in the past produced and sold perfumes and scented oils.

When I was a child living in a village in Bihar, a 'Gundhi' (pronounced like Gandhi but with slightly less stress on the 'a') used to visit our area every summer to sell perfumes. The villagers treated them with respect, offering them a place to stay overnight. We children would run behind them, asking for perfumes. The Gundhi would gently dab the cork of a small perfume bottle on our wrists and shower us with smiles. These Gundhis came from Gujarat.

Years later, I asked people from my village whether the Gundhis still visited, and I found out that the tradition had stopped in the late 1990s when the gap between Hindus and Muslims began to widen. This means that, despite the massacre during the Partition of India, the poison of communal hatred had not yet deeply penetrated our villages until more recent decades. In those days, it was difficult to differentiate between a Hindu and a Muslim hamlet in our villages. However, today, the growing sizes of temples and mosques, as well as shamashans (cremation grounds) and kabristans (graveyards), now declare from a distance whose area you are entering.

Modi's father, Damodardas, ran a teashop near Vadnagar railway station. Modi dabbled in theatre during his school days and completed his matriculation from Bhagwatacharya Narayanacharya High School before joining Visnagar College in Vadnagar. Later, as he claimed, he wandered into the Himalayas before briefly returning home for two days, after which he left for Ahmedabad.

In Ahmedabad, he grew close to Lakshmanrao Inamdar, also known as Wakil Sahab, the RSS prant pracharak, and found something that piqued his interest.

During his 2014 campaign, he presented himself as a humble tea seller, creating an image of a young man running from street to street and office to office, selling tea in glasses. This portrayal was widely accepted as the truth.

Modi began living in the RSS office in Ahmedabad at the age of twenty-one. He attended the Sangh Shiksha Varg, an educational programme of the RSS, at several locations, including Nadiad, Bajwa (Baroda), and later Nagpur in 1978. In addition to other duties, he was assigned the task of managing correspondence. Some of his older colleagues in Ahmedabad allege that he would alter the content and destination of letters those days.

Modi grew close to Madhukar Rao Bhagwat, a senior RSS functionary, and spent a month with him at a camp in Nagpur, where he was introduced to Madhukar Rao's son, Mohan Bhagwat. Mohan became the sarsanghchalak in 2009, five years before Modi rose to become the top leader of the BJP. He supported Modi as the party's prime ministerial nominee.

While Madhukar Dattatraya Devras, sarsanghchalak, and other senior leaders were arrested in June 1975 after Indira Gandhi imposed the Emergency, Modi managed to evade capture and continued working for the RSS underground. The Sangh and its twenty-five subsidiaries were banned, but the organization continued to function, as Govindacharya, a former RSS and BJP functionary, would later compare it to a centipede—unstoppable even if some of its legs were broken. This was because there were more RSS men operating outside the official structure than within it. For instance, Morarji Desai was deeply impressed by the role played by the underground pracharaks and often spoke of how effectively they carried out their responsibilities in secrecy. Morarji's sympathy for the RSS and the Mahasabha leaders was widely open—he was more pracharak than most pracharaks.

A pracharak typically devotes their entire life to the expansion of the Sangh without having a family, though there are exceptions. Modi was one such exception, as the RSS 'outsourced' him to the BJP in 1986.

Modi grew significantly by associating with grassroots leaders, such as Karpoori Thakur, who served twice as chief minister of Bihar, though he never completed a full term. Initially a Gandhian, Thakur became a socialist before eventually aligning with the Hindutva movement. Despite initiatives like implementing 26 per cent reservation for backward castes in government jobs and prohibiting liquor in the state, he was never seen as a serious leader of the state. It surprised many when Modi's government posthumously honoured him with the Bharat Ratna. Thakur was largely erased from public memory, but Modi didn't forget him. Thakur had served as the chief minister of Bihar for six months in 1970–71, but during the Emergency, the fear of arrest forced him to go underground. During this period, he attended several secret RSS meetings, including one in Ahmedabad in November 1975. This meeting, organized by Modi, was attended by leaders such as Mohan Dharia, a confidant of Morarji, among others. Thakur, a socialist leader, saw beyond the obvious in aligning with the Sangh, a move that ultimately proved beneficial.

Arun Sinha, a researcher, states:

> Located on the western fringes of Patna, in the Braj Kishore Memorial, 235 legislators of Janata Party had met to elect their leader … Even before the voting was completed, it was clear that Karpoori Thakur was winning. With the solid support of about 50 BLD [Bharatiya Lok Dal] legislators and about 68 belonging to Jan Sangh [the first political handle of the RSS], he had a head start over the other candidates … Despite those foregone conclusion, the air was thick with speculation while the voting was in process. Karpoori Thakur was a barber by caste, wasn't he?[2]

The barber caste had historically been associated with efficiency in surveillance during the monarchy. Thakur's involvement in Modi's meeting opened the door for him into the Jan Sangh, further solidifying his political connections.

Initially, Thakur enjoyed broad support from various castes, thanks to the RSS. Over time, however, he shifted focus to become an exclusive leader of the OBCs. Eventually, even this base eroded.

Bihar has yet to recover from the damage inflicted by Karpoori Thakur when, as the education minister of the state in 1967–68, he removed English from the matriculation examinations. The people of Bihar, relieved at being freed from the burden of the 'alien language', soon realized that an entire generation had failed, as career-oriented education without English had become impossible. Enlightened parents quickly began sending their children to Delhi and other states for their studies.

The Jan Sangh and the RSS, which supported Karpoori in every decision, didn't have the same attitude towards English in their own lives.

N.C. Kelkar, who served as the editor of the *Kesari* newspaper when Tilak was in jail in 1897 and 1908, wrote about the popularity of English language and English education in Konkan: 'In 1858, Edwin Arnold wrote most of the advanced students are better scholars in English than in Marathi.'[3]

In 1979, a derogatory slogan surfaced against Thakur: 'Karpoori, *kar pura*, *chhor kursi uthao chhura* (Karpoori, finish your task, leave the chair and pick up the razor)', a reference to his barber caste.

What happened in Bihar those days is happening to India now. A certain cycle of mechanical religiosity begins with a remark and subsides once the political target is achieved. This disturbs the working class. I hear many aware parents from humble backgrounds saying that they encourage their children to go abroad to study any course.

From 907,404 Indian students studying abroad in 2022, the number rose to 1.32 million in 2023 and 1.33 million in the first half of 2024.[4]

The most recent data from the German Academic Exchange Service reveals that 49,483 international students from India were studying in Germany during the 2023–24 winter semester, reflecting a 15.1 per cent increase from the previous year.[5]

Normally, such matters don't bother politicians. What troubles them is the fear of losing voters. This generation doesn't know Thakur. With the chicanery of Jawaharlal Nehru on his lips, to suggest that he was not a typical power-hungry politician, Modi attempted to secure the OBC vote by giving the highest civilian award to the forgotten leader.

By 1992, Modi had established himself as 'an impressive Hindu political personality' in Gujarat. The following year, 'the US Government too paid heed to him, and he was invited to America as a youth leader at its centenary celebration on the World's Parliament of Religions, which Swami Vivekanand had attended in 1893 in Chicago'.[6]

The interest that Barack Obama and Donald Trump showed in Modi during their time in the White House always amazed his followers in India. Some Indians believed that their country's premier was given such importance because India had grown into a powerful nation under his leadership. However, when Joe Biden cold-shouldered him during the Quadrilateral Security Dialogue, or the QUAD summit, in Tokyo in 2022, this perception was shattered, frustrating many Indians who had dreamed that after winning over Pakistan with US support, Modi would also make America bow before him—the 'Vishwa Guru' ('Global Preacher'). Trump is back as president, but we have to wait to see how he treats India now.

Since 2014, India had been hearing that Modi was destined to attain the status of a spiritual master. His publicity team continued to hail him as 'the most popular leader of the world', even after the 2024 parliamentary election results, where he became prime minister for a third consecutive term with only 240 BJP seats—down from 303 in 2019.

While the White House assessed India's reliability under Modi on issues related to China in 2022–23, right-wing media at home attempted to salvage his image with superficial praise. One such effort took place in June 2023. Reports in India depicted a private and state dinner hosted by Jill and Joe Biden at the White House as evidence of personal bonding between Biden and Modi. On 21 June, several Indian newspapers prominently reported that the meeting would lead to 'stronger and deeper' ties between the US and India. They quoted Modi telling the *Wall Street Journal* that 'there is an unprecedented trust' between the leaders of the two nations. However, India's newspaper also carried a smaller piece in which John Kirby, coordinator for strategic communications at the National Security Council, was quoted saying that Biden would raise 'human rights issues' with Modi during the visit, hinting that the US is still concerned about human rights practices in India.

When Rishi Sunak became the UK prime minister in October 2022, right-wing media in India trumpeted his unverified ancestral ties to the RSS, suggesting that his election was a victory for India over the British, all under Modi's leadership. When a British MP raised the issue of Modi's 'direct involvement' in the Gujarat riots of 2002 and accused him of fostering a 'climate of impunity', Indian media reported that Sunak had defended his Indian counterpart and addressed him as 'honourable'. In reality, Sunak used the word to refer to the questioner and clarified that the UK government's position was 'clear and long standing'.

The UK Parliament held a thirty-minute debate on 9 February 2022, marking the 20th anniversary of the Gujarat riots. Kim Leadbeater, a Labour Party politician, stated, 'All we can say with certainty is that, at the very least, 1,000 people lost their lives and the majority of them were Muslims.'[7]

Kim spoke from personal experience, as her sister, Jo Cox, a parliamentarian, was tragically shot and stabbed in Birstall, West Yorkshire, in 2016 by Thomas Mair, a far-right extremist.

Modi's pivotal moment came on 27 February 2002, when the Sabarmati Express was set on fire near Godhra railway station in Gujarat, following disputes between passengers. Many travellers, returning from Ayodhya, were tragically charred to death. Much has been written about what transpired afterward with Modi as the chief minister of the state. His destiny to lead India towards a semi-Hindutva state began from that point.

Sonia hastened this trajectory by being overtly apolitical. She famously branded Modi a '*maut ka saudagar*' ('merchant of death'), a remark that backfired and propelled him to an elevated political standing. 'There was a relation of love and hatred between Media and Modi for many years after 2002. Modi attained his status because of the hatred of his detractors for him. He got benefitted by the manner in which the Congress and the media targeted him so badly. Modi faced them with zeal. The media couldn't ignore people's attraction towards him, his charismatic personality and the power to pull the crowd.'[8]

The making of Modi can be traced through the legacy of many leaders who were active during and after the time of Gandhi and Nehru. He is, in many ways, a continuation of the past.

Indira, a transient dictator, had her band of bureaucrats, along with leftist and centrist authors, to publicize her. She created intellectuals who shamelessly stood by her during her misdeeds, which even surpassed her larger-than-life image.

The 1977 election was a festival in our villages, despite widespread ballot rigging. My fellow villagers still recall the day they seated some kids on wooden chairs and asked them to stamp '*haldhar-chaap*' ('a farmer carrying a plough on his shoulder') on voting slips laid out on a table. This was the election symbol of the Janata Party, founded by J.P.

After their victory, J.P. and his colleagues in the consortium of political parties, including the BJS of the RSS, gathered at Rajghat and pledged to carry forward Gandhi's work. However, the chaos caused by many ambitious leaders in the group led to the election of Morarji Desai as the leader of the Janata Parliamentary Party. He went on to become the prime minister.

Modi, by most accounts, is a blend of all those he either loved or hated. On 31 March 2014, in Itanagar, he declared, 'The country needs a servant, not a ruler. I am a servant, not a ruler.'

This echoed Jawaharlal Nehru's words from 1949, when he said, 'Today I address you for the first time officially as the First Servant of the Indian people, pledged to their service and their betterment.'[9]

Compared to the 1977 election, the 2014 campaign was on a much grander scale. In Banaras, around 200 giant mobile screens were displayed. I spent several days covering Modi's campaign, immersing myself in the atmosphere. One evening, I went with some local friends to an upmarket restaurant for dinner. Our lively conversation made it clear we were journalists. Later, the clerk at the counter informed me that someone had paid my bill, leaving behind a saffron-coloured visiting card. It was an experience that went beyond that of just a journalist.

Apparitions: The Guides

The history of modern India and its prominent leaders remains incomplete without examining the real ghosts and resurrections of the period. Many within the RSS believed that Vajpayee was their third prime minister, following Morarji Desai as the first and P.V. Narasimha Rao as the second. For them, the elections of Morarji and Rao shattered the myth that one couldn't hold the top post in the country without the consistent support of the Nehru–Gandhi family. This belief was further bolstered by the fact that both prime ministers aligned with Hindutva. Morarji secured his position after giving it his best effort.

Three days after Nehru's death, a front-page headline in *Hindustan Standard* declared: 'After Nehru, Desai and Shastri in Close Race'. Morarji, believing himself to be Nehru's natural successor, faced a setback when Shastri was elected prime minister. Despite this failure, the West was confident that this Anavil Brahmin from the Surat region (Valsad) would eventually ascend to the top post.

Two months after Indira Gandhi imposed the Emergency, the International Institute of Strategic Studies in London organized a seminar to discuss the situation in India. During the event, Peter Lyon from the Institute for Commonwealth Studies, University of London, remarked:

> It was an act of political suicide by Mrs Gandhi and that it would be only a matter of years, if not months, before like the indestructible Lucifer, Morarji Desai would rise from what many thought was his political grave.[10]

Lyon's statement made it clear that the West had a sharper focus on Morarji than on any other Indian leader.

Two months before the Emergency, Morarji began a fast at his New Delhi residence to pressure the Centre into holding elections in Gujarat. Unlike Gandhi, he wore a vermillion mark on his forehead, though he still tried to present himself as a Mahatma-like figure. He listened to prayers from the Gita, Quran, and Bible, and spun yarn on a wheel. History shows that Morarji's actions sparked hope within the RSS, becoming a topic of discussion at its office in Ahmedabad. Lakshmanrao Inamdar, a pracharak, saw this event as a remarkable turning point in Indian politics. It signalled that the political landscape of India was shifting away from Nehru–New Gandhi family. Moreover, it marked a movement away from Uttar Pradesh, though this shift was perhaps an illusion—because when Modi eventually became prime minister, he chose to represent Varanasi.

We have seen in Chapter 3 how the Congress Party settled the Jallianwala Bagh scam after a truce between Nehru and Jayakar.

The second major financial controversy of the post-Independence era, following the tax evasion scandals involving mill owners and the ousting of the then finance minister, Chetty, from Nehru's cabinet in 1948, was attributed to Morarji Desai. Madhu Limaye, a socialist leader, accused Morarji's son, Kantibhai, of using his father's influence as deputy prime minister and finance minister for undue gains in his insurance business. At the time, Kantibhai served as his father's private secretary. Limaye further alleged that Kantibhai had leaked a budget proposal and claimed that the deputy prime minister's son was receiving Rs 2,500 per month from a former business associate.

Another allegation involved Viswanath Toupe, the personal secretary to the finance minister from 1958 to 1963, who reportedly wrote to the Ministry of Industry requesting favours for Kantibhai's firm.

Morarji believed that Indira Gandhi used the controversy to undermine him. She allegedly presented him with an incomplete photocopy of a letter from Toupe, suggesting there was some merit to the allegations.

Although the case was transferred to the Central Bureau of Investigation, the agency never actively pursued it.

Peter Lyon's forecast carried more weight than Indira's alleged attempt to weaken Morarji. The animosity towards Indira ran so deep that during the elections following the Emergency, her rivals popularized the slogan, '*Dekho* Indira *ka ye khel, kha gai rashan, pi gai tel*' ('See the game of Indira; she ate all the food and drank all the oil').

While Indira lost the elections, she returned to power in 1980, as the perception that non-Nehru–Gandhi leaders couldn't effectively run the government had not entirely disappeared.

The first question Khushwant Singh asked Indira during an interview three months before the mid-term elections was about the two years of Janata government. He inquired, 'I heard people from all walks of life, all over the country, say, "*Inko raj karna nahin ata* [They don't know to rule]."'[11]

Singh noted, 'This was precisely her own view of the [Janata] government.' He quoted Indira's response, 'There was no rule of government in the sense I understand these works. Whatever decision they took were taken from the very narrow point of view of what would benefit them immediately.'

She claimed that caste wars had erupted, her previous efforts to integrate the border states into the national mainstream had been neutralized, and the Janata regime's decision to auction gold 'served no purpose except [to increase] the price of gold'. The Reserve Bank of India had auctioned about 12,000 kg of gold.

The experience to date has been that people form a democratic government, which takes unilateral decisions and suppresses those who question it. However, Indira opened the doors to autocracy in India. Her lust for absolute power led her to promote extremism in Punjab, resulting in massacres that ultimately culminated in her assassination by her Sikh security guards.

Her eldest son, Rajiv, surrounded himself with a group of businessmen, technocrats, politicians, and friends who helped shape his public image as a good human being. In December 1987, when Rajiv jumped into the ocean in Kavaratti, Lakshadweep, to save a beached whale, cameramen were conveniently on hand to capture the moment.

But Rajiv couldn't control his ambition to be recognized as an international statesman. It drove him to interfere in Sri Lanka's internal affairs by sending Peace Keeping Force and secretly meeting the Liberation Tigers of Tamil Eelam (LTTE) chief, Velupillai Prabhakaran, in New Delhi. However, Rajiv was too naïve to realize that his advisors were leading him into a dangerous situation.

While we criticize Modi for being dictatorial and taming the press and media, it was Indira who exercised absolute control over them during the Emergency. The situation didn't change when the Janata government took power. Khushwant Singh explains:

> The record of the Janata [government] in the matter of freedom of expression had been deliberately underplayed. A large number of editors and journalists had been quietly eased out of their jobs, many had been blacklisted by the official media, and ministers of several states, probably Punjab and Haryana, had made public speeches threatening to cut off the hands of recalcitrant journalists.[12]

Rajiv, too, sought to curb the media by introducing the Anti-Defamation Bill, driven by his desire to prevent the Bofors scandal from gaining public attention.

Rajiv's calculations regarding the Babri issue failed to deliver the expected results in 1989, as people believed he and his cronies had received kickbacks in the supply of 155 mm field howitzer from Sweden's Bofors AB.

Despite the Congress coming to power at different intervals, the frustration that had begun to build against the party eventually compressed and solidified.

In 1984, when Amitabh Bachchan contested the Lok Sabha election in Allahabad at the request of his friend Rajiv, girls would lay their dupattas on the road where he was expected to pass. However, by 1989, those same girls tore down the canopy where Amitabh was scheduled to campaign for a Congress candidate. They stood waiting, shoes in hand, ready to greet the superstar. Fortunately for him, he didn't show up. A true friend, Amitabh later went on to become a publicist for Modi.

Rahul may criticize Modi's disinterest in building up higher education in India, but he would likely resent being reminded that his father, Rajiv, was prime minister when it often took five years to complete an undergraduate degree at many universities in Uttar Pradesh and Bihar, an additional three to four years for a post-graduate degree, and five to six years to become a lawyer or earn a PhD. Anarchy and the absence of academic sessions were the norm during that period.

Currently, Rahul seems caught between secularism and Hinduism, with the two poles pulling him in opposite directions. His social media team and aides have tried to mould him into a cohesive figure, but the attempt appears to have failed. The result of the 2024 parliamentary elections reflected not an embrace of Rahul, but rather a rejection of Modi.

One possible reason for Rahul's lack of understanding might be that, unlike his great-grandfather, grandmother, and father, he struggles to bring genuine people close to him. Instead, he is surrounded by half-baked minds, some centrists, and others who are pseudo-leftists.

In March 2022, I asked a former ultra-leftist why he had joined Rahul's team, and he replied, 'I am here to strengthen the left.' This man had used leftist ideologies for over two decades to secure jobs of his choosing, and now he was in the Congress, influencing what Rahul would say and do. I was curious to know how he managed to impress Rahul. He explained it to me:

> Rahul often sits with us and discusses world history. Mostly it happens that the discussion turns to Bolshevik Revolution or Boston Tea Party or international affairs. We have studied all this very well and talk to him in length. There are also National Students Union of India [the Congress' students wing] members in the meeting. They remain silent. Once Rahul asked one of them what was his point of view and his replied, 'Sir, I am from the NSUI.'

Rahul's ancestral etiquette prevents him from indulging in self-praise, and he lacks people who can guide him properly. Modi, on the other hand, has learned from nearly every political figure of his era. He is the product of a unique cocktail of Gandhi, Nehru, Savarkar, Indira, Morarji, and many other contrasting personalities.

Despite facing criticism for following the Savarkarian ideology that led to the assassination of Mahatma Gandhi,

Modi's speeches are often incomplete without a fond mention of Gandhi. He frequently claims to follow Gandhi's principles. While he targets Jawaharlal Nehru, he simultaneously imitates him in many ways. The accumulation of power that Modi believes in had echoes of Indira Gandhi's approach to governance.

At the same time, his training in the RSS has instilled in him a natural disdain for leftists and centrists.

During an investor summit in Lucknow on 29 July 2018, Modi portrayed himself as a modern-day Mahatma, proudly stating that he was not afraid to stand alongside industrialists. He said:

> I am not one who is shy of standing with industrialists. You cannot have a blot on you simply by standing with anyone if your intentions are good and clear. Gandhiji's intentions were so pure that he never hesitated in staying with Birla family.

Gandhi, too, addressed his association with wealthy people in an article in *Harijan Sewak* on 31 March 1946. 'I take benefit of motors and other facilities from wealthy people. But I am not in their control. I can keep them at bay immediately if it is needed in the interest of common people,' he wrote.

Self-Appraisal

Although Modi's supporters often praise him before admiring themselves, he compliments himself even more earnestly. This approach worked well for a decade, as he spoke with élan and compared himself to past leaders.

In 2019, Modi laid the foundation stone for the Kashi Vishwanath Corridor, a Central government project to renovate the shrine in Varanasi, and said:

> The almighty had perhaps preordained me to do this work after 250 years [since Ahilyabai Holkar, the 18th-century queen of the Maratha Malwa kingdom]. A voice came from within me when I was here in 2014 to contest the election and I didn't come here on my own; I was brought here [by the almighty]. Today I think that I was summoned [by God] for such a work.

It was unique in the sense that no other world leader has spoken so longingly about themselves. However, repetition can lead to fatigue.

'Modi fatigue' began to surface when, during the 2024 election campaign, he kept giving the people 'Modi's guarantee'. His overdose of cultural schism, religious nationalism, and self-canonization began to wear thin.

But this is not something that will stop him in this lifetime. He is among those who enjoy the luxury of saying anything and everything. Take, for instance, his claim in Dhaka during the fiftieth anniversary of Bangladesh's independence, where he said he 'must have been twenty to twenty-two years old' when he and his colleagues 'did Satyagraha for the freedom of Bangladesh'.

Unlike his predecessors, Modi's double-edged strategy is to elevate himself as a transcendental figure while ruthlessly dismantling his rivals. It was not a random political move when, during the 2014 Lok Sabha elections, the BJP crafted the narrative that supporting Modi was synonymous with standing by the country. Even a future loss of parliamentary seats or dethronement is unlikely to deter such a protagonist from his self-admiration.

While Ambedkar defended Savarkar without pretence, the Dalit leader's so-called follower, Mayawati, is a secret admirer of Modi. Secret, because she believed that her mild criticism of him would keep her politically relevant, and perhaps he might reward her with something extraordinary.

The four-time UP chief minister also attempted an extreme form of self-promotion, but she lacked the support of the elite. Her self-admiration was mostly confined to the volumes of her autobiography, which are unavailable anywhere except in her own library.

In the fourth volume of her book, *Mera Sangharshmai Jeevan ewam Bahujan Movement ka Safarnama* (*A Travelogue of My Struggle-Ridden Life and BSP Movement*), she writes that the changes she sought for India's downtrodden and oppressed were extraordinary and that her struggle should be placed above the lives and legacies of Queen Victoria and Babar.

She released the book in Lucknow on her fifty-third birthday but made sure it didn't reach the hands of reporters or party workers. Her security guards quickly took charge of it. I managed to glimpse the pages during its transfer from the hall, getting to hold the book for less than twenty minutes.

In the preface, Mayawati referenced *Babarnama: Journal of Emperor Babar* and the diary of Queen Victoria. She wrote in Hindi:

> When I first thought of compiling my life and my struggle, I was not aware of *Babarnama* or the life of Queen Victoria ... Babar and Queen Victoria were rulers right from the beginning ... But my journey was a story of endless struggles. It was an extraordinary event that I mustered courage to collect the details. I was born in a Scheduled Caste, which has

> been an oppressed class for several thousand years. They didn't have the freedom to study because of religious discrepancies.

The influence of Victoria and Babar is evident in Mayawati's decisions regarding her statues and monuments. I was told that every time she commissioned a life-size statue of herself, she asked the sculptor to match its grandeur to that of Victoria's statues.

During her fourth term as the chief minister, between 2007 and 2012, Mayawati instructed officers to ensure the extensive use of pink sandstone in the memorials and monuments dedicated to Ambedkar, Rama Bai, and her own mentor Kanshi Ram, where she also had statues of herself installed. Today, many treat her statue as an idol. Although she rejects Sanatan culture and Hinduism, her statue is worshiped by many. It wouldn't be surprising if, in a few decades, she is eventually incorporated into Hinduism as some form of incarnation, becoming a goddess for a section of people.

'Don't go to temples to offer to the gods and goddesses. Your goddess is here before you,' Maya once told her party leaders when she was serving her fourth term as chief minister, brimming with confidence.

Explaining her motivation to write the book, Maya remarked:

> This effort was necessary because every day, every moment of my life is a page of history. It was my responsibility to collect the details in their true form. People wouldn't forgive me if I left these scattered pages of contemporary history.

Her first book, *Mera Sangharshmai Jeevan ewam Bahujan Movement ka Safarnama,* was released in 2006 to mark her fiftieth birthday. Since then, she has released a new volume annually.

While Maya opposed Modi verbally, her actions and writings bolstered the type of politics Modi championed. Clearly, she has evolved from Ambedkar, who was a friend of Savarkar and never an admirer of Gandhi. However, efforts are now being made to portray Gandhi and Ambedkar as having complemented each other.

Indira, too, enjoyed being called 'Mother India' and embraced the slogan coined by Dev Kant Barooah: 'India is Indira; Indira is India'. In return, Indira rewarded him with the position of Congress president.

Modi's Precision

Modi's strength lay in his clarity of thoughts and words. He didn't waste time on those whose education distanced them from him. He had conducted extensive research to identify where to focus for political gain. Instead of following the complex ideas of historical figures, he distilled what was simple and easily understood by the masses—a rare quality.

Readers of Gandhi, on the other hand, may occasionally find themselves confused. This can happen when someone is well-intentioned and flexible enough to adapt to different situations. No such ambiguity existed with Modi.

When the people of Kheda district in Gujarat asked Gandhi during the First World War why a 'votary of nonviolence' was urging Indians to take up arms for a government that had done nothing good for the country, he responded:

> Partnership in the Empire is our definite goal . . . We should suffer to the utmost of our ability and even lay down our lives

> to defend the Empire. If the Empire perishes, with it perishes our cherished aspirations.[13]

He was willing to send Indians to war but didn't tolerate any cruelty toward cows, which he considered 'the most important object of Hinduism'.[14] Gandhi even refused to drink milk on a doctor's advice because of 'the cruel manner of milking cows and buffaloes had impelled [him] to abjure milk for ever'. However, he eventually agreed to drink goat milk at Kasturba's suggestion.

Louis Fischer noted:

> Gandhi wanted to live. He was not immune, he confessed, to that 'subtlest of temptations, the desire to serve'. Had he been up to par physically, his will might have been strong enough to reject Kasturba's suggestion. But the very fact that he could not resist the suggestion showed how badly he needed the milk.[15]

For Gandhi, the Gita was both a 'mother' and 'a dictionary of daily reference'.[16] 'But his commitment to non-violence [ahimsa] made him reject absolutely their invocation of the Gita to justify the use of violence in a righteous cause, while his belief in a unified India denied their claim that the Gita was an exclusive "Hindu Bible".'[17] Mahatma Gandhi believed that the Gita could be read by a person of any faith because it was fundamentally about ethics.

For the common Hindu, and for those aligned with Hindutva, cow milk is seen as 'mother cow's milk' and is not prohibited. In contrast, Golwalkar followed the Hindu Mahasabha's stance on militarization but didn't support a blanket ban on cow slaughter. Once, some people approached the RSS leader for his signature to prevent killing of 'useless cattle' only because some Muslims wanted the practice to continue. Reflecting on this, Golwalkar remarked:

> What does this show? We are to protect the cow not because the cow has been for ages an emblem of Hindu devotion but because the Muslims kill it! This Hinduism is born out of reaction, a kind of 'negative Hinduism'.[18]

Golwalkar's liberal stance didn't win Gandhi's confidence when they met in 1947. Gandhi accused RSS men of killing Muslims, which the then sarsanghchalak denied. Later, Nehru wrote to his home minister, stating that, according to Gandhi, Golwalkar's words couldn't be trusted, even if he swore that his group was never involved in violence.

Scholars were surprised by Indira's decision to include Golwalkar in a committee formed to determine whether the country needed a law against cow slaughter. Headed by Justice A.K. Sarkar, the committee existed for twelve years before being disbanded by Morarji during his tenure as prime minister. Like the other members, Golwalkar was also in no hurry to make a decision.

The Gita and the cow have now become political tools for Modi. He gifted *Bhagavad Gita According to Gandhi*, the simplest version of the Gita, to Barack Obama during his visit to the White House after becoming prime minister. He also presented the same book to Emperor Akihito of Japan and other world leaders.

Under Modi's leadership, an initiative was launched in 2017 to develop several provinces as 'cow welfare states' with Rs 613 crore approved for Uttar Pradesh alone to fulfil this goal. Between 2018 and 2023, police in Uttar Pradesh shot and injured over a hundred criminals involved in cow smuggling or slaughter. Punishment came swiftly, even before the judicial process began, sending an unmistakable message to the public. Modi wanted to convey that he was a staunch supporter of cows, and his action in this regard was both clear and bold.

When Modi needs to quote someone, he opts for simple references. While paying tribute to Golwalkar, he echoed Indira's words from the Parliament in 1973: 'He was a scholar, a powerful man and a believer. He holds an important place in the national life because of his influential personality and confidence in his ideas.' Modi also referenced the *Deccan Chronicle*, comparing Golwalkar to Vivekanand.[19]

In his book, *Jyotipunj*, Modi compared Hedgewar with Vivekanand, stating that both, in the final phases of their lives, focussed on uplifting the lives of the nation's people.

Modi's words serve a clear purpose. He understands that comparison is an effective way to elevate someone. As chief minister of Gujarat, he frequently spoke about the similarities between Hedgewar and Vivekanand. He quoted Vivekanand, asking, 'What kind of hitch is there in introducing yourself as a Hindu?' and Hedgewar's assertion, 'I say this is a Hindu nation.'[20]

One of Modi's biographers noted a resemblance between him and Vivekanand, recalling that the former chief minister of Gujarat was invited to America to attend the centenary of the World Parliament of Religions; '[the] same time one hundred years ago in 1893, Swami Vivekanand had brought India to the fore as the world leader'.[21]

Many writers on Modi have claimed that he went to Belur Math, the headquarters of the Ramakrishna Mission in Howrah, after leaving home as a youth. However, he was sent back with the suggestion to follow the teachings of Vivekanand and devote himself to social work.

His meditation at the Vivekanand Rock Memorial in Kanyakumari on 31 March and 1 June 2024 reaffirmed his Savarkarian aspirations. His supporters and the media drew comparison between Vivekanand and Modi.

Modi's image-building has been a continuous process. Since he took over as prime minister, over half a dozen books about him have been published. These are not intellectual discourses; they are mere appreciations. While the intellectual class might dismiss those books as cheap or pulp literature, Modi's supporters read them carefully.

In the past, Modi worked smartly to position himself as a greater symbol of Hindutva than anyone else. He justified the 2002 Gujarat riots in simple terms, explaining that Ahmedabad was engulfed in Hindu–Muslim violence both before and after Independence, leading Hindus to feel they had no one to stand up for them. 'A large number of Hindus were killed in these riots … As if the Hindu society had accepted this situation … The Muslim society considered it a weakness of the Hindus.'[22]

Such views prevented genuine intellectuals from finding common ground with Modi, which is why his supporters labelled them 'urban Naxalites' out of sheer frustration.

But there are genuine intellectuals throughout every phase of India's history who have continued to admire

Nehru. Even today, no serious seminar on modern India in Indian universities is complete without acknowledging his contributions.

Celebrated scientist D.D. Kosambi expressed great trust in Nehru, recognizing his 'distinguished record in the struggle for India's freedom, and by his active share in the struggle against war', declaring himself a 'humble admirer of the author' of *The Discovery of India*.[23]

Modi would always fall short of such admiration. When an author within his camp wrote a book about him, he compared the 2014 election to the '*dharmyuddha*' (war for religion) described in the epic Mahabharata, devoting numerous pages to disparaging the leaders of the rival camp. Such parallels are drawn when there is nothing substantial to say about someone.

A Message from Pakistan

In his 2014 election campaign, Modi promised a New India with better days ahead for the people. After becoming prime minister, he introduced the slogan '*Ek* Bharat, *Shreshtha* Bharat' (One India, Best India).

The RSS also employs the slogan of One India, signifying an undivided India that includes Pakistan and Bangladesh. Even today, one faction of the RSS presents a map that portrays not only Bangladesh and Pakistan but also Myanmar (Burma) and Nepal as a single administrative entity.

The fantasy surrounding Pakistan has permeated India's tea-stall conversations. This sentiment became especially pronounced during the Kargil conflict.

I recall hearing such trivial remarks in Allahabad during the latter years of the Rajiv Gandhi government (1984–89), which coincided with Benazir Bhutto's first term in Pakistan

(1988–90). The atmosphere in the city was such that university students made light of even the most challenging situations. Amidst frequent tensions along the Line of Control, students would gather at tea stalls on University Road, jokingly claiming, 'Rajiv and Benazir are having an affair, and that's why India and Pakistan will soon be one again.'

Tragically, both Rajiv and Benazir were assassinated in 1991 and 2007, respectively. It is not that the RSS or the BJP are unaware that a pre-1947 demographic India is unattainable; rather, they believe India should dominate the lives of its neighbouring countries.

When we tune into news channels, we often witness Pakistan's political and economic collapse. However, these discussions seldom address the pressing issues within India—extreme poverty in many regions, farmer suicides, the COVID-19-induced lockdown that devastated lives, religious hatred, and the erosion of democracy.

Officially, India has fought three wars against Pakistan. In the first war in 1947, Pakistan lost Jammu and Kashmir but gained control of Gilgit, Baltistan, and Azad Kashmir, which India refers to as Pakistan-Occupied Kashmir. During the second war in 1965, sparked by Pakistan's Operation Gibraltar, India successfully forced the adversaries to retreat. The third war in 1971 led to India assisting East Pakistan in gaining independence from West Pakistan, resulting in the birth of Bangladesh.

However, Modi's first national election campaign created the perception that India lost to Pakistan under the Congress and that he would reclaim those territories. This tale appeals to Hindutva pride, which thrives on the freefall of information. A mere virtual sentiment that India is at war with Pakistan excites many, though his exhilaration tends to dissipate when the rival is China.

Advani, one of the founding members of the BJP, was unable to achieve the same level of influence, power, or recognition that Modi eventually did; he missed the stature that Modi ultimately attained. In 2013, while Advani was preparing to be projected as the prime ministerial candidate, Modi's supporters allegedly began writing letters to the RSS and other senior BJP leaders. As this letter-writing campaign continued for months, the illusion of Modi's popularity grew disproportionately. He came to be seen as the embodiment of Hindutva and progress.

The names of Pakistan and Jinnah inadvertently cleared the path for Modi, removing Advani from his route to 7, Race Course Road, the prime minister's residence, which was later renamed 7, Lok Kalyan Marg.

Karachi is Advani's birthplace, where he initially worked for the RSS. Rumours circulated that he was implicated in a plot to assassinate Jinnah shortly after the partition of India. According to reports, Karachi police registered a case against eighteen Hindus, including Advani, for conspiring to eliminate Jinnah. Six were convicted and extradited to India in 1948, while the others absconded.

While this allegation could hold some truth, there is also a possibility it was a rumour spread by Advani's supporters to showcase his communal stance. Past reports indicated that the Mahasabha considered assassinating Jinnah, and such rumours served as a kind of medal decorating the chest of Advani. However, he distanced himself from this darker narrative at Jinnah's mausoleum.

During a week-long tour of Pakistan in 2005, he wrote in the mausoleum's guest register:

> 'There are many people who leave an inerasable stamp on history. But there are very few who actually create history. Quaid-e-Azam Mohammed Ali Jinnah was one such rare individual. In his early years, Sarojini Naidu, a leading luminary of India's freedom struggle, described Mr Jinnah as an 'ambassador of Hindu-Muslim unity'.

The RSS and the BJP didn't anticipate such unbigoted and thoughtful remarks from their leader. As a result, they were prepared to sideline Advani if a viable alternative emerged. Mohan Bhagwat threw his support behind his father's disciple. Even when the Government of India awarded him the Bharat Ratna in 2024, it was clear that he was not embraced wholeheartedly. The prime-time news headline read: 'Modi gave the award to Advani'.

Gandhian-UnGandhian

While interviewing a senior RSS leader in Allahabad in 1999, our conversation somehow turned to Gandhi's assassination. Suddenly, he became furious and shouted, 'Why did they arrest my father for Gandhi's murder?'

I disliked his outburst and left without completing the assignment. The next morning, I heard a knock on my door and opened it to find him standing there, holding two food packets. 'I thought we could have breakfast together, so I brought curd and jalebi,' he said.

A year later, I visited his office in Delhi and accidentally entered his room. A life-size picture of Gandhi hung on the wall. I didn't ask him about it, but I realized then that if the

New Gandhis didn't change their ways, Mahatma would soon become one of the heroes of the RSS–BJP.

Despite Hindutva's anti-Gandhian actions, portraits of Gandhi and Savarkar hang near each other in the old Parliament. We know that this symbolic gesture of bringing two leaders with such contradictory temperament close—if only metaphorically—began during the Vajpayee government. Gandhi was complete in himself, while Savarkar had to be placed near him to be elevated.

A sense of futility loomed large over Modi without Gandhi. Much of his writing and speeches were incomplete without invoking the Father of the Nation. He often cited the well-known saying about 'Gandhiji': 'My life is my message.'[24]

This preoccupation runs so deep that Gandhi often surfaces effortlessly in Modi's words. Once, recalling Anantrao Kale, a senior RSS functionary, he mentioned that when Kale was an eleven-year-old living in Deogarh, Sindhudurg district (which was carved out of Ratnagiri in Konkan), 'he put his gold bracelet in the hand of Mahatmaji'.[25]

Modi noted that the 'symbolic rose and chapati' in the freedom struggle of 1857, the 'Bhakti Yuga of 19th century', 'Ganeshotsav of Lokmanya Tilak', or 'the message of Ramrajya from Gandhiji' were all forms of 'India's internal energy'.[26]

He even equated the Ramraj (Ram Rajya) of Gandhi and Savarkar, a clever way to draw a comparison between the two. However, one's Ram Rajya embraced all humans, while the other excluded those who didn't accept Hindustan as both their fatherland or motherland and sacred land.[27]

In most of his speeches, Modi included at least a sentence or two about Gandhi's qualities. In one such speech in Varanasi, he remarked:

> All of you know that Rashtrapita (Father of the Nation), Mahatma Gandhi had worked a lot to eliminate leprosy. As he was living in Sabarmati Ashram, he received an invitation to inaugurate a leprosy hospital in Ahmedabad. Gandhiji told them that he wouldn't come to inaugurate it. He said he would be happy when called to put a lock on that leprosy hospital.

Remember, this appreciation comes from a follower of Savarkar. For some, it may appear as a cryptic form of playing seesaw, but those who engage in it know that confusing the public is the easiest task at their disposal.

Modi remains silent when a leader of his party demonizes Gandhi or calls for a temple to be built for Godse. He doesn't respond when a leader from his camp or a sadhu advocates for the genocide of Muslims. His followers have even called for the conversion of the Taj Mahal, the 17th-century Mughal mausoleum, into a Shiva temple, and he listens in silence.

Even if the Hindutva group manages to take Gandhi away from the Congress, they would only exploit him for political gain. In March 2024, Modi stated in Ahmedabad that while his government had developed Gandhi's Sabarmati Ashram, previous Congress-led governments had neglected it. Yet, in May 2024, he stunned the nation with his narrow political agenda, claiming that no one knew Gandhi before Richard Attenborough's 1982 biopic.

Many years ago, Manas Mukul Das, the former head of the English department at the University of Allahabad, enlightened me that while what the Mughals did to the Hindus might be painful for those fixated on the past, we also need to consider Dara Shikoh, the eldest son of Shah Jahan. Manas Da pointed out that 'Shikoh translated fifty-one Upanishads into Persian' and its 'Latin translation first introduced the Upanishads to Goethe, Schiller, Schopenhauer, and Southey'.

Manas Da wrote letters to Modi and other key BJP politicians, urging them to talk about Dara Shikoh if they were interested in Shah Jahan, the builder of the Taj Mahal. Shah Jahan's other son, Aurangzeb, allegedly destroyed temples to build mosques. Manas Da's letters went unanswered. He had quoted Dara Shikoh as saying, 'Their [the Hindus'] Vedanta is like our Tasawwuf.' He gave me a copy of the letter, hoping that I would forward it to the intended recipients. However, I didn't pass it on, as I believed such communications are one-way.

Whenever furious with Modi, some people who disliked him referred to him as Hitler, the dictator who was 'represented as a sort of European Gandhi: a vegetarian, simple, ascetic who slaved night and day for the benefit of the country'.[28]

Manas Da's ideology is not beholden to anyone. He held up a mirror to the Congress as well and remarked, 'Mahatma Gandhi wanted the Congress to dissolve itself and go to the villages to mingle with the people and help create an entirely different society. A deep social transformation doesn't emerge from the barrel of guns, terrorists or states.'

I often attempted to engage Manas Da in discussions about Modi's politics, but each time he gently steered the conversation back to Gandhi, seeking solutions to every problem through the lens of Mahatma.

What Is in a Name

We know that Tees January Marg was once Albuquerque Road, Mumbai was Bombay, Chennai was Madras, Kolkata was Calcutta, Deen Dayal Upadhaya Nagar was Mughalsarai, and Prayagraj was Allahabad. We know that Modi's hometown, Vadnagar, was known by several names: Skandpur, Kanakpur, Chamatkarpur, Arksthali, Anantpur, and Vridhnagar. Whenever we discussed the 'Amrit Udyan' in the president's palace in New Delhi, we remembered that it was originally the 'Mughal Garden'.

You can rename these places, but you cannot erase the memory of their original essence. The oral history of something is always stronger than the written word; this is how India's ancient history has survived.

My professor of modern poetry at the University of Allahabad, Arvind Krishna Mehrotra, was born in Lahore in 1947. At just four weeks old, he came to India with his maternal grandfather, Amolak Ram Mehta, his parents D.K. Mehrotra and Promila Mehrotra, and others. Amolak Ram was a senior health department officer in undivided India and built a house in Lahore in 1926.

A Shia family that migrated from Panipat in Haryana lived in that house, along with many other families. In 2009, Arvind Krishna discovered that the lane was still called Temple Road, the street remained Mehta Gullie, and the plaque honouring Amolak Ram Mehta was still intact. Begum Badar Hassan and her two daughters, who lived there, had no desire to replace it with another marble tablet. Fatima, Badar's granddaughter-in-law, remarked that this was 'because they were not in the business of erasing history, they were people who just moved on with time'.

This is beyond the understanding of a majoritarian mind. Interestingly, even Savarkar was not in favour of changing names. While declaring that Hinduism is only a fraction of Hindutva, Savarkar referenced *Romeo and Juliet*, 'What's in a name? That which we call a rose. By any other name would smell as sweet …'

He then emphasized the significance of a name, saying, 'Ah! Call Ayodhya, Honolulu, or nickname her immortal prince [Lord Rama] a Pooh Bah, or ask the Americans to change Washington into Chengizkhan or presume a Mohammedan to call himself a Jew, and you would soon find that "open sesame" was not the only word of its type.'[29]

Let alone the fact that *Essentials of Hindutva* was first published under the pen name 'A Maratha' rather than his real name. Savarkar was also known by other pseudonyms, such as Tatya, Chhadam, and Chitragupta. Modi himself used the pseudonym Prakash during the Emergency and even lived disguised as a Sikh to avoid being captured. These changes were situational.

Some people claim that Gandhi's name will also be erased from the country in the future. This assertion has been categorically denied by the BJP government. However, it is saffron party leaders who have spread this rumour. A BJP minister from Haryana stated in 2017 that while they had already replaced Gandhi's picture with Modi's on the calendars and diaries of the Khadi and Village Industries Commission, Mahatma's photos would be gradually removed from currency notes. Although he later retracted his statement and a Union minister in Modi's government denied any such plans, the purpose of the remark was served. They initiated a debate on the subject, which is how public opinion is shaped slowly and steadily before any plan is implemented. Replacing a

'Himalayan figure' like Gandhi with someone else would undoubtedly be a violent idea, promoting further violence and diminishing Gandhi's legacy.

Gandhi had once expressed his desire to live for 125 years, but Godse, in his own way, pledged to see how Bapu could live that long. Eventually, Gandhi was unable to prevent the escalating Hindu–Muslim conflict and, as a result, he stated that he no longer wished to live for 125 years. Later, he remarked, 'I wouldn't like to stay in India if India accepted violence as its religion and I am alive at that time.'[30]

Finally, a Hindu's bullet silenced Gandhi, and the ideology of his killers continues to mock him. However, it would be premature to conclude that that marks the end, especially with the rise of the Hindutva government.

In his lifetime, there was a time when Muslim newspapers referred to Gandhi as the 'greatest enemy of Islam in India'.[31]

Although certain sections of both Hindus and Muslims anathematized Gandhi, his legacy endures. On the other hand, Savarkar's ideology remains inconsistent, and the educated find it insupportable. Nehru and his successors consciously worked to establish Gandhi as an immortal figure, but his legacy could be effaced if his detractors remain in power for too long. Godse, an aberration in history, will be invoked by clowns in every generation. Only time will tell the length and trajectory of Modi's story—before and after.

6

Rahul Gandhi

The Search for Identity

Passing through Lalit Kala Academy in Lucknow on a pleasant April day in 2015, I noticed a scrawny bloke of average height riding a scooter with a young woman on the pillion. She leaned in from behind and kissed his right cheek.

What caught my attention was a slogan written on the number plate of his two-wheeler: '*Mujhe Brahmin hone par garva hai* (I am proud of being a Brahmin).' This phrase distilled the essence of '*Garv se kaho hum Hindu hain* (Say with pride that I am a Hindu)', a slogan that originated in the late 1940s and was fervently repeated in the 1980s when the RSS passed the political baton to Advani at the height of the movement against the Babri Masjid.

Mahant Digvijaynath initiated this campaign in the 1940s.

This raises a few questions: Why was Digvijaynath, a Kshatriya, assigned this role? Was it merely because he was anti-Muslim and a leader of the Mahasabha, or was there something more? There is no definitive answer. Poona was considered the Vatican of the Mahasabha during those days, and most directions likely came from there. The enterprising mahant of Gorakhnath temple recognized a potential issue for Poona, allowing them to make the temple one of their centres of activity and accepting them as his superiors.

It is also said that the Gorakhpanthis have strong ties to Poona. George Weston Briggs, in his book *Gorakhnath and the Kanphata Yogis,* noted that followers of Siddha Handi Pharang Nath, a failed disciple of Gorakhnath, resided in Poona.

It is no secret that a significant number of Shiv Sena members travelled from Poona to Ayodhya during the movement against the Babri Masjid. Balasaheb Thackeray claimed in 1992 that his men had demolished the structure. Whether this claim is accurate or not, there is no denying that his party and followers were integral to the movement. Prior to that, Thackeray had spent many years convincing the Konkanasth Brahmins that he was meant to advance their agenda.

The Babri incident has been mentioned frequently in this book due to its magnitude. Its enormity is such that no single piece of writing could fully encompass the entire story. Moreover, its impact is so profound that future generations will continue to feel its repercussions if the country fails to acknowledge the obvious.

Abhiram Das, the member of Mahasabha who planted an idol in the Babri Masjid on the night of 22 December 1949, claimed that the idol emerged on its own from the abyss of the earth. The people of Ayodhya know the truth, but it remains entombed in their hearts—either because it frightens them or because they support the fiction. The situation is such that nobody wants to hear the reminders from Congress leaders that everything the BJP boasts about regarding the Ayodhya temple was, in fact, the handiwork of their ancestors. Nehru and Rajiv both played significant roles in advancing the issue. Rajiv allowed the shilanyas (foundation) programme of the Vishwa Hindu Parishad at the disputed site in 1989.

However, this didn't deter Rahul from claiming in Deoband (home to Darul Uloom, the oldest Islamic seminary after Cairo's Al Azhar University) that if anyone from his family had been prime minister at the time, they would have stood between the Babri Masjid and the mob that demolished it.

Even though Rahul tried to assert that only his family members could have saved Babri, it was under Congress leader Narasimha Rao's government that fanatics were allowed to bring it down.

In 2013, Rahul tore up a copy of an ordinance passed by his own party's Manmohan Singh government, which had provided a three-month reprieve for convicted lawmakers facing disqualification. This kind of dialectical tension is characteristic of him. It goes without saying that the sense of family history within the high-hatting New Gandhis is quite poor.

Rahul's tendency to view his surroundings through the eyes of his faceless courtiers leaves his sense of history half-baked. What else could explain why he lectured at the Congress office in Lucknow in 2012 on how to win an election, just months after his party lost the UP elections?

During the 2012 assembly election campaign, one of Rahul's attendants informed journalists that they were heading to Barabanki, where a huge crowd awaited him. The reporters rushed to the location, only to find fewer than forty people there. The attendant who lured the journalists to the rally stood proudly behind his master, gazing at the ground. Rahul, too, was unfazed.

When Sanjay Gandhi died in a plane crash in 1980, his body was kept in the prime minister's bungalow, and Indira was receiving visitors. Ravi Shankar, a Congressman at the time, stated, 'There were some women in salwar-kurta and some men donning white turban. They would start crying to see her. They would be filmed [by the videographers] ... stop [crying] the moment Indiraji went away from their view.'[1]

At that time, there were only a few around the family, but today, it is only such individuals who form the coterie around Rahul, advising him on matters concerning the Congress, the country, Hinduism, Hindutva, or the Bolshevik Revolution. However, these sidekicks have matured over time and now stay away from the cameras.

His frequent verbal blunders on sensitive issues reveal a lack of political shrewdness and balance. While addressing a rally in Indore in 2013, Rahul mentioned intelligence input that the ISI was in touch with riot-affected youths from Muzaffarnagar. 'An officer walked into my room and said that there were ten or fifteen riot-affected youths in Muzaffarnagar's refugee camps whom the Pakistani intelligence agency was trying to recruit,' he claimed, just days before meeting the families of the riot victims.

A few years ago in Bareilly, he stated, 'Once my family decides something, it doesn't go back. Be it about India's freedom, dividing Pakistan or taking India to the 21st century.' Both Muslims and Hindus were displeased by his remarks, and this was how Modi secured the lion's share of India's politics for over a decade.

The youth wearing his caste with pride on his scooter was obnoxious. As I jotted this down in my diary, I couldn't help but think that he or his offspring likely wouldn't struggle the way Rahul has to become part of the 'holy superlative class', the superior Brahmins. It is a generational struggle that he inherits from Nehru, rooted in their indecision to either fully embrace or reject Hindutva, or adopt Hinduism in its entirety.

The predominant and hyperactive holy class had formed a cartel in pre-independent India, and it has since embedded itself further into the country's psyche. Anyone with ambitions can gain acceptance from them, but only by yielding to their authority. This is where Modi's acceptability comes into play and where Rahul falters.

Rahul, hedged in and on the fence, remains unable to break into this consortium—much like Jawaharlal, who was similarly confined under Gandhian compulsion. Rahul is there now, trapped by Nehruvian obligation.

Trying to shed that burden without being branded a Hindutva admirer, Rahul wrote in the visitor's register of Pushkar temple:

> I, Rahul Gandhi, son of Shri Rajiv Gandhi, am happy to come to Pushkar for puja ceremony on 26/11/2018. After offering puja with the help of our family priest [Dinnanath Kaul and Rajnath Kaul], I feel contented and happy. I have prayed for peace and harmony in India and the world.

Dinnanath told reporters, 'His gotra is "Dattatreya", and he is a Kashmiri Brahmin. Motilal Nehru, Jawaharlal Nehru, Indira Gandhi, Sanjay Gandhi, Maneka Gandhi and Sonia Gandhi have come and offered prayers here and we have a record of it. [Rahul] Gandhi came and offered prayers here … Dattatreya are Kauls and Kauls are Kashmiri Brahmin.'

It was an exercise by Rahul, in collaboration with a priest, to convey to the Hindus, particularly the Brahmins, that he too was one of them. The Congress leader's temple visit was not a private matter, the media was invited to witness him portraying himself as a Hindu.

The conflict within Rahul's mind, or his desire to remain in everyone's good graces, took him from Pushkar to the Ajmer Sharif Dargah.

Back in Delhi, one of his aides declared, 'Rahul Gandhi is a 'janeudhari' [sacred thread holder] Hindu.' Meanwhile, thousands of social media operatives from the rival camp, ever ready to pounce on Rahul's missteps, sprang into action. Hundreds of photos of him wearing a skullcap flooded every virtual platform, aiming to undermine the claim that he belonged to the sacred class. The other side fears what might happen if Rahul is politically accepted as a Brahmin.

Some genuinely believe he is naïve. This perception has helped Hindutva groups portray him as a fool on social media. After the 2024 parliamentary election results, when the Congress gained forty-seven seats compared to 2019, many were quick to say that he had matured. But those who know him well understand that he could be back to square one at any moment.

Motilal knew exactly what he wanted and had no inhibition. He never cared for the Kaul Brahmins who ostracized him for crossing the Arabian Sea, nor did he ever try to reclaim his caste badge. Rahul, however, carries the legacy badge of Jawaharlal, who was never accepted by the Konkanasth Brahmins, yet persistently sought their approval through his colleagues—Mookerjee, Gadgil, Morarji, and many other ghosts of the past.

Jagan Phadnis highlighted the misconception that Gandhi was eliminated solely due to the partition of India or his decision to pay money to Pakistan. Phadnis argued that the 'tendency or idea to kill Gandhi was born and developed in Maharashtra'. He further adds:

> The social and political condition of Maharashtra was in its root … The reign of Maharashtra was in the hands of Brahmins when the English unfurled Union Jack at Poona's Shaniwar Wada … The British took power in their hands in Maharashtra from the Brahmins … The English granted Rai Bahadur and Sir Bahadur to some of the Brahmins of Poona after the establishment of the British government. This kindness didn't reach some of the Brahmins and unrest started growing in them. Vishnushastri Chiplunkar gave this discontent the form of anti-English discontent; tried to invoke nationalism.[2]

Phadnis observed that the rise of Gandhi pushed the politics of the Tilakites into the background. 'Here lies the seed of Gandhi's murder. There is a slight difference between the Hindutva of Maharashtra and the Hindutva of the rest of India.'[3]

Clearly, for some freedom fighters, the nation was not the first priority. They rejected anyone outside their community who didn't submit to their authority, believing that leadership of the party or the country was their exclusive birthright.

Explaining the history more clearly, another author writes, 'Social inequality had taken a grave shape because of unlimited benefits bestowed on the Brahmin caste during the Peshwa's rule.'[4]

He explains that the Brahmins enjoyed wealth and security during the Peshwa's time:

> The upper class criticised the foreign rulers after the end of Peshwa's regime only till Elphinstone, an Englishman, didn't play the trick of inviting them to a place for alms and charity giving. It is not that all Brahmins became supporters of British rule. But one thing certainly happened that they felt it unnecessary to keep intense feeling of discontent for those who provided them the guarantee of security of economy and life.[5]

A few months after I saw the youth with his girlfriend in Lucknow, I received a call from a Congress leader. He informed me that a former Union minister wanted to meet me, and the meeting was scheduled for the next day.

The former minster was the son of a former vice president of the Congress Party, a man who had been very close to two Congress prime ministers, Rajiv Gandhi and Narasimha Rao. Yet, he had challenged Sonia's supremacy in the party.

I met him in his cosy dining hall in Lucknow, where everything, from the walls to the sofa, was draped in white. He wore his usual white linen kurta-pyjama. 'Rahulji has given me a list of people,' he said, 'and told me to ask them whether the Congress should shift to Hindutva politics to beat the BJP?'

I didn't have any strong opinion to offer. My belief was that politicians understood their own politics better than any journalist. But since the leader insisted I share my thoughts, I tried to be as honest as possible. I told him that every person or organization bases its existence or ideology on something tied to its past, and any significant deviation might harm them irreparably. The Congress had long been known for its secular politics, claiming support from every caste and religion. They might adopt a soft-Hindutva approach, as Rahul seemed to be doing for a shift, but embracing Hindutva fully would mean aligning with the killers of Gandhi. The BJP, after all, was known for its sectarian and Hindutva politics, dominated by a Brahmanical, anti-Muslim, and anti-Dalit mindset.

In the words of Gandhi, 'The ruler and the ruled cannot become the same by killing the king. The worker cannot be the master after cutting the head of the master. This is true for everything.'[6]

I don't know what happened to that survey.

For the Congress, secularism was mainly about the inclusive majority, which had aligned with Gandhi. This was why the party had ruled over the country for more than six decades, even though Muslims had drifted towards regional parties.

The Hindutva forces consistently tried to reverse the Congress's politics. They quickly eliminated Gandhi and marginalized the smoke-filled rooms of the New Gandhis when Modi took charge. Modi was assimilated into the holy order because of his personal submission to the RSS. Eventually, some right-wing leaders went so far as to dub him the 'Eleventh Avatar of Lord Vishnu'.[7]

There was a process to this sort of contrived canonization, and Modi understood it well.

Congress leaders hailed Rahul as a 'tapasvi' and circulated pictures of him in saffron attire on social media during his 'Bharat Jodo Yatra'. Soon after, Rahul himself declared, 'This is a land of tapasvis, but the government is targeting them.'

Around the same time, he worshipped at the Brahmsarovar Temple in Kurukshetra, Haryana, and emerged with a tripuṇd (a set of three horizontal lines made with sacred ash) on his forehead and a kesariya (saffron) shawl draped over his shoulders.

But on 17 March 2024, Rahul made it abundantly clear that he didn't understand what he was saying. 'There is a term, "Shakti" in Hindu religion. We are fighting against Shakti,' he said in Bombay while concluding his Bharat Jodo Nyaya Yatra. He intended to convey that the Congress was battling the power (Shakti) of the RSS backing the BJP or the misuse of government machinery against political rivals. However, he mistakenly used the metaphor 'Shakti', which is widely revered as a synonym for Goddess Durga.

He acted as a Hindu but lacked even a superficial grasp of the religion. He would have been better off true to his original self because making such errors is inexcusable when facing political sharks. This faux pas led to a cynical view among the people that Rahul doesn't need a rival—he was his own worst enemy.

Rahul struggled to convey his thought to the public but failed to recognize that the time and mood were not in his favour. His religious shortcomings and misplaced words only made things worse.

Rahul had another limitation. He couldn't support figures like Savarkar or Godse, even indirectly, and he couldn't criticize Gandhi or Muslims, even symbolically. The BJP, however, had no such restrictions. They picked up, dropped, and revived figures like Godse and Gandhi as the situation demanded. If necessary, they would even quietly set Savarkar aside.

In the end, Rahul will likely settle for what the Congress has always claimed as its policy. In its manifesto for the 2024 parliamentary elections, the Congress summed it up:

> The plurality of religions represents the history of India. History cannot be altered. All people living in India and all children born in India are equally entitled to enjoy human rights that includes the right to practice one's religion … the Congress believes that there is no place for authoritarianism or majoritarianism.

Perhaps influenced by an ill-informed reader of Ghalib and Mir, or a mediocre *charba* player (duplicate of a shayar), Rahul said he had opened a '*Mohabbat Ki Dukan* (A Shop of Love)' against '*Nafrat Ka Bazaar* (Market of Hatred)'. Initially, it didn't resonate, but over time, it gained some traction as signs of his rival's decline became apparent.

Politics Through Godman

We are familiar with the association of Swaroopanand Saraswati (former shankaracharya of Jyotir Math and Dwarka Sharada Peetham), Dhirendra Brahmchari (yoga guru), and Sathya Sai Baba (spiritual guru and mystic) with the Congress Party. When we postulate that Modi played a particular kind of politics, we must also remember what the Congress has done. One example is enough to illustrate how politics has evolved under Rahul Gandhi.

Modi kicked off the BJP's election campaign in Kanpur, Uttar Pradesh, on 12 October 2013. Just a few days earlier, Charan Das Mahant, then the agriculture and food processing minister in Manmohan Singh's government, wrote a letter to the Archaeological Survey of India (ASI). In the letter, Mahant conveyed that Shobhan Sarkar, a godman from Kanpur, had a vision of 1,000 tonnes of gold buried beneath the palace of Rao Ram Baksh Singh, a local chieftain in Daundia Khera, Unnao district, 70 km southeast of Kanpur and 630 km southeast of New Delhi.

Mahant expressed belief in Sarkar's power. Consequently, the ASI deployed a team to excavate the site. Huge trucks were stationed nearby, ready to transport the gold to New Delhi.

Sarkar, originally named Viraktanand, had the perfect secular tale to support his hallucination. He reminded people of a piece of history: In 1857, some freedom fighters led by Maulvi Liyaqat Ali looted gold from Allahabad Fort and handed it to Nana Sahib Dhondu Pant, the adopted son of Maratha Peshwa Baji Rao II, to hide. When Brigadier General James George Smith Neill began searching for the gold, it was allegedly taken to Daundia Khera and buried on the grounds of Baksh Singh's fort.

Two days before Modi's rally, Sarkar publicly declared that Modi was 'a leader of thieves' and 'shouldn't be voted to power at any cost'.

Soon, men and women, vendors and smugglers, thieves and saints, politicians and journalists began flocking to

Daundia Khera. As a result, the crowd there ended up being larger than the one at Modi's rally.

Modi issued a statement saying that 'millions of people trust[ed] saint Shobhan' and expressed respect for 'his penance and sacrifice'. The response Modi received during his campaign after the Kanpur rally was a clear indication of his party's impending victory.

Sarkar, in turn, responded to Modi, saying, 'All I hope is that whichever party comes to power uses the treasure wisely for the development of the country.'

No one was prevented from reaching the excavation site while Modi's rally was underway. The inquisitive crowd preferred a gold spot in place of the PM-in-waiting. However, a large paramilitary force dispersed them in Daundia Khera after Modi finished his speech in Kanpur. In the end, nothing was found beneath the palace except for some broken earthen tiles, and the ASI withdrew after a month.

During the height of the excitement, one of Sarkar's disciples confined in me that he and some members of the saint's ashram had met Indira Gandhi in the past. He also hinted that Sarkar and a few of his close aides had also met Sonia and Rahul Gandhi a few months before the drama began.

The New Gandhis failed to see the writing on the wall and continued with their smugness. The gold evaporated in Daundia Khera, and the Congress, along with its allies, secured only 44 parliamentary seats. In contrast, the BJP and its allies won 282 seats.

I met Sarkar while covering a routine newspaper story, but it quickly escalated into a major controversy, causing me many sleepless nights. Sarkar refused to be photographed, claiming that only a shadow would appear if anyone tried to snap his picture. However, my photographer, Naeem Ansari, secretly captured his image, which was published in the newspaper the next day. The following morning, one of Sarkar's disciples called to inform me that the seer was furious. He had smeared black ash on his face and body and ran all over his ashram. When I asked the disciple what this signified, he said it meant that the earth would turn upside down, as Sarkar was preparing to unleash his ultimate spiritual power. Later, the disciple, and subsequently an editor of a Hindi newspaper in New Delhi, warned me that I would soon be eliminated.

Rumours Versus Truth

As Modi became prime minister, Hindutva followers began receiving good news regarding the Ram Temple and citizenship rights. Another significant event occurred in 2014: a new phase of undermining Gandhi began, fuelled by rumour-mongering. While Gandhi had always faced harsh criticism, an organized effort emerged after Modi's rise in national politics to erode his standing in the public eye. Certain writings about Gandhi's experiment with brahmcharya, already in public domain, were rehashed in magazines and newspapers as if they were new revelations. These accounts conveniently omitted Gandhi's own perspective on the matter.

Speaking on sex education, Gandhi once remarked:

> Its aim should be to win over this disorder and utilize it well. The natural use of this education should be to ingrain in the hearts of the children the difference between a human and a demon. Who will impart this true sex-education? Clearly one who has won over his anomalies.[8]

The New Gandhis made no effort to minimize the damage being done to Mahatma's legacy. They showed no inclination to defend him as this new phase of demonization started. They were too busy protecting their own power, politics, and pleasures—much like how Nehru was preoccupied elsewhere when Gandhi's assassination was being planned.

I have covered Rahul as a journalist since 2005, often spending nights outside guest houses and hotels in Rae Bareli, Amethi, and other places, waiting for him to come out and say a few words. Occasionally, I succeeded and found him to be both educated and well-informed. On one such occasion, we discussed the Bolshevik Revolution. During that conversation, he claimed that Modi was merely a pawn in the hands of the RSS. His discourse was impressive, and he also appeared to be a good listener.

However, minutes later, he was shouting at some panchayat-level leaders who had complained that the Congress president's (Sonia's) representatives in Rae Bareli expected certain gratifications before allowing them to meet him. Rahul declared that anyone making such complaints would be suspended from the party.

The notion that Rahul wanted to make or break the party has always haunted many. People hoped he was ready to take up the mantle of leadership, but he continually disappointed them.

Those close to his inner circle have told me that despite everything, he has personally remained distant from any form of financial corruption. For instance, in 2019, when industrialists from Gujarat approached him through Ahmed

Patel—the then political secretary of Sonia and treasurer of the Congress Party—he refused to meet them. I cannot say the same for his sister, Priyanka Gandhi Vadra, who quickly agreed to the meeting.

In 2017, during an election rally in Rae Bareli, her mother Sonia's parliamentary constituency until 2024, Priyanka declared from the dais, 'We are Sanatani Hindus.' However, she doesn't emphasize this much, possibly due to her husband Robert Vadra's family background. She also avoids addressing the charges against her husband, instead reiterating that they are part of a political vendetta.

Someone once remarked, 'Vadra is like a caged bird. A princess breathes in the heart of this Janus-faced bird, but his life is in control of a monster. What will the princess do?'

BJP leaders target Vadra for his alleged involvement in land scams in Haryana and Karnataka, usually just before an election, but once the polling is over, they return to their abodes.

A section of Congress members believe she refrains from commenting on the Vadra issue because she understands him in the right proportion.

During a rally in Srinagar at the conclusion of his Bharat Jodo Yatra, Rahul recalled receiving a phone call when his grandmother was assassinated, and another when his father was killed. He acknowledged that the families of terrorism victims must have received similar calls. 'Those who organize violence … cannot understand this. They cannot understand the pain; I can understand this. My target is to stop this phone call.' He sought to present himself as a complete politician.

But why does he remember the two assassinations yet fail to mention Mahatma Gandhi, on whose legacy his family stands? How can he afford to lose Gandhi, especially when his grandfather, a Parsi, and his mother, a Catholic of Italian origin, are often viewed as antithetical to his public image and frequently come up in general discourse?

To those who remember Mulayam Singh Yadav, often regarded as the most liberal of liberals, Rahul's background may seem like a weak point. Mulayam had promised to support Sonia Gandhi in April 1999, only to change his mind overnight, declaring that 'a foreigner shouldn't be the prime minister of India'.

Regrettably, Rahul heavily banks on Mulayam's son and seems to take Gandhi for granted.

Things have become more complicated since Nehru's time due to interfaith marriages, but they could still be managed with some smart moves. While some initial rituals after Feroze Gandhi's death followed Parsi traditions, most of the Hindu ceremonies were performed. Part of his remains was buried in a Parsi cemetery in the Mumfordganj area of Allahabad, but the majority was immersed in the Sangam.

Sonia has lived like any Hindu widow since Rajiv's assassination. Uma Bharati, a senior BJP leader, once told me in Rae Bareli that this made her respect Sonia.

A wry question arises: Why do the New Gandhis or the Congress fail to capitalize on this, that is, their affinity to Hinduism? Is it due to a lack of intelligence or willpower?

Gandhi, the Nehrus, and the New Gandhis were never fully accepted by the holy class, but Gandhi had such a vast following that they failed to sideline the Anglicized son of an ostracized Kashmiri Brahmin.

Unwilling to accept defeat, Nehru's detractors reiterated, during the final phases of the freedom struggle, that the Nehrus's ancestor, Raj Kaul, was a Persian. Their association with the tenth Mughal emperor made the rumourmongers' task easy.

In the past, Lala Lajpat Rai accused the Congress of opening a branch in Kabul. In reality, under Nehru's secretaryship, the Congress had formed a Kabul Committee at the behest of Deshbandhu Das. 'I do not know how Lalaji was misled in the matter. He may have relied on various rumours …' Jawaharlal observed.[9]

The foundation of such lies run deep. RSS volunteers used to sing in their shakhas, '*Suno re bhai gup, suno re bhai shap, ki naav me nadiya dubat jai* [Listen to the tattle; listen to the gossip, that the river is sinking in the boat].' It may have been for fun, but it also served as a guide for mealymouthed politicians to follow for a better future.

For example, when Rahul claimed in a rally in Gujarat's Patan in 2017 that Modi had promised a machine to farmers that would 'produce gold if potato is put into it', the BJP's social media team edited the video to depict it as a promise from the Congress leader to convert potato into gold.[10]

The Ramification of the Dilemmas

One winter morning in 2023, I woke up to a light-hearted interview of Rahul by an actor-journalist flashing on my phone screen. The interviewer asked if he had bullied his sister since he was older. He responded that they used to fight a lot because of the violence they had witnessed around them. 'But we stopped fighting after my father's death,' Rahul said.

So, they fought due to the psychological trauma of the violence around them but stopped after witnessing yet another tragedy. This contradiction between mind and words mirrors how many people perceive Rahul.

His temple-hopping, embracing Savarkarian Modi—a mascot of the Sangh—in the Parliament, forming a government in Maharashtra with Shiv Sena, and saying he would never visit the RSS office, even if his throat were cut are some of his most serious political paradoxes.

'You have hatred for me,' Rahul told the BJP and the government before walking over to Modi in the Lok Sabha.

> You have anger against me. I am Pappu [fool] for you. You can hurl all sorts of diatribes at me, but I don't feel even the slightest anger or hatred toward you. I am Congress, we are Congress, and this sentiment has formed the country. Never forget this. You all have this sentiment, and I will bring it out of you. One by one, I will bring out the love that you have inside you. I will convert all of you into the Congress.

Modi remained unmoved, not getting up when Rahul hugged him. The government's cronies were quick to seize any opportunity to ridicule him and support Modi, whose response was cold. That opportunity came soon enough. After returning to his seat, Rahul winked at his then-colleague Scindia, an action that seemed inappropriate or awkward in the situation, causing others to mock him or not take the hugging gesture seriously. The entire episode was like reading the Bible with devotion, only to throw it into a culvert afterward.

Rahul was almost mystical in Srinagar in 2023. He mentioned that during his yatra from Kanyakumari to Jammu and Kashmir, he faced many challenges, and all his ahankara (pride) evaporated.

He invoked religion in his speech, displaying a manufactured preternatural or spiritual inclination towards Hinduism. 'As per the thought of Shivji, it is called shunyata [void],' he said, didactically, in an attempt to capture people's attention. Such a discourse could help him if his mind and lips coordinated well.

However, during his Bharat Jodo Nyaya Yatra in 2024, he generalized the youth of Varanasi in excitement, calling them 'drunkards', thus filling his own 'void' with a disparaging remark. This instantly annoyed the residents of Varanasi, the ancient seat of Lord Shiva.

A section of intellectuals who had placed their hopes in Rahul called it a 'need of the time' when he befriended Shiv Sena. They saw a saint in him when he spoke of shunyata, and a statesman when he declared his intent to 'convert everybody into the Congress'.

An academician can remain in their ivory tower, gazing at Rahul with motherly love, unburdened by the harsh realities, but real results will only come when the Congress leader learns to mix religion and politics in the right proportions. This balance is only possible if he understands both politics and religion. Unfortunately, it seemed too late for him to achieve what Modi has already mastered with ease.

Many RSS leaders confided that, despite all this, they were certain of one thing: none of Modi's team members possessed Rahul's potential. They couldn't match what Rahul accomplished—walking 135 days from Kanyakumari to Srinagar in the name of uniting India, and again for 66 days from Manipur to Bombay in the name of justice.

They admitted in their meetings that the Congress leader had outshone them through his yatras. They acknowledged that Rahul had the drive to undertake something even larger. Somewhere, defeat had settled in their minds.

Hopping from place to place, Rahul often appeared with sandalwood paste on his forehead, sometimes dressed in saffron and wearing a rudraksh. He revisited the concept of the 'void' and told reporters in Haryana during his first yatra, 'Rahul Gandhi *aapke dimag mein hai, main maar diya usko. Woh hai hi nahin . . . Baat nahi samjhe*? Hindu *dharm ko padho baat samajh mein aa jayegi* ... Shiv*ji ko padho . . . Image ka mujhe kuchh lena dena nahin hai* [Rahul Gandhi is in your mind; I have finished him off. He is non-existent . . . You didn't understand the message? Read Hindu religion, read about Lord Shiva . . . I am not concerned with image building].'

By saying all this, Rahul was trying to convince Hindus that he belonged to the Sanatan culture and the holy caste. Hinduism teaches the curbing of ego, making oneself a void, becoming nothing—a journey toward self-mortification, which Gandhi had followed. It is from this tradition that Rahul picked up the concept of 'shunyata', claiming '*gaya woh* (Rahul is gone)'. But he failed to resonate with the people, as they found little coherence between his words and actions. Many might not agree with this after the 2024 election results, but the truth was that the outcome was more a result of anger against Modi in Uttar Pradesh than any love for Rahul.

The Hindu seers who received proper training don't mention their real names and avoid using the word 'I', as they have ostensibly destroyed the ego and assimilated themselves into the cosmos.

Religion has become fast food for politicians and their voters. However, Rahul made it less digestible with his convoluted rhetoric. When discussing yoga or Shiva, Modi delivered straightforward speeches, often pointing his index finger at the audience. This gesture symbolized his unyielding ego. Such tendencies were either aligned with the innocent people or opposed to Gandhi, but in both cases, it was Gandhism that suffered.

Gandhi effectively confronted the issues that Rahul is currently battling, which stem from his social maladroitness. The forces that once challenged Gandhi and Nehru can be understood from the interactions between Glorney Bolton, R.S. Sapru, and K.S. Jayakar.

Bolton, Sapru, and Jayakar were aboard the ship that took them and Gandhi to the Second Round Table Conference. Sapru and Jayakar attended all three round table conferences in London, while Gandhi and the Congress opted to stay away from the first and the third conferences.

Bolton was unaware of the complexities of Indian realities, and Sapru and Jayakar fuelled his misconceptions, suggesting that 'when the time was ripe, the Congress might expel him [Gandhi]'.[11]

He began his book with a quote: 'Of John Stirling, his friend, Thomas Carlyle has written: It is better to be unknown than misknown.'[12]

To Bolton, Gandhi was 'like a Pope surrounded by ambitious Cardinals who have twice his knowledge and diplomacy … When old Cardinals found the Pontiff pliable, younger Cardinals are finding him obstinate'.[13]

It is also possible that the rumour was circulated among Bolton's circles to reach Gandhi, hoping he would become furious and distance himself from Nehru upon returning to India. They failed to understand that Gandhi was never in haste.

Rahul lacked the fortune of having a Gandhi physically present, and he didn't possess the qualities of Nehru. His struggles are not only against the Saprus and the Jayakars but also against his own lack of wisdom and judgement.

I wrote an examination for the National Law School of India University, Bangalore, at a government school in New Delhi in 2020. While sitting in the examination hall, we overheard a female teacher telling the children, 'Children, you should ask your parents to vote for the BJP.'

One of the examinees reacted, but our invigilator didn't respond. Later, I told an editor of a news channel about this campaign. He instantly replied, 'I know the BJP is working very hard to win this time.'

Recently, someone brought me a scoop. He showed me a letter from a grandson of Gandhi, which claimed that Feroze's father was one Badshah Khan. I browsed the internet and found the original letter, which discussed a different subject and made no mention of Feroze or Badshah.

I don't know if Rahul will ever be able to tackle this situation, nor am I sure whether he is interested in dealing with it. In a small meeting of students and academicians in Lucknow on 10 May 2024, Rahul said, 'Once I asked my grandmother [Indira] how should the people remember you after you are gone? She said she doesn't want to be remembered at all. I also don't want to be remembered. I want to work till I have time.'

Some people who worked closely with Rahul claimed that he had a theory to save the Congress Party from extinction. He believed that for this to work, the party should stay out of power for fifteen years or even longer. This approach, he argued, would help Congress members learn to struggle as they had during the freedom struggle.

Someone in the Congress told me that Rahul was aware of the deadwood in the party and wanted them to exit. However, what happened thereafter didn't support this theory.

Ghulam Nabi Azad followed Rahul's hunch, but the Modi government lured him away far too easily. In contrast, other leaders had promising potential. Jitin Prasada, one of Rahul's close friends, served as the Union minister of state for human resources in the Manmohan Singh government. Scindia held the position of minister of state for communication and commerce and industry during the Congress rule, while R.P.N. Singh was minister of state for home affairs in the Congress government. He wanted the deadwood to leave, but some promising leaders also deserted the Congress.

Later, Scindia, Prasada, and Singh joined the BJP. They were followed by Nallari Kiran Kumar Reddy, the former chief minister of Andhra Pradesh, and C.R. Kesavan, the great-grandson of Rajagopalachari. The list continued to grow.

Why couldn't Rahul continue as the Congress president, a position he held for nineteen months? To put it in the words of a family chronicler, 'Even his mother, who is the most powerful Congress leader, is not able to stabilize her son at the top post of the party.'

There is no denying that the contradictions in Rahul stem from his inconsistent past. His mother may consider this, but voters are unlikely to have such affection for him.

Born on 19 June 1970, he attended St. Columba's School in Delhi and the Doon School in Dehradun. He also studied at St. Stephen's College. Later, he attended Harvard University for a year and obtained his BA degree from Rollins College in Florida. He ultimately gained admission to Trinity College, Cambridge, for an MPhil before joining the Monitor Group, a management consulting company in London.

Rahul shifted from Harvard to Florida for security reasons after his father's assassination, living there under the pseudonym Raul Vinci.

After returning to India, he started Backops Services Private Limited, a technology consultancy firm involved in legal, accounting, bookkeeping, and auditing services.

He entered politics in 2004 and was elected as an MP from Amethi. Soon, the people of Amethi began saying that he visited the constituency as if it were a picnic.

Hit and Run

We have seen Rahul eating with a poor family or having tea at a roadside dhaba. He sits with labourers to understand their struggles and sows paddy on occasions. Reporters frantically write about what he tells the boy who serves him samosas and tea and how an old victim of police brutality feels when the New Gandhi scion hugs him. But did he ever revisit them? Did he or any of his team members ever look back to see how the woman in Amethi or any person across the country, at whose house he had stayed, is doing?

Rahul and former British foreign secretary David Miliband slept on rope cots in two adjoining huts belonging to two scheduled caste women in a village in Amethi. Cows and buffaloes roamed throughout the village, and he posed with a calf for the delight of the cameras. The entire village congratulated the two hosts of Rahul and David, believing that fortune had descended on the two poor families. As days, months, and years passed, the villagers began to look down on the two women and questioned them what Rahul and the white man were doing in their huts.

There are many such women, men, and youths all over the country who have memories of Rahul, while he has moved on.

A large number of impoverished families in Amethi, which he represented in the Parliament for fifteen years, and from where his office assistant won after a break of five years, are not below the poverty line and do not qualify for the benefits the government extends to the poor. Indira allocated agricultural lands to those families in 1970s and 1980s under her 'Garibi Hatao' ('Eradicate Poverty') programme. However, these families have become poorer than before. The pieces of land allotted to them were barren, but by virtue of being from a landed class now, they were no longer considered poor in government records.

It might have been a well-intentioned plan by Indira, but she depended on the cold-hearted Sanjay to execute it. He allowed his local henchmen to manipulate the orders and allotted fertile land to their cronies. There is a famous anecdote about Indira wanting to install hand pumps along the roads in Sultanpur district, but Sanjay's men buried water canisters just below the ground and fixed hand pumps above them. Indira passed along the road, checked the hand pumps, and thanked Sanjay.

Rahul ignored the villagers' requests to review the situation.

During his two yatras in 2023–24, Rahul covered over 10,000 km but never returned to the places to see if he had truly made any change in anyone's life. This doesn't reflect on his intention but definitely highlights his disconnect from the people. He has learnt nothing from Gandhi, whose surname he uses.

Ostrich Syndrome and Other Stories

Feroze graduated from Edwin Christian College in Allahabad and joined Gandhi's freedom movement. Some people say that during this time, he changed his surname from Ghandy to Gandhi. However, it was Gandhi himself who suggested the surname to Feroze when Nehru confessed that he was uncomfortable with his daughter's name as Indira Ghandy. Feroze died in 1960, eighteen years after their marriage.

Family sources and older people in Rae Bareli claim that Feroze didn't respect Indira. He was also known for refusing to meet with party leaders. Close family friends had seen her sitting on the stairs of Feroze's house, crying.

Feroze was elected an MP from Rae Bareli twice. The Congress veterans shared interesting stories about him, including one from 1957 when he thoroughly dressed down Chaudhary Charan Singh for refusing to give election tickets to two female candidates he had recommended.

Rahul has inherited much from his grandfather. In Rae Bareli in 2012, I ran into a Congress campaign manager from Delhi, whom Rahul refused to meet. While looking at the manager's sneakers, he remarked, 'Your shoes are so costly; what is there for you to say?'

The campaign manager had seen me interviewing Priyanka in the past and requested that I communicate his desire to join her team instead of working with Rahul. I felt incapable of facilitating this and couldn't help him. His annoyance was a testament to Rahul's political callowness.

This naivety was sometimes evident in Rahul's uncle Sanjay. During a visit to Amethi in 1980, Sanjay saw Saccharum ravennae, known as sarkanda in Hindi, and declared, 'We have done so much for Amethi that large-scale farming of sugarcane is taking place in the area.'

Rahul also speaks on various subjects without conducting thorough research on them.

I don't know if Rahul ever read the books written by Nehru. Sanjay once 'boasted to a newspaper editor that he read only comics and never anything serious such as his grandfather Jawaharlal Nehru's books'.[14]

Despite his ignorance about India, Sanjay possessed the ability to superimpose himself onto others, an essential quality in politics. He appointed Praveen Kumar Prajapati, a tribal from Chhattisgarh (then part of Madhya Pradesh), to the Rajya Sabha, despite opposition from his own associates.

One day in early 1980, during her visit to Ambikapur, Indira spotted Prajapati, who was wrapped in a Congress banner. Curious, she inquired about him and instructed her aides to offer him a government job. They informed her that he was thirty-two years old, making him over the age limit for employment. Indira then asked Sanjay if he could find a position for him.

Sanjay met with Prajapati for about ten minutes and decided to send him to the Rajya Sabha. The decision was so unbelievable that when Prajapati called his friend Ram Chavi Dubey to share the news, Dubey urged him to stop talking and quit drinking too much arak (local liquor).

Prithvi Pal Singh, a Congress leader, who previously had Prajapati sit on the floor, was instructed to welcome the tribal worker at Bhopal railway station.

Rahul seldom mentions Feroze or Sanjay in his speeches or conversations, and he rarely speaks of Gandhi. Although he once admitted that the Emergency was a mistake, he compared that period to the present activities of the RSS, claiming that the Congress never captured institutions in the same way as is being done now. The Congress leader made this statement during an online interview with Kaushik Basu, the economic advisor to the Manmohan Singh government and a professor of economics at Cornell University. Newspapers reported it briefly the next day in their inside pages.

His perfunctory confession revived my memory of Modi's scepticism. He took home a model of the Grand Zayed Mosque from the United Arab Emirates and placed it in a corner of the Nehru Memorial Museum and Library Society in New Delhi. Modi also brought replicas of the Ulugh Beg, Sher Dor, and Tilya Kori Madrasahs—the Registan ensemble built during the Timurid Empire in Samarkand—and donated them to the museum.

The officials positioned these replicas in a dark and dusty corner of the museum, which spans 30 acres, as if tasked with ensuring that they remained unseen. In his role as president of the museum and library, Modi added a new building to the premises and, in 2022, replaced the nameplate of the institute with Pradhan Mantri Sangrahalaya (Prime Minister's Museum). The name was officially changed to Prime Ministers' Museum and Library Society a year later.

Nehru had lived there as the prime minister of India, and the museum was dedicated to him by the Congress government after his death. We can only imagine the extent to which Nehru can be erased from public memory and knowledge.

Rahul lost his membership in the Lower House in 2023 after a court in Gujarat sentenced him to two years in jail for calling some 'Modis' 'thieves', referring to financial criminals who shared a common surname with the prime minister. He was specifically talking about bank-defaulter businessmen who fled India.

Rahul was granted bail, and the Supreme Court eventually stayed the punishment. He attempted to rally sentiment against Modi in Santa Clara, claiming that the prime minister considered himself above God. At Sanford University, he criticized the 'concentration of wealth' and 'inequality in India'. However, back home, he avoided discussing why the situation had persisted during the decades his party was in power.

Rahul and his family consistently shied away from addressing the incarceration of 1,50,000 people during the Emergency, as well as the high-handedness of Sanjay, Vidya Charan, and others. Vidya, perhaps the most notorious figure in this context, told Nikhil Chakravarty, the editor of *Mainstream*, 'If you like to go and attack the government ... For God's sake, keep off Sanjay.'[15]

There was a time when Indira would personally meet and ask every visiting resident from Rae Bareli or Amethi about their journey, their needs, and whether they were comfortable in Delhi. However, everything changed in 2004. The most senior Congress leaders from Uttar Pradesh and many other states, who once could easily meet Rajiv, were now made to wait for hours at Rahul's door in New Delhi, hoping he would exchange pleasantries with them.

Frustration among these leaders peaked in 2014 when they witnessed Rahul's 'Sanjay moment' unfold without any political strategy. He decided to field Prem Chand Jayasi, an unknown leader from Chhattisgarh, as the candidate for the Janjgir-Champa Lok Sabha seat simply because he was active on WhatsApp.

Jayasi managed to meet Rahul in person in 2013 and requested a ticket for Masturi Assembly seat. Eyewitnesses noted that Rahul gave him a hard look, and the request was clearly turned down. Undeterred, Jayasi purchased a smartphone and began sending messages to Rahul and other Congress leaders in the Centre about his day-to-day activities. He was eventually declared a Lok Sabha candidate but lost to the BJP.

Today, there are thousands of Congress members, both big and small, who message Rahul every day.

We have the famous stories of Rahul's canine companion, Pidi, who picked up a biscuit before it was offered to the Congressmen, yet Rahul expected his colleagues to eat from the same plate. During interviews with domestic journalists, Rahul has often been seen responding more to Pidi's antics than to the questions posed.

In October 2023, Rahul flew Noorie, a female dog, from Goa to his home in New Delhi as gift for his mother on World Animal Day. Let's see what surprises this pup has in store. Pidi has already created many headlines for the Congress, but Noorie has yet to.

The future Edward VII, then a sixteen-year-old Bertie, once answered a question about whether kings should be elected by saying, 'It is better than hereditary rights because you have more chance of having a good sovereign, if it goes by hereditary rights if you have a bad or a weak sovereign, you cannot prevent his reign.'[16]

Edward VII wrote this in 1857, yet became king forty-four years later by hereditary right, despite facing his greatest opposition from none other than his mother, Queen Victoria. In a letter to her daughter Alice, she wrote that Bertie 'shows more and more how totally, totally unfit he is forever becoming King'.[17]

Sonia used her authority to make Rahul the president of the Congress in December 2017, but unable to handle the responsibilities, he resigned in July 2019.

A mother once wished that her incapable son was never a king, yet he ruled over the United Kingdom and India for nine years (1901–10). Similarly, another mother handed her son the top post of her party, but he failed to manage it for even two years.

If we consider the country as a democracy, we cannot entirely rule out the possibility of Rahul becoming prime minister in the future. He is, after all, the leader of the main opposition party and anti-incumbency sentiment against Hindutva may continue to grow.

The Last New Gandhi

Nehru was prime minister for sixteen years, Indira for more than fifteen, and Rajiv for five. During his ten years in office, Manmohan Singh repeatedly stated that he would step down the day Rahul asked him to.

It was often argued that Congress fatigue and anti-incumbency allowed other parties and leaders, like Morarji Desai and Vishwanath Pratap Singh in the past, and more recently Modi, to wrest power from the Congress. The Congress under the New Gandhis failed to deliver in proportion to the years of power they enjoyed, forgetting that their hold was not eternal.

It seems futile now to remind them of the words of 20th-century British philosopher-politician, Richard Burdon Haldane: '[The] State must see to – the living wage and a decent home – and I can add a third, and that is sufficient knowledge ... People who live under good condition have larger ideals.'[18]

The Nehrus and the New Gandhis made little effort to fulfil these essentials in Indian democracy. For many years, the average daily earning of a poor person remained under Rs 20 and never crossed Rs 100. While knowledge was available in universities and schools, the poor lacked the means to educate their children. Though Manmohan introduced the National Rural Employment Guarantee Act (NREGA) in 2005, providing menial jobs to the poor, the reality on the ground seemed of no concern to Rahul.

Take, for example, the case of the Amethi parliamentary constituency. Before 2005, over 400 of the 749 village chiefs were financially strained and unable to send their children to school. After the act was introduced, they became the wealthiest people in their villages. Each panchayat received between Rs 40 lakh and Rs 2 crore annually. Most of them used the funds to dig community ponds in front of their houses, which they then kept for their exclusive use.

While Rahul's team previously avoided staying even a single night in Amethi, they began camping there after the act was introduced. Many Congress members were suspended from the party for speaking out against the corruption in the programme.

Rahul, too absorbed in his own hereditary greatness, seems uninterested in scrutinizing the flaws within his inner circle, content to enjoy the privileges that came with this legacy.

The Last New Gandhi only remembers Gandhi when he or his party needs him for political purposes. Too conscious of their lineage, most of Bapu's descendants live largely out of the public eye, surfacing only occasionally to protect the Mahatma's legacy.

Priyanka's children won't even carry the Gandhi name; they are Vadras. And so ends the history of the New Gandhis. Mahatma Gandhi has not vanished entirely, because every country needs a hero, and Savarkar has yet to fully occupy that space in the Indian consciousness.

Rahul could still learn something from Cecil Delisle Burns, a priest-turned-atheist, who said:

> The best system of government is one which makes a larger number of citizens understand what government is. The dictator may tell his faithful followers how hard his task and how noble he is to undertake it for their sake; but they cannot understand what he is talking about if they can only cheer. But the alternative is not traditional democracy. The alternative is a much greater participation in the art of government than is involved in an occasional vote at an election . . .[19]

Modi and Rahul both have a message here to reflect on, if they have the time and the intention to grasp it, and the wisdom to respect such a sterling view. Age is still on Rahul's side, and he has Gandhi to draw upon if he truly understands this. But his inaction when Gandhi is attacked or appropriated suggests a political dysfunction, a reluctance to fight back.

Mahatma Gandhi had no true disciples in the conventional sense, except for those who assisted him in his day-to-day life. The poor people of the country loved him and believed that he could drive the British away. They trusted him not because he practised a particular ideology, but because he was one of them.

In a letter dated 21 January 1940, Jinnah wrote to Gandhi: 'Events are moving fast, a campaign of polemics, or your weekly discourse in the Harijan, or metaphysics, philosophy and ethics, or your peculiar doctrines regarding khaddar, ahimsa and spinning are not going to win India's freedom.'[20]

In contrast, Savarkar never made any effort to connect with the masses; he mostly confined himself to his Hindutva club members, attempting to influence them. Meanwhile, Motilal Nehru sent his son, Jawaharlal, to Gandhi to learn the art of politics. With the help of his own intelligence and the influence of the Mahatma's name, Jawaharlal Nehru established himself and set the stage for future generations in his family.

There is little to remember about Nathuram Godse except that he was a mindless follower of his leader.

Modi, on the other hand, is a politician who seeks to align himself with both Gandhi and Savarkar. However, many criticize him for lacking genuine intention. His close ties with corporations, some of which have been accused of being 'intentionally bankrupt' or of flourishing at the expense of the common people, suggest his reliance on economic policies akin to those of Chetty and Patel. These policies, as we have discussed before, seem to benefit the rich and the powerful rather than the masses.

Some corporate reports even suggest that under Modi's rule, the middle class has shrunk, while the ranks of the poor have grown.

Rahul Gandhi, too, hails from a political family that ruled India for many decades, largely because of the legacy of Gandhi. However, any future return to power for the Congress may not be due to their merit or political capability, but because of the nature of India's electoral system, where the lesser evil, or the candidate with less partisan baggage, often prevails.

Go quickly, then, quickly, and bring him here.
Some enemy else may snatch him,
as one would a lion cub torn from its lonely mother.
Hurry and lose no time!
When a man lies dead and helpless,
all the world delights to mock and injure him.

Teucer in Sophocles' *Ajax*
(Translation by John Moore)

Notes

Chapter 1: Mahatma Gandhi

1 Rolland, R., 1948, *Mahatma Gandhi: The Man who Became One with the Universal Being*, translated by Catherine D. Groth, Agra: Shiva Lal Agarwal and Co. Ltd, p. 2.

2 Ibid., p. 185.

3 Nietzsche, F., 1968, *Twilight of the Idols: The Anti-Christ*, translated by R.J. Hollingdale, Harmondsworth, p. 141.

4 Mishra, P., 2004, *An End to Suffering: The Buddha in the World*, Picador, p. 344.

5 Birla, G.D., 1977, *Bapu: A Unique Association*, Volume I, Mumbai: Bharatiya Vidya Bhawan, p. 7.

6 Sheean, V., 1954, *Mahatma Gandhi: A Great Life in Brief*, Publication Division, Government of India, p. 173.

7 Gandhi, M.K., 1927, *An Autobiography* or *The Story of My Experiments with Truth*, translation by Mahadev Desai, Ahmedabad: Navajivan Publishing House, pp. 74–75.

8 Rolland, R., 1948, *Mahatma Gandhi: The Man who Became One with the Universal Being*, translated by Catherine D. Groth, Agra: Shiva Lal Agarwal and Co. Ltd, p. 7.

9 Gandhi, M., 1949, *Bapu, My Mother*, translated by Chitra Desai, Ahmedabad: Navajivan Publishing House, p. 14.

10 Government of India, 1986, *The Collected Works of Mahatma Gandhi*, Volume 95, New Delhi: Publications Division, Ministry of Information and Broadcasting, p. 7.

11 www.golwalkarguruji.org, 23 October 2017.

12 https://www.mkgandhi.org/mynonviolence/chap157.htm

13 https://indiankanoon.org/doc/1627588/

14 Bachchan, H., 1963–70, *Neer ka Nirman Phir*, Rajpal and Sons, pp. 283–84.
15 Bose, N.K., 1953, *My Days with Gandhi*, Calcutta: Nishana, p. 146.
16 Ibid., pp. 149–50.
17 Doke, J.J., 1909, *M.K. Gandhi: An Indian Patriot in South Africa*, London India Chronicle, reprinted in 1967, p. 38.
18 Bose, N.K., 1953, *My Days with Gandhi*, Calcutta: Nishana, p. 150.
19 *The Statesman*, 16 October 1946.
20 Wolpert, S., 2001, *Gandhi's Passion: The Life and Legacy of Mahatma Gandhi*, New York: Oxford University Press, p. 8.
21 Bose, N.K., 1953, *My Days with Gandhi*, Calcutta: Nishana, p. 152.
22 Gandhi, M., 1949, *Bapu, My Mother*, translated by Chitra Desai, Ahmedabad: Navajivan Publishing House, p. 16.
23 Wolpert, S., 2001, *Gandhi's Passion: The Life and Legacy of Mahatma Gandhi*, New York: Oxford University Press, p. 7.
24 Ibid., pp. 7–8.
25 Gandhi, M.K., *Young India*, 7 May 1931.
26 Gandhi, M., 1949, *Bapu, My Mother*, translated by Chitra Desai, Ahmedabad: Navajivan Publishing House, p. 30.
27 *The Collected Works of Mahatma Gandhi*, Volume 95, p. 8.
28 Gandhi, M., *Gandhi: My Mother*, pp. 17–18.
29 Bose, N.K., 1953, *My Days with Gandhi*, Calcutta: Nishana, p. 14.
30 Ibid., p. 148.
31 Gadgil, N.V., 1965, 'Government from Inside', Government of India; reprint by Meenakshi Prakashan (Meerut), p. 147.
32 Jayakar, M.R., 1958, *The Story of My Life*, Bombay: Asia Publishing House, p. 361.
33 Ibid., p. 362.
34 Gadgil, N.V., 1965, 'Government from Inside', Government of India; reprint by Meenakshi Prakashan (Meerut), p. 146.
35 Ibid., p. 147.
36 Wolpert, S., 2001, *Gandhi's Passion: The Life and Legacy of Mahatma Gandhi*, New York: Oxford University Press, pp. 254–55.
37 Bose, N.K., 1953, *My Days with Gandhi*, Calcutta: Nishana, p. 209.
38 Ibid., p. 291.

39 National Archive of India, Identifier: PR_000004014963, File No. 181-G/47.

40 Kripalani, J.B., 1970, *Gandhi: His Life and Thought*, New Delhi: Publication Division, p. 99.

41 Ibid.

42 Ibid.

43 Savarkar, V.D., *Hindu Rashtra Darshan*, Pune: Maharashtra Prantik Hindusabha, p. 48.

44 Nehru, J., 1936. *An Autobiography*, New Delhi: Jawaharlal Nehru Memorial Fund, p. 73.

45 Ibid., p. 458.

46 'History of Hindu Mahasabha', Savarkar.org, p. 365.

47 Pujari, V.K., 1946, *Congress, League aur Hindu Mahasabha*, Delhi: Ratan and Co., p. 251.

48 Ibid., p. 251.

49 Gadgil, N.V., 1965, 'Government from Inside', Government of India; reprint by Meenakshi Prakashan (Meerut), pp. 147–48.

50 Nehru, J., 1936. *An Autobiography*, New Delhi: Jawaharlal Nehru Memorial Fund, p. 290.

51 Ibid.

52 Bolton, G., 1934, *The History of the Indian National Congress*, London: George Allen and Unwin, p. 256.

53 Savarkar, V.D., *Hindu Rashtra Darshan*, Pune: Maharashtra Prantik Hindu Mahasabha, p. 14.

54 Ambedkar, B.R., 1940, *Pakistan or The Partition of India*, Thacker and Co., p. 142.

55 Ibid., p. 91.

56 Ibid., p. 92.

57 Ibid., p. 32.

58 Ibid., p. 139.

59 Ibid., p.143.

60 Bose, N.K., 1953, *My Days with Gandhi*, Calcutta: Nishana, p. 165.

61 Ibid.

62 Gandhi, M.K., *Young India*, 13 July 1921.

63 National Archive of India, Identifier: PR_00004047540

64 Kalelkar, K., 1950, *Stray Glimpses of Bapu*, Ahmedabad: Navajivan Press, p. 14.

65 *Young India*, 13 July 1921.

66 Ibid.

67 Gandhi, M.K., *Young India*, 13 July 1921.

68 Gandhi, M.K., 1921, 'Gokhale: My Political Guru', *Young India*, pp. 48–51.

69 Birla, G.D., 1977, *Bapu: A Unique Association*, Volume I, Bombay: Bharatiya Vidya Mandir, p. 37.

70 Gandhi, M., *Harijan*, 2 November 1934.

71 Gandhi, M., *Harijan*, 29 August 1936.

72 Ibid., p. 44.

73 Ibid., p 10.

74 Doke, J.J., 1919, *M.K. Gandhi: An Indian Patriot in South Africa*, Publication Division, Government of India.

75 *The Collected Works of Mahatma Gandhi (Vol. I)*, p. 285.

76 Power, P.F., 1969, 'Gandhi in South Africa', *Journal of Modern African Studies*, p. 442.

77 Ibid., p. 443.

78 *The Collected Works of Mahatma Gandhi (Vol. V)*, p. 419.

79 *The Collected Works of Mahatma Gandhi*, p. 127.

80 Ibid., pp. 12–13.

81 Jones, E.S., 1948, *Gandhi: Portrayal of a Friend*, p. 8.

82 https://www.gandhiashramsevagram.org/gandhi-articles/influence-of-mahatma-gandhi.php

83 Toit, B., 1996, 'The Mahatma Gandhi and South Africa', *Journal of Modern African Studies*.

84 Rolland, R., 1948, *Mahatma Gandhi: The Man Who Became One with the Universal Being*, translated by Catherine D. Groth, Agra: Shiva Lal Agarwal and Co. Ltd.

85 Oak, A., 2022, 'Political Ideas of B.G. Tilak: Colonialism, Self and Hindu Nationalism', Universiteit Leiden, The Netherlands,12 April, p. 251. (https://hdl.handle.net/1887/3283505)

86 Tilak, B.G., 1922, *Bal Gangadhar ki Jivani,* Pune: Kesari Press, p. 232.

87 Ibid., p. 234.

88 Ibid., p. 234.
89 Bharatiya, B.L., 1987, *Swami Shraddhanand Granthawali*, Delhi: Govindram Hasanand, p. 155.
90 Chaturvedi, U., 1989, *Samaj Sudharak Swami Shraddhanand*, Delhi: Anil Prakashan, p. 117.
91 Kashyap, S.C. and M.C. Shah, 1985, *Govind Ballabh Pant*, New Delhi: Publications Division, Ministry of Information and Broadcasting, GOI, p. 202.
92 Wahi, Dr S., 2010, *Acharya Narendra Dev and his Ideas,* Kolkata: Raja Rammohun Roy Library Foundation, p. 8.
93 Ibid., p. 120.
94 Ibid., p. 123.
95 Patwardhan, A., 'Socialist plea for united work', *Janata*, 1 June 1947.
96 'Congress Socialist Party's Separation from the Congress (1946–48): A Socialist Point of View' was presented by Narendra Kumar Singh and Anand Prakash Singh at the Indian History Congress, 2002.
97 Wahi, Dr S., 2010, *Acharya Narendra Dev and his Ideas,* Kolkata: Raja Rammohun Roy Library Foundation, p. 120.
98 Singh, H.K., 1959, *A History of the Praja Socialist Party*, Lucknow: Narendra Prakashan, p. 225.
99 Kashyap, S.C. and M.C. Shah, *Govind Ballabh Pant*, p. 204.
100 Ibid., p. 205.
101 Gandhi. M.K., *The Collected Works of Gandhi XXXII*, p. 453.
102 Doke, J.J., 1919, *M.K. Gandhi: An Indian Patriot in South Africa*, Publication Division, Government of India, p. 106.
103 Gandhi, M.K., 1927, *An Autobiography or The Story of My Experiments with Truth*, Ahmedabad: Navjivan Publishing House, pp. 29–30.
104 *Mahatma Gandhi: His Life, Writings and Speeches*, Madras: Ganesh & Co., p. 60.
105 Gandhi, M.K., *Harijan Sewak*, 28 April 1946.
106 Ibid., 2 June 1946.
107 Nehru, J., 1936, *An Autobiography*, New Delhi: Oxford University Press, p. 72.
108 Lester, M., 1931, *My Host: The Hindu*, London: Williams and Norgate Ltd, p. 28.
109 Ibid., p.34.

110 Savarkar, V.D., 1963, *Six Glorious Epochs of Indian History*, Bombay: Savarkar Prakashan, p. 255.

111 Macdonell, A.A., 1922, *Hymns from the Rigveda*, New Delhi: Oxford University Press.

112 Savarkar, V.D., 1925, *Hindu Padpadashahi* (A Review of the Hindu Empire of Maharashtra), Madras: B.G. Paul and Co., p. 6.

113 Savarkar, V.D., 1923, *Hindutva*, Nagpur: V.V. Kelkar, p. 99.

114 Ibid., p. 101.

115 Savarkar, V.D., 1949, *Hindu Rashtra Darshan*, Bombay: Savarkar Prakashan, p. 302.

116 Gandhi, M., 1949, *Bapu, My Mother*, translated by Chitra Desai, Ahmedabad: Navajivan Publishing House, p. 37.

117 Gadgil, D.R., *Government from Inside*, p. 150.

118 Golwalkar, M.S., 1960, *Bunch of Thoughts*, Bangalore: Vikram Prakashan.

119 Venkata Rao, M.A., 1960, 'Introduction', *Bunch of Thoughts* by M.S. Golwalkar, Bangalore: Vikram Prakashan, p. xxi.

120 Deshmukh, N., 2020, *Rashtriya Swayamsevak Sangh*, Prabhat Paperback, p. 373.

121 Bhai Paramanand, 1934, *The Story of My Life*, Lahore: Central Hindu Yuvak Sabha, p. 31.

122 Ibid., p.180.

123 *Telegraph*, Kolkata, 7 February 2024.

124 Bajwa, Dr K.K., 2004, *Sri Guruji: Vyaktitva evam Krititva*, New Delhi: Suruchi Prakashan, p. 36.

125 Khan, N.A., 2018, *Shaikh Mohammad Abdullah's Reflections of Kashmir*, Palgrave Macmillan, p. 197.

126 Nene, R. and N. Modi, 2001, *Setubandh*, translated by Subhas Bhatia, Prabhat Prakashan, p. 45.

127 Kapur Commission's Report

128 https://indiankanoon.org/doc/383735/

129 Golwalkar, *Bunch of Thoughts*, p. 273.

130 Elst, K., 2001, *Gandhi and Godse: A Review and a Critique*, New Delhi: Voice of India, p. 16.

131 Martin Luther King's remark put up in the National Gandhi Museum, New Delhi.

132 Birla, O., *Antim Jan*, December 2022.

Chapter 2: Vinayak Damodar Savarkar

1 *Dainik Bhaskar*, 22 July 2016.
2 Mankekar, D.R. and K. Mankekar, 1977, *Decline and Fall of Indira Gandhi*, New Delhi: Vision Books, p. 30.
3 BBC, 24 April 2020.
4 *The Telegraph*, 30 March 2020.
5 The Telegraph, 7 July 2024.
6 *L'Humanite*, Marseilles, 12 April 1910.
7 Jayakar, M.R., *The Story of My Life*, p. 103.
8 Ibid., p. 109.
9 Savarkar, V.D., *Mera Ajeevan Karavas*, p. 8.
10 Ibid., p. 24.
11 Ibid., p. 24.
12 Mulayam's speech in the lower house on 13 February 2019.
13 Khan III, A., 1954, *The Memoir of Aga Khan*, Cassell and Company Ltd, p. 153.
14 Ibid., p. 154.
15 Ibid., p. 155.
16 Savarkar, V.D., 1963, *Samagra Savarkar Wangmaya: Hindu Rashtra Darshan*, Volume 6, Poona: Maharashtra Prantik Hindusabha, pp. 479–80.
17 Savarkar, V.D., 1963, *Samagra Savarkar Wangmaya: Hindu Rashtra Darshan*, Volume 6, Poona: Maharashtra Prantik Hindusabha, pp. 479–80.
18 Savarkar, V., *Hamarai Samasyayen*, New Delhi: Rajpal & Sons, p. 50.
19 Srivastava, H., 1989, *Udit Martand Veer Savarkar*, New Delhi: Anmol Publication, p. 12.
20 Garg, K., a booklet on Veer Savarkar, p. 6.
21 Sanyal, S., *Bandi Jeevan*, p. 151.
22 Gandhi, M.K., 1909, *Indian Opinion*, Johannesburg. In B. Srinivasa Murthy (ed.), 1987, *Mahatma Gandhi and Leo Tolstoy Letters*, California: Long Beach Publications, pp. 41–42.
23 Savarkar, V.D., 2015, *Six Glorious Epochs of Indian History*, translated by S.T. Godbole, Prabhat Prakashan, p. 272.
24 Nehru, J., *An Autobiography*, p. 36.
25 Ibid., p. 36.

26 M.P.T. Acharya's review of Angelica Balabanoff's memoirs, *Erinnerungen und Erlebnisse* (*My Life as a Rebel*) in 1927. (theanarchistlibrary.org)
27 Khan, A., 1954, *The Memoirs of Aga Khan*, New York: Simon and Schuster, p. 96.
28 Ibid., p. 229.
29 Gadgil, V.N., 1965, *Government from Inside*, p. 148.
30 *Samagra Savarkar Vangmaya*, Vol. 3, p. 483.
31 *Samagra Savarkar Vangmaya*, Vol. 4, p. 710.
32 Savarkar, V., *Hamarai Samasyayen*, New Delhi: Rajpal & Sons, p. 14.
33 (Ashtekar, G.T., 1984, *Bharatendu Harishchandra Evam Vishnushastri Chiplunkar*, Jaipur: Panchsheel Prakashan, p. 78.
34 Tilak, B.G., *Bal Gangadhar Tilak,* p. 30.
35 Gandhi, M.K., 1927, *An Autobiography or The Story of My Experiment with Truth*, Ahmedabad: Navajivan Publication House, p. 3.
36 Kelkar, N.C., 1928, *Life and Times of Lokmanya Tilak,* translated by D.V. Divekar, Madras: S. Ganesan Publisher, p. 12.
37 Savarkar, V.D., *Six Glorious Epochs of Indian History*, p. 330.
38 Shanmukham Chetty's speech in the Parliament on 26 November 1947.
39 Savarkar, V., *Hamarai Samasyayen*, New Delhi: Rajpal & Sons, p. 15.
40 Ibid., p. 480.
41 Savarkar, V.D., *Mera Aajeevan Karavas*, p. 290.
42 Ghosh, B.K., *The Tale of My Exile*, Pondicherry: Arya Office, p. 119.
43 Ibid., p. 265.
44 Ibid., p. 290.
45 Kelkar, N.C., 1928, *Life and Times of Lokmanya Tilak*, Madras: S. Ganesan Publisher, p. 287.
46 'Letters from Andaman', Savarkar.org, p. 7; and 'Hindu Rashtra Darshan', Savarkar.org, p. 54.
47 Goyal, K.S. *Main Savarkar Bol Raha Hun*, New Delhi: Pratibha Pratishthan, p. 12.
48 Savarkar, V. *Hamarai Samasyayen*, Rajpal & Sons, p. 12.
49 leaflet.in, 23 October 2024.
50 Barandbench.com, 16 July 2024.
51 Oak, A. 2022, 'Political Ideas of B.G. Tilak: Colonialism, Self and Hindu Nationalism', Universiteit Leiden, The Netherlands, 12 April, p. 251.

52 Ibid., p. 232.
53 Clausewitz, C., 1940, *Vom Kriege* (On War).
54 Savarkar, V.D., 1971, *Six Glorious Epochs of Indian History*, translation by S.T. Godbole, p. 144.
55 Ibid., p. 274.
56 Ibid., p. 33.
57 Adolf Hitler to Otto Strasser on 21 May 1930. It was published by Oxford University Press. Volume II, p. 989.
58 Nehru, J., 1936, *An Autobiography*, p. 173.
59 Savarkar, V.D., *Essentials of Hindutva*, p. 41.
60 Savarkar, V.D., *Inside the Enemy Camp*, Savarkar.org, p. 33.
61 Singh, Dr S.K., 2015, *Life and Work of Veer Savarkar*, New Delhi: Apple Academic Press, p. 8.
62 Ibid., p. 14.
63 The pamphlet of the Hindustan Socialist Republican Army they threw in the assembly hall.
64 *The Collected Works of Mahatma Gandhi*, Volume XLV, p.133.
65 Ibid., p. 349.
66 Gandhi, A.G., 2008, *The Life and Time of Veer Savarkar*, Prabhat Books, p. 59.
67 Ibid., p. 58.
68 Savarkar, V.D., 2015, *Mera Ajeevan Karavas,* Prabhat Prakashan, p. 286.
69 https://organiser.org/2023/03/23/125458/bharat/bhagat-singh-and-veer-savarkar-trough-each-others-pen/
70 *shahidbhagatsingh.org*
71 Majumdar, R.C., 1975, *Penal Settlements in the Andamans*, Publications Division.
72 www.shahidbhagatsingh.org
73 Bhagat Singh's letter to one of his friends published in the *People* in June 1931 (www.shahidbhagatsingh.org).
74 Savarkar, V.D., *Hindutva: Who is a Hindu?* p. 64.
75 Savarkar, V.D., 1971, *Six Glorious Epochs of Indian History*, translation by S.T. Godbole, p. 480.
76 Ibid., p. 275.
77 Ghosh, B.K., 1922, *The Tale of My Exile*, Pondicherry: Arya Office, pp. 108–09.

78 Ibid., p. 22.
79 Ibid., pp. 78–79.
80 Savarkar, V.D., 2015, *Mera Ajeevan Karavas,* Prabhat Prakashan, p. 291.
81 Ibid., p. 284.
82 Ibid., p. 288.
83 Ghosh, B.K., *The Tale of My Exile*, p. 16.
84 Sanyal, S., 1922, *Bandi Jeevan,* edited by Banarasidas Chaturvedi, Delhi: Atmaram and Sons, p. 190.
85 Ibid., p. 192.
86 Ibid., p. 16.
87 Letter No. 836-PMO/80.
88 'Biography of Babarao Savarkar', savarkar.org, p. 58.
89 Abhilesk Patal, 1921, identified: PR_000004009466, File No. 354, National Archive of India.
90 Mitra, H.N. (ed.), July–December 1924, *The India's Quarterly Register*, Calcutta: Annual Register Office, p. 238.
91 'Report of Bombay Legislative Council', Vol. XII, Part 1, 1924, p. 735.
92 *Collected Works of Gandhi*, Volume, 38, Publication Division, Government of India, p. 138.
93 *Collected Works of Gandhi*, Volume 86, p. 86.
94 Nehru, *An Autobiography*, p. 50.
95 Heyst, A., 1940, *After Hitler*, M. Publishing Co., p. 33.
96 Abhilesk Patal, identifier: PR_000002027114, File No. 238, National Archive.
97 Abhilesk Patal, 1949, Identifier-PR000004009616, File No. 54/6/49, National Archive.
98 'J.L. Kapur Commission Report', Part 2, 2017, Notion Press, pp. 187 –88.
99 Payne, R., 1969, *The Life and Death of Mahatma Gandhi*, London: The Bodley Head, p. 615.
100 Inamdar, P.L., 1979, *The Story of the Red Fort Trial (1948–49*), Popular Prakashan, p. 141.
101 Ibid., p. 143.
102 Ibid., p. 25.

103 Gandhi, A.K., *Life and Times of Veer Savarkar*, p. 60.
104 Ibid.
105 National Archives of India: Private Papers; 27, Mahatma Gandhi Papers (1880–1948); 12.D, Gandhi Murder Trial Papers; File 26, Printed Records of Mahatma Gandhi Murder Case, Volume II; Written Statement of Nathuram Godse, Accused No. 1, Para 149.

Chapter 3: Jawaharlal Nehru

1 Neruda, P., 1978, *Memoirs*, Penguin Books, pp. 199–201.
2 Neruda, P., 1978, *Memoirs*, translated by Hardie St Martin, Penguin Books, p. 202.
3 Ibid., p. 204.
4 Nehru, J., 1936, *An Autobiography*, New Delhi: Oxford University Press, p. 5.
5 Bose, S.K., 1985, *Adhunik Bharat Ke Nirmata: Tej Bahadur Sapru*, translated by Shakuntala Mathur. Publication Division, p. 206.
6 Ibid., p. 209.
7 Ibid., pp. 22–23.
8 Nehru, J., 1985, *The Discovery of India*, New Delhi: Oxford University Press, p. 325.
9 Ibid., p. 392.
10 Singh, N., 2019, *Khooni Vaisakhi*, translated by Navdeep Puri, Harper Perennial, p. 11.
11 Jayakar, *The Story of My Life*, Bombay: Asia Publishing House, p. 332.
12 *Navajeevan*, 18 November 1920.
13 Jayakar, *The Story of My Life*, Bombay: Asia Publishing House, p. 340.
14 Nehru, J., 1977, *Wangmay*, Volume 8, New Delhi: Jawaharlal Nehru Memorial Fund, p. 173.
15 Bandopadhyay, C.R., 1994, 'Anandamath', *Bankim Chandra Chatterjee: Essay in Perspective*, Sahitya Academy, p. 224.
16 Sengupta, S.C., 1994, 'Bankim Chandra and the Bengal Renaissance', *Bankim Chandra Chatterjee: Essay in Persepective*, Sahitya Academy, pp. 138–39.

17 Nehru, J., 1977, *Wangmay*, Volume 8, New Delhi: Jawaharlal Nehru Memorial Fund, p. 173.

18 'The Indian War of Independence', savarkar.org, pp. 24–25.

19 *Jawaharlal Nehru Vangmay*, Vol. 8, p. 173.

20 Ibid., p. 348.

21 Bose, 1953, *My Days with Gandhi*, Calcutta: Indian Associated Publishing Co. Ltd, pp. 98–99.

22 Golwalkar, 1960, *Bunch of Thoughts*, Bangalore: Vikram Prakashan.

23 Rau, M.C., 1967, *Gandhi and Nehru*, Bombay: Allied Publishers Pvt. Ltd, p. 77.

24 Savarkar, *Six Glorious Epochs of Indian History*, p. 348.

25 Deshmukh, N., 2020, *Rashtriya Swayamsevak Sangh*, New Delhi: Prabhat Books, p. 111.

26 An article by Mohanlal Saksena, a Congressman, featured in *Motilal Nehru*, a birth centenary souvenir published by Motilal Nehru Centenary Committee in 1961, with patrons Rajendra Prasad, President of India, and S. Radhakrishnan, vice-president (p. 35).

27 *Nehru: A Bunch of Old Letters*, 1958, Bombay: Asia Publishing House, p. 339.

28 Ibid., p. 348.

29 Dansana, A., 2020, 'Hirakud Dam Oustees and the Proclamation of Justice in India'.

30 Parliament Proceedings, Central Information Commission, CIC/SH/A/2016/001055.

Chapter 4: Nathuram Godse

1 Godse, G., 2019, *Gandhi Vadh aur Main*, New Delhi: Surya Bharati Prakashan, p. 139.

2 *A Bunch of Old Letters*, 1958, Bombay: Asia Publishing House, p. 58.

3 'Mahatma Gandhi Assassination: J.L. Kapur Commission Report', Part 1, Notion Press, 2017, p. 141.

4 Deshmukh, N., 2020, *Rashtriya Swayamsewak Sangh*, Prabhat Paperback, p. 88.

5 Abhilekh Patak, Identifier: PR_000004076826, File No.40/18/53-JUDL, National Archive of India, 1953, pp. 4–6.

6 Godse, G., 2015, *Gandhi Vaddh aur Main*, Delhi: Surya Bharati Prakashan, pp. 301–2.
7 National Archive of India, File No. 21/6/58-JUDL.
8 Godse, G., 2019, *Gandhi Vaddh aur Main*, Delhi: Surya Bharati Prakashan, p. 301.
9 Gadgil, D.R., 1968, *Government from Inside*, p. 148.
10 Khosla, G.D., 1965, *The Murder of the Mahatma*, London: Jaico Publishing House, p. 13 (https://www.mkgandhi.org/ebks/the-murder-of-the-mahatma.pdf).
11 Godse, G., *Gandhi Vadh aur Main*, introduction.
12 Godse, N., 2019, *Gandhi Vadh aur Main*, compiled by Gopal Godse, New Delhi: Surya Bharati Prakashan, pp. 11–12.
13 Wolpert, S., *Gandhi's Passion*, p. 159.
14 NDTV (Meerut), 19 August 2016.
15 Godse, G., 2019, *Gandhi Vadh aur Main*, New Delhi: Surya Bharati Prakashan, p. 139.
16 Ibid., p. 141.

Chapter 5: Narendra Modi

1 Surti, A., 2020, *Gujarat ki Lokapriya Kahaniyan*, Prabhat Prakashan, p. 3.
2 Sinha, A., 1977, 'Janata Elects a Leader', *Economic and Political Weekly*, Vol. 12, No. 26, 25 June 25.
3 Kelkarp, N.C., 1928, *Life and Times of Lokmanya Tilak*, translated from Marathi by D.V. Divekar, Madras: S. Ganesan, p. 64.
4 *Economic Times*, 1 August 2024.
5 *India Today*, 18 September 2024.
6 Makwana, K., 2014, *Modi: Common Man's PM*, Prabhat Books, pp. 121–22.
7 https://hansard.parliament.uk, Vol. 708.
8 Balashankar, R., *Rashtra Sadhak Narendra Modi*, Prabhat Prakashan, p. 54.
9 'Jawaharlal Nehru's Speeches', Vol. 1, 1946–49, Publication Division, p. 29.
10 Bhargava, G.S., 1977, *Morarji Desai: Prime Minister of India*, Hind Pocket Books, p. 9.

11 Singh, K., 1979, *Indira Gandhi Returns*, New Delhi: Vision Books, p. 179.
12 Singh, K., 1979, *Indira Gandhi Returns*, Vision Books, p. 182.
13 Gandhi, M.K., *Harijan Sewak*, 21 September 1940.
14 Ibid.
15 Fischer, L., *Mahatma Gandhi: His Life and Times*, Bharatiya Vidya Bhawan, p. 120.
16 2019, *Bhagavad Gita According to Gandhi*, Quignog Books, p. 244.
17 Ibid., pp. 241–42.
18 Golwalkar, 1960, *Bunch of Thoughts*, Bangalore: Vikram Prakashan, p. 63.
19 Modi, N., 2010, *Jyotipunj*, translated by Sangita Shukla, Delhi: Prabhat Prakashan, p. 16.
20 Ibid., p. 11.
21 Makwana, K., 2014, *Modi Common Man's PM*, Prabhat Books, pp. 121–22.
22 Nene, R. and N. Modi, 2001, *Setubandh*, Delhi: Prabhat Prakashan, p. 52.
23 Kosambi, D.D., 1957, *Exasperating Essays*, New Delhi: People's Publishing House, pp. 10–11.
24 Modi, N., *Jyotipunj*, p. 44.
25 Modi, N., 2012, *Samajik Samrasta: A Collection of Speeches and Writings*, edited by Kishor Makwana and translated by Prem Shankar Bhatt, Delhi: Prabhat Prakashan, p. 21.
26 Ibid., p. 30.
27 Savarkar, V.D., *Hindutva*, Prabhat Prakashan, p. 65.
28 Heyst, A., *After Hitler*, p. 33.
29 Savarkar, V.D., *Hindutva*, Prabhat Prakashan, p. 9.
30 Gandhi, M.K., *Young India*, 6 April 1921.
31 De, A. (ed.), 1999, *Gandhi–Jinnah Correspondence and Communal Question*, Calcutta: Ratna Prakashan.

Chapter 6: Rahul Gandhi

1 Shankar, R., 1986, *Rajiv Gandhi Amethi Me*, Lucknow: Sulabh Prakashan, pp. 10–11.

2 Phadnis, J., 2010, *Gandhi ki Shahadat*, Varanasi: Sarva Sewa Sangh, pp. 5–6.
3 Ibid., p. 13.
4 Ashtekar, G.T., 1984, *Bharatendu Harishchandra Evam Vishnushastri Chiplunkar*, Jaipur: Panchsheel Prakashan, p. 25.
5 Ibid., p. 31.
6 Gandhi, M.K., *Harijan Sewak*, 13 July 1947.
7 Ndtv.com, 13 October 2018; jagran.com, 18 December 2023; *Deccan Herald*, 29 May 2024.
8 Gandhi, M.K., *Harijan*, 21 November 1936.
9 Nehru, J., *An Autobiography*, p. 159.
10 amarujala.com, 11 November 2017.
11 Bolton, G., *The Tragedy of Gandhi*, London: George Allen and Unwin Ltd, pp. 256–57.
12 Ibid., p. 11.
13 Ibid., p. 16.
14 Abbas, K.A., 1985, *Indira Gandhi: The Last Post*, Bombay: Popular Prakashan, p. 11.
15 Mankekar, D.R. and K. Manekar, 1977, *Decline and Fall of Indira Gandhi*, New Delhi: Vision Books, p. 81.
16 Wilson, B., 'Review of Jane Ridley's *Bertie: A Life of Edward VII*', *London Review of Books*, Volume 34, Number 18, 27 November 2012, p. 12.
17 Ibid., p. 12.
18 R.B. Haldane's speech on challenges to democracy given at the Workers Education Association at Coventry, London, on 13 April 1918.
19 Burns, C.D., 1934, *The Challenges to Democracy*, London: George Allen and Unwin Ltd, p. 23.
20 De, A. (ed.), 1999, *Gandhi–Jinnah Correspondence and Communal Questions*, Calcutta: Ratna Prakashan, p. 80.

About the Author

Piyush Srivastava is an Indian mainstream journalist with over two decades of experience. He has a postgraduate degree in English literature from the University of Allahabad. Currently with *The Telegraph*, he has worked in the past with the India Today Group, *The Indian Express, Hindustan Times* and *The Times of India*. He has covered politics and society in almost all major states of India including Maharashtra, Delhi, Madhya Pradesh, Chhattisgarh, Uttarakhand, and Uttar Pradesh. The floods of stories around him have recently prompted him to try his hand at screenplay writing.